Jewish
Perspectives
on the
Experience
of
Suffering

Jewish Perspectives on the Experience of Suffering

edited by
Shalom Carmy

Robert S. Hirt, Series Editor

The Orthodox Forum Series
A Project of the Rabbi Isaac Elchanan Theological Seminary
An Affiliate of Yeshiva University

JASON ARONSON INC.
Northvale, New Jersey
Jerusalem

This book was set in 11 pt. Newbaskerville by Hightech Data Inc. of Bangalore, India and printed and bound by Book-mart Press, Inc. of North Bergen, NJ.

10 9 8 7 6 5 4 3 2 1

Library of Congress Cataloging-in-Publication Data

Jewish perspectives on the experience of suffering / edited by Shalom Carmy.
    p. cm.
    "The Orthodox Forum series."
    Papers presented at the Orthodox Forum 7th conference, held Apr. 2–3, 1995, in New York City.
    Includes bibliographical references and index.
    ISBN 0–7657–6050–9
    1. Suffering—Religious Aspects—Judaism—Congresses.
2. Holocaust (Jewish theology)—Congresses. 3. Theodicy—Congresses. I. Carmy, Shalom. II. Orthodox Forum (7th : 1995 : New York, N.Y.)
BM645.S9J49 1999
296.7—dc21   98–36383

Printed in the United States of America. Jason Aronson Inc. offers books and cassettes. For information and catalog write to Jason Aronson Inc., 230 Livingston Street, Northvale, NJ 07647-1726, or visit our website: http://www.aronson.com

THE ORTHODOX FORUM

The Orthodox Forum, convened by Dr. Norman Lamm, President of Yeshiva University, meets each year to consider major issues of concern to the Jewish community. Forum participants from throughout the world, including academicians in both Jewish and secular fields, rabbis, *rashei yeshiva*, Jewish educators, and Jewish communal professionals, gather in conference as a think tank to discuss and critique each other's original papers, examining different aspects of a central theme. The purpose of the Forum is to create and disseminate a new and vibrant Torah literature addressing the critical issues facing Jewry today.

The Orthodox Forum
gratefully acknowledges the support
of the Joseph J. and Bertha K. Green Memorial Fund
at the Rabbi Isaac Elchanan Theological Seminary.

THE ORTHODOX FORUM
Seventh Conference

April 2–3, 1995, 2–3 *Nisan* 5755
Congregation Shearith Israel, New York City

LIST OF PARTICIPANTS

Rabbi Elchanan Adler, Yeshiva University
Dr. Norman Adler, Yeshiva University
Rabbi Marc Angel, Congregation Shearith Israel, New York
Professor David Berger, Yeshiva University
Dr. Michael Berger, Emory University
Rabbi Saul J. Berman, Yeshiva University
Rabbi Jack Bieler, Hebrew Academy of Greater Washington
Dr. Rivkah Blau, Shevach High School
Rabbi Yitzchak Blau, Yeshivah of Flatbush High School
Rabbi Yosef Blau, RIETS/Yeshiva University
Dr. Judith Bleich, Touro College
Rabbi Shalom Carmy, Yeshiva University
Rabbi Zevulun Charlop, RIETS/Yeshiva University
Rabbi Mark Dratch, Shaarei Shomayim Congregation,
    Toronto
Rabbi David Eliach, Yeshivah of Flatbush High School
Dr. Yaffa Eliach, Brooklyn College
Dr. Yaakov Elman, Yeshiva University
Rabbi Barry Freundel, Kesher Israel Synagogue, Washington,
    D.C.

Let not desire assure you that the grave is your ref-
uge, for unwillingly were you created, and unwillingly
were you born, unwillingly do you live, and unwillingly
do you die, and willy-nilly are you destined to give an
account before the Supreme King, the Holy One,
blessed be He.

—*Avot* 4:29

[The Greek philosophers] contract the heart and
harden the thoughts, provide empty joy and miserable
consolation, denying the future and despairing of the
past . . . for [Socrates] said that whoever knows the
world will not rejoice in his good or be troubled over
the bad. And they said that the unfortunate is he who
is troubled by anything at all.

—Ramban

Life must be seen, before it can be known.
—Samuel Johnson

Who is for me in heaven but You? I want none other
on earth. My flesh and heart are consumed, O rock
of my heart, and my portion is God forever.

—Ps. 73:25–26

****

To the martyred memory of
my maternal grandparents
Shalom Yaakov and Dreizel Birnbach
Hy'd
I dedicate this volume
for my friends and students
the *Mishpaha ha-Lomedet*
with abiding affection

Contents

Preface

Shalom Carmy

This book is not meant to be a gentle book. The essays collected here, as the title indicates, strive, above all else, to be faithful to the *experience* of suffering as it is encountered from the perspective of normative Judaism. Samuel Johnson wrote: "Life must be seen, before it can be known."[1] In the spirit of his words, let us recall that the work of the intellect, be it philosophy or literature, history or psychology, is an integral aspect of experience, one that, properly conceived and conducted, is a valuable pathway to truth and sometimes to consolation. But the intellectual

---

[1]Samuel Johnson, "Nature and Origin of Evil: Review of a Free Enquiry" (in *Works of Samuel Johnson*, Troy, 1903, vol. XIII 217–255) 227.

gesture cannot serve as a substitute for experience. In organizing this volume, the analysis of experience has taken precedence over the experience of analysis.

This book originated in the papers circulated to the Seventh Orthodox Forum, convened by Dr. Norman Lamm from April 2–3, 1995. In it, the intellectual disciplines that are brought to bear on the experience of suffering are varied. Rabbis Aharon Lichtenstein and Moshe Tendler undertook the task of applying the data of Halakha. The former addresses the question of the right human response to suffering; the latter analyzes halakhic definitions of pain. My own essay, while anchored in the classic texts of Torah and Jewish medieval and modern thought, draws heavily on Western philosophy and literature. Dr. Yaakov Elman deepens and expands his work on rabbinic theology and literature, uncovering the variety of responses in the sources. The extreme experiences with which Dr. Moshe Spero's paper struggles are those of his psychiatric patients. Dr. Nehemia Polen builds on his previous writing to present the theological reflections produced during the destruction of European Jewry in the 1940s, and Dr. Yaffa Eliach tells more about what it meant to make sense of life in the shadow of death in the vale of slaughter. The volume is rounded out by Rabbi Yitzchak Blau's annotated bibliography, which is intended to assist the reader's attempts to think further about the subject of the book and to confront independently some of the theological and other intellectual resources that affected the minds of the authors. My opening chapter sets the stage for the others and presents some ideas about issues not fully treated in the rest of the book.

****

Before explaining the dedication I have chosen for this collection, let me take advantage of this opportunity to acknowledge those who have been instrumental in its production. Dr. Norman Lamm, president of Yeshiva University and convener of the Orthodox Forum, deserves the thanks of all who have benefited from the forum's work, not least in the present volume, where his own writing has so fruitfully informed the discussion. As always, I enjoyed working with Rabbi Robert Hirt, vice president of the Rabbi Isaac Elchanan Theological Seminary. His commitment was fully reflected in that of his staff, in particular Mrs. Marcia Schwartz, whose assistance made my work easier. I cannot forgo thanking the entire staff of the Mendel Gottesman Library and Mrs. Ceil Levinson of the Yeshiva College Dean's Office, without whose supererogatory commitment over many years it would have been impossible to combine writing and editing for publication with my primary responsibilities as a *mehanekh*. The Steering Committee of the Orthodox Forum has been, for me, the very model of collegial academic work, with special mention this time going to Dr. Judith Bleich and Dr. David Shatz.

****

It has been my great good fortune to have studied with outstanding mentors and to be blessed with wonderful friends and students. The participation of my revered teacher, Rabbi Aharon Lichtenstein *shlita*, was for me, and for his other students, a highlight of the conference; many of us sensed the almost palpable influence of his teacher and ours, *maran ha-Rav* Joseph Soloveitchik *zt"l*, on our deliberations. Yet it is a special joy to mention my friends and students, who have sustained and inspired me, both spiritually and intellectually, throughout my career. Rabbi Joseph Wanefsky commented trenchantly on matters of which he has specialized knowledge, as did Rabbi Moshe Wohlgelernter. Several former students attended the forum, including Rabbi Nathaniel Helfgot, Rabbi Benjamin Samuels, Rabbi Alan Stadtmauer, and Dr. Jerry Zeitchik; the involvement of Rabbi Yitzchak Blau, Rabbi Mark Gottlieb, and Rabbi Kenneth Waxman extended far beyond their participation in the sessions. Members of the younger generation whose remarks substantially enhanced this book include Rabbi Yaakov Blau, Uri Etigson, Asher Friedman, Dovid Gottlieb, and Aaron Liebman. At the risk of omitting names, let me mention others with whom I have had valuable discussions bearing on the content of this volume: Erica Brown, Judah Dardik, Rabbi Emanuel Feldman, Rabbi Adam Ferziger, Elisha Goldberg, Dr. Roald Hoffmann, Dr. Mark Kirschbaum, Rachel Leiser, Rabbi Jeffrey Sacks, Meir Soloveichik, and Bernard Stahl. Seth Farber and Chaim Motzen helped with some of the editorial responsibilities. Last but not least, my gratitude for many searching conversations with Rabbi Yamin and Dvora Levy: it seems fitting that most of the first chapter was written in their home.[2]

This book is intended to commemorate and to perpetuate aspects of the legacy of my maternal grandparents. My grandfather, who was in the United States for two extended periods, despaired of the future of God-fearing Judaism in this country and returned home. My grandmother, by contrast, with a keen awareness of the circumstances facing Polish Jews, urged her children to get out. Her last reported conversation took place during the transport to Plaszow and was devoted to persuading a young man that his only chance to survive, slim as it might be, was to abandon the old people and run away.[3] Working on the questions that

---

[2]See also Yamin Levy, *Confronting the Death of a Baby* (Hoboken, N.J., 1998).

[3]My cousin Jonathan Feldstein has heard the story from the successful escapee, Mr. Bernard Schanzer.

are central to this book, I have time and again wondered what my grandparents would have made of it and of the long and winding road that has led me to that veritable oxymoron of the late twentieth century, an American *mekom* Torah.

Elsewhere in this book I stated, in the name of Rav Kook, that an act of construction is deemed valuable in itself, even when it does not produce an object more valuable than what is being replaced. The world of my grandparents was destroyed. The uncompromising quest for a life of integrity, a life governed by the love of God and the love of Torah, continues, wherever their spiritual and physical descendants engage in acts of construction. The dedication of this volume is thus not only a monument to the past, it is also a commitment to the future.

Shalom Carmy
17 Tammuz 5757

1

The Long and Winding Road: By Way of Introduction

Shalom Carmy

In the waning years of the twentieth century, the most profound and fateful division separates the religion of reality from the religion of comfort. The distance is that between devotion to a religious teaching because one assents to its truth and is committed to the realization of its ideals and the view that religion is to reliably fulfill our demands; it is supposed to "work for us" or "work for me," as the requirement might be. It is the distance between experiencing the encounter with God, first and foremost, as the infinite demand that we bring our lives into conformity with His will and involvement in religion as if it were one more brand of therapy, a convenient weapon in the service of our endless desire to have favorable feelings about ourselves. To

1

borrow the vernacular of America's civil faith, we must choose between believing in God and believing in Santa Claus.

Cicero spoke for the Stoic comforters, who see it as their duty "to do away with distress root and branch, or allay it, or diminish it as far as possible, or stop its progress and not allow it to extend further, or to divert it elsewhere,"[1] equipped with a variety of philosophical diversions, chief among which is an insistence on the insignificance of this world and its happenings. Many devout people deny or minimize evil, thus adopting the God's-eye perspective of redeemed eternity as if the ultimate reconciliation already had been achieved. And where the sentiments of piety are attenuated and religion has become a pleasant avocation, even as the consolations of mere human reasoning have lost their ancient power to persuade, well-worn words yet might furnish the weary with a tender-minded bubble of metaphysical elevator music, a therapeutic haven amid the harshness of human reality and what we have made of it.

Judaism is not a tender-minded religion. Therefore Ramban scorns the Stoic mentality of the generic "Greek philosophers" and their followers, for they "provide empty joy and miserable consolation, denying the future and despairing of the past."[2] Prolonged, undisciplined indulgence in sorrow is, of course, rejected by Halakha: it is incompatible with our belief in the omnipotence and benevolence of God. Yet are we required, in the name of simple theological and moral honesty, to take the evils of this world

---

[1]Cicero, *Tusculan Disputations* III, 75 (trans. J. E. King, Harvard [Loeb Classical Library], 1950, 315f). See also Seneca, *To Marcia on Consolation* II–III (in Seneca, *Moral Essays,* trans. J. W. Basore, Harvard [Loeb Classical Library], 1951).

[2]Ramban, "Preface to *Torat haAdam,*" in *Kitve Ramban,* ed. Chavel (Jerusalem, 1964), I, 14.

seriously, to mourn when sorrow is called for and rejoice in moments of joy.[3] It is simple honesty to acknowledge the ineluctable element of sadness in our lives, even in happy lives, and in the lives of others. It is simple honesty to remember that misfortune sometimes threatens to crush the human being.[4] Nor can we be insensible of the experience of estrangement that may pass between man and God: at times terribly incomprehensible; and when comprehension strikes, even more terrible in accusation.

Simple psychological honesty also compels the frank recognition of our own "natural consciousness" and its legitimate role in religious experience.[5] We stand in relation to God, not only when we are confronted by His Truth, but also when we seek Him in the quest for self-fulfillment and, yes, in our hopes for ordinary human happiness. Indeed, men and women who have chosen truth over happiness frequently get both, while those whose preferences are reversed often end up with neither. Yet simple moral honesty tells us that we stand in relation to God, not only when we are pleased to do so, but also when we would rather not.

---

[3]See Rambam, *Hil. Avel* 13:11–12 and Ramban to Deut. 14:1, where he strikes a more otherworldly note than in the passage quoted.

[4]Recall, for example, the scene in which the narrator of Conrad's *Under Western Eyes* witnesses the "motionless dumb" desolation of Mrs. Haldin, whose world has been shattered by Razumov's confession that her dead son was betrayed by one regarded as a trusted friend. He observes: "There was nothing absurd in that cry, no exaggeration of sentiment." That judgment, with its implied suspicion of exaggerated grief subordinated to the recognition that there are situations to which undiluted distress is the only honest response, captures something of the ethical and psychological reality I am trying to describe. (Joseph Conrad, *Under Western Eyes* [New York, 1925] 324.)

[5]The term *ha-vaya tiv'it* and the idea derive from Rabbi Soloveitchik's *U-Vikkashtem miSham*.

Nowadays there is a tendency, common even among the Orthodox and rife among others, to reduce Jewish religiosity to external behavior and vague emotion. As far back as 1937 Germany, Rabbi Alexander Altmann argued for the necessity of Jewish dogma rooted in authentic religious experience. While the nostalgic aspect in his depiction of the past is open to debate, his statement about the general duty of theology and its relation to Jewish practice is one that can well-define the specific task of this volume:

> At best, theological concepts are enjoyed as edifying homiletics, but they are no longer understood or carried further in disciplined thought. To be sure, Halakha is the cornerstone of Jewish existence. . . . But Judaism, too, is more than law. The law itself needs the religious conception of the world so that, based on it, it can be practiced organically. We lack this religious conception of the world. We had it once, but we have lost it. Philosophy of religion, kabbala, and Hasidism are systems of thought that supported the law. We need the dogma, but it can be created only by the power of *emunah.* We need a genuine Jewish piety, a deep re-rooting in the soil of *emunah* in order to speak a legitimate Jewish word and to be able to confront the diverse problems of the Jewish present. Is there a way?[6]

* * *

One of the advantages and pleasures of taking part in the Orthodox Forum is the opportunity to benefit from the criticisms and insights of other participants. Ordinarily these remarks are incorporated into the final text. In the case of the present publication, several of the questions raised

---

[6]Alexander Altmann, "Are There Dogmas in Judaism?" in *The Meaning of Jewish Existence: Theological Essays 1930–1939*, ed. A. Ivry and trans. E. and L. Ehrlich (Brandeis, 1991), 111.

during and after the conference demand further elaboration. I deem it worthwhile to devote attention to some of these key points, if only to show the need for further reflection in the spirit of this book and the directions such work might take.

Meaning and Ambiguity

Several of the papers state or imply that human beings suffer without knowing why. Suffering, according to Halakha, precipitates the obligation of repentance and regeneration, but it does not unambiguously indicate where we stand in relation to God, whether the suffering is to be construed as punishment, as the absence of special providence, or in terms of the many other categories discussed throughout the book. The objection is that uncertainty makes repentance impossible: you can't repent unless told exactly what, if anything, you have done wrong. It is as if you wished to compensate the victim of an injury without knowing the nature of the injury or the address of the wronged party, or to treat a disease in ignorance of its etiology and character.

Like many analogies, this one betrays misleading assumptions. Thinking of the repentance owed God along the lines of tort law or medical cause and effect omits the crucial dimension of our relationship to God: its *personal* quality. As God, in His wisdom, has called upon us to formulate our relationship to Him as one between persons, human relations might offer a more appropriate model.

Imagine that I come to the reasonable belief that my closest friendship inexplicably has cooled. The first step is self-examination. Have I done something to hurt the other person? Can I surmise what it is? Have we simply grown apart without any specific offense on my part? In the final analysis, I am uncertain as to the cause of the estrangement.

Moreover, it would be presumptuous of me to be confident
that another person's heart is transparent to me. Yet—and
this is the important point—I need not be paralyzed by the
uncertainty. The deeper my probing of the relationship as
it was, as it is, and as I would want it to be, the more capable I am of a subtle and realistic response that takes into
account the ambiguous aspects of the situation. In order
to "renew our days as of old," I must express remorse at
what has been ill-done or not done, appreciate the value
of the friendship, show sorrow about the present state of
affairs, and so forth. My purpose is less to classify and weigh
possible causes of estrangement than to penetrate the meaning of a relationship and to animate its substance. Even
when I have the opportunity to confront my friend and
thoroughly clear the air, much will be left in the shadows.
The deepest and most dynamic reconciliation is achieved
only in the future that remains unfinished and undefined.

What is true of our significant connections to other human beings is pertinent to the God-relationship as well. God
reveals and conceals Himself at one and the same time. The
belief that our situation before God can be comprehended
and pinned down diminishes Him, and by interpreting a
living relationship in static categories, we diminish ourselves
as well. Whether we are standing before God in prayer,
seeking to plumb the depths of our needs and aspirations
in the light of his will for us, crying out our dependence
on his providence, expressing gratitude and praise, or confronting incomprehensible pain and the frustration of our
desires, we never can reduce our experience of God to a
transparent formula. Ambiguity, the dialectic of divine ac-
cessibility and hiddenness, is not an impediment to the
quest for God. On the contrary, it is a mark of the complexity and profundity that distinguishes confrontation with
God from comforting but ultimately empty gestures, that
separates genuine religious experience from intellectual and

emotional sterility.[7] While this emphasis on the complexity of religious life is apparently disquieting to some individuals, I believe that this account is closer to the concrete experience of prayerful, repentant human beings, including the experience of those religious individuals whom the idea troubles.

"He Was With Us"

The comforting, yet unsettling, reality of our existence before God characterizes the experience of the religious individual who senses God's presence in the midst of suffering. Rabbi Lichtenstein writes:

> A neighbor of ours, Leib Rochman, who had lived through the Holocaust and had written about it, was once asked by a pseudo-philosopher guest where the *Ribbono shel Olam* had been at the time. Looking her straight in the eye, he responded calmly [in Yiddish], "He was with us." And, as he repeated the story, one sensed how much awareness of that presence had sustained him.

To this way of thinking, it was objected that speaking of divine sympathy with human suffering is philosophically egregious, insofar as it ascribes human pathos to God, and dangerously reminiscent of Christian notions.[8] Rav Lichtenstein's excursus grapples with the question of how

---

[7] I have discussed this aspect of the religious life with special attention to prayer in "Destiny, Freedom and the Logic of Petition" (*Festschrift* for Rabbi Walter Wurzburger, *Tradition* 1989), 17–37.

[8] The discounting of Jewish thinkers who are "soft on anthropopathism" on the grounds of Christian affinity is old hat in modern Jewish thought. See the scathing chapter on A. J. Heschel in Eliezer Berkovits, *Major Themes in Modern Philosophies of Judaism* (New York, 1974), and my partial defense of Heschel in "Modern Jewish Philosophy: Fossil or Ferment" (*Tradition* 15:3, Fall 1975, 140–152), 147–151.

we can speak of divine involvement in our pain and sorrow, in line with biblical and rabbinic formulations, despite
the problems raised by medieval rationalist philosophy. His
discussion is instructive and inspiring in its effort to balance
conflicting textual and experiential data, striving to do justice to each factor without avoiding the responsibility of
choice, which condemns us to misrepresent, as is inevitable
with fallible man, the infinite Truth. In a more technical
vein, let me add the following considerations, which might
be of significance:[9]

The problem of ascribing human feelings to God is not
the most pressing one in formulating an account of human
experience. After all, the same question comes up with
respect to all anthropopathism, not only to suffering. The
Torah invites us to use personalistic language to describe
God's relationship with us, and while the problems raised
by such language deserve philosophical attention, we need
not bring religious existence to a halt while we wait for the
philosophers to come up with airtight theories to explain
this linguistic practice.[10] If there is an insurmountable difficulty here, it must be specifically connected to the idea
of divine *sympathy.*

The difficulty is often based on the intuition that sympathy entails suffering: to sympathize with a person suffering from headache, it is necessary to have headache oneself or some experience sufficiently like having headache.[11]

---

[9]This section was written before I received the final version of Rav
Lichtenstein's essay. Despite a reluctance to repeat points that he makes
with greater precision and eloquence, I have retained most of my comments.

[10]Cf. Rav Soloveitchik's *U-Vikkashtem miSham,* note 2.

[11]See Max Scheler, *The Nature of Sympathy,* for such a notion. The
difficulties attendant upon any attempt to identify the feelings of one

The intuition is fallacious. To be sure, it might be difficult for a human being to sympathize with someone without having access to his experience. From this perspective, for example, a young, healthy doctor might be unable to respond to an older patient until he shares the patient's limitations. But this is a consequence of the doctor's ignorance, not the ontological structure of sympathy. A man suffering headache may be singularly unsympathetic to other sufferers, if only because he is wrapped up in his own misery. More often than not it is the wholesome individual who can more readily extend sympathy to others. Suffering, then, is not a necessary condition of sympathy, and its contingent role in spurring sympathy is a function of human limitations, irrelevant to the divine.[12]

Classical forms of christology indeed require divine suffering because atonement for human sin can be accomplished only through the suffering of the Second Person in the Trinity. The Jewish idea of *Immo anokhi be-tzara* (I am with him in distress, Ps. 91:15) means that God offers man companionship and sympathy. It does not require God to suffer.

Yet the Rabbis of the Mishna, who, as Rav Lichtenstein remarked, are presumably above suspicion of crypto-Christianity, did not repine from ascribing suffering to God. *Sanhedrin* 6:5, for example, depicts the Shekinah's partici-

---

person with those of another have been notorious at least since Wittgenstein's comments on "private language" in his *Philosophical Investigations*. They hardly need to be rehearsed here.

[12]It is a commonplace of pastoral psychology that suffering and sympathy frequently are connected for another reason: because the person extending sympathy is more credible to the sufferer if he or she is speaking from personal experience. This, too, is a contingent relation and is not pertinent to divine sympathy.

pation in man's pain.[13] Whoever insists on rejecting the possibility of divine suffering would have to take such language as a metaphor for divine sympathy. Either Hazal were not afraid that Jews would go too far with a literal reading of the image, or they were willing to take the risk for the sake of a more vivid articulation of God's presence.[14]

There is another set of spiritual obstacles that prevent us from relying on the comforting power of divine companionship when we experience distress. We are not always aware of God's nearness to us and solicitude for us. Sometimes, as Job, Lamentations, and many Psalms remind us, the God-fearing person feels abandoned by God. And in moments of loneliness and desolation, the individual is tempted to wonder if all thoughts of God's concern are not fantasy and self-deception. If, as Iris Murdoch once wrote, "Almost anything that consoles us is a fake,"[15] then it often will be the most intense spirits whose distrust of that which promises to console obliterates, for them, the crucial distinction between "anything" and "almost anything." Frequently the seductiveness of the popular Nietzschean dictum, "What does not destroy me makes me stronger," leads us to value suffering and to disdain, without further probing, that which would disclose a horizon beyond unrelieved misery. Hence, too, the perennial attraction of the literary hero who is stripped of every vestige of dignity, the Job or the Lear whose suffering is naked, as it were, without the

---

[13]On the text of the Mishnah, particularly the word "Shekinah," see E. E. Urbach, *Hazal* (Jerusalem, 1969), 50 n. 94.

[14]With respect to the talmudic statement about God weeping (*Hagiga* 5b), see Polen's essay and add to it Rav Kook, *Orot hakodesh* III (Jerusalem, 1964), 105 and 243.

[15]*The Sovereignty of Good* (London, 1970), 59, quoted by Vincent Brümmer, "Can a theodicy console?" in *Speaking of a Personal God* (Cambridge University, 1992), 128–51 and 148.

protective padding of worldly diversion, unanesthetized even for an hour by sedative illusion, and when the theme is taken to its limit, bereft even of the attention of God.[16] There are terrible moments when even the individual who firmly believes in the majesty and benevolence of God despairs of the hope that God's benevolence may extend to him or to her. Although simple honesty knows that neither despair nor hope hold sway over reality, the hard-boiled exterior of despair may glitter with a dark verisimilitude that initially obscures the calm, persistent truth of men and women such as Leib Rochman.

No formula or technique can reliably assure the sufferer of God's authentic presence in his or her pain. Individuals who know this presence in their own lives generally do not pontificate about it: Leib Rochman's testimony was not spontaneous; it was elicited only by the pseudo-intellectual's provocation. What is required—and this is a worthy subject for further study—is a greater affinity for the virtues and the way of life that make the human being worthy of God's presence. The Talmud, for example, interpreting Isa. 57:15,

---

[16]Within a traditional religious framework, the desire to be tested by God reflects a similar hunger for the strenuous, unpadded life. Rabbi Moshe Eisemann's essay, "Looking Through the Frosted Window: When Things are Hard to See and Understand—Some Reflections Upon Chronic Pain" (*Tradition* 31:1, Fall 1996, 11–21), concludes with a consideration of the paradox that the Jew prays not to be put to the trial yet identifies with David's request that God test him (Ps. 26:1). His eloquent answer, deriving from a discourse of R. Hutner, is that "one who loves God would want to demonstrate his loyalty by plunging into the fray. But that urge must be tempered by a sober awareness of what failure would mean. . . . We do not seek to expose ourselves to battle since we are afraid of failure, but we will not shrink from it when we are called. We crave the heady sense of service loyally performed." R. Hutner's discussion is presumably the one published in *Pahad Yitzhak, Rosh haShana* (Brooklyn, 1986), ch. 7.

teaches that God is with "the lowly and humble of spirit" (*dakka u-shefal ruah*). One *Amora* holds that the lowly dwell with God, and another that God dwells with the lowly. The Talmud is inclined to the latter view, for God descended to Mount Sinai rather than elevating the mountain.[17]

When the Wicked Prosper

Professor David Berger has noted the virtual absence of attention, in the essays comprising this book, to the problem that the success of the wicked poses to the religious believer. The Bible, rabbinic thought, and the standard medieval philosophical literature are concerned with the prosperity of the wicked, as well as the suffering of the righteous. The traditional agenda of theodicy, the justification of God's governance of the world, must confront both challenges. If anything, as many Jewish thinkers have acknowledged, the flourishing of the wicked is harder to explain than the tribulations of the good, for it is far more likely that the public saint is secretly corrupt than that the outwardly vicious deserves his good fortune by virtue of his concealed life.[18]

One partial answer is that the authors have gravitated naturally, whether consciously or unconsciously, toward strands of Jewish thought that place less emphasis on the calculus of justice and more on the quest, by the devout individual or the community, to discover meaning in their

---

[17]*Sota* 5a. Maharal, in his commentary *ad. loc.*, explains why the second opinion is superior to the first. When God descends to the human situation, he is making himself available according to the human being's capacity (*ke-fi koho*).

[18]For representative examples, see R. Yosef Albo, *Sefer haIkkarim* 4:7; Ramban, "Rosh haShana Sermon" (in *Kitvei Ramban* I), 224–5; *Torat haAdam* II, 275; and Commentary on Job 11:1 (I 52).

suffering. The success of the flagrant evildoer is thus peripheral to their spiritual endeavor. Surely the Rambam casts a giant shadow, even where his views are controversial, and his philosophy is centered on the nature of divine providence as it pertains to human individuals rather than on considerations of fairness. Rav Soloveitchik's influential articulation, with its emphasis on man's creative response to suffering, reflects the Maimonidean derogation of "forensic theodicy" (as the traditional argument is called in my essay below).[19]

This may be correct, as far as it goes, but it does not fully reflect the importance of the demand for justice in normative Jewish sources, the sheer sense of outrage expressed by psalmists and prophets when they contemplate the wicked triumphant. Hence, the displacement of this impulse in the present volume requires further explanation and, in the name of theological integrity, the outline of a corrective.

To begin with, it is not at all clear whether—and how—bringing the wicked to bay improves the situation of decent people. When I am consoled with the assertion that a vicious individual who has attempted to harm me or those I care about is much more miserable than his victims, my instinctive response is that I would not begrudge his happiness, that I would positively rejoice in it, if that kept him

---

[19]Ramban (Nahmanides) (*Torat haAdam* 282–283) explains Rambam's (Maimonides') neglect of the flourishing wicked problem with the suggestion that divine loving kindness (*hesed*) requires less explanation than divine rigor. While this interpretation locates a significant presupposition for a theodicy in the spirit of the Maimonidean approach, I would venture to say that Rambam's entire system is less rooted in the primacy of *hesed* than in a conception of spiritual excellence that is, in a sense, beyond consideration of either mercy or severity.

out of my way. Is it the least comfort to anyone in our family that by the time my grandparents were murdered, Hitler, who would not survive them for long, was already a physical and mental wreck?

The desire to see the books balanced, and the frequently allied desire for vengeance, often go rancid. "More substance in our enmities/Than in our love"[20] makes for felicity neither in this world nor in the next. Retributive rage can blot out other legitimate moral feelings; revenge is liable to violate proportionality. Too much of what the contemporary world recognizes as moral energy is more destructive than upbuilding. Too much of what passes for moral passion owes its motivational force and its very substance to envy and *schadenfreude*, a lust and fury bespeaking spiritual passivity and lack of creative resources.[21] Retribution and revenge have gotten a bad name, and not without reason. Consequently it is not surprising that normative theodicy will find little use in discussing the fate of the wicked and that contemporary religious psychology will avert its eyes from examining our feelings and judgments in this area.[22]

----

[20]W. B. Yeats, "Meditations in Time of Civil War," VI.

[21]Among the many biblical texts that highlight the success of the wicked, Ps. 37 is distinctive in taking as a point of departure the envy or jealousy to which the righteous is tempted.

[22]Do not misunderstand. I do not mean to exclude retribution, or even revenge, from the realm of moral feelings. Judaism endorses the justification of punishment as retribution. While Halakha sharply circumscribes the legitimacy of revenge, there is a place for it in Jewish moral psychology. For purposes of such an analysis, revenge is defined as "taking retribution personally." I hope to elaborate on this concept, its significance and halakhic basis, in future writing. The need for such analysis is all the greater in view of the conspicuous dangers with which I am concerned in the present context. The modern and post-modern critique of retribution and revenge can be found in the work of

How can one properly confront the existential offense presented by the flourishing of the wicked and the psychological challenge posed by the potential perversions of the feelings aroused by the vision of evil rampant? Part of the difficulty, it seems to me, stems from the fact that revenge, by its very nature, entails "taking evil personally," regarding it as a personal affront: consider the difference between the appropriate attitude of an officer of the law tracking down a criminal and the reaction of the murder victim's family. That very personalization, which is inherently a healthy moral phenomenon, opens the door to excess and to an obsession that leaves no room for growth in other directions, certainly with regard to revenge and likewise with regard to the other justice-hungry feelings. The solution, which is perhaps easier formulated than realized, is to separate the *content* of our desire to balance the books (which, as just noted, embraces personalization) from the *motivation* of that desire, which must be emancipated from the impulse to destroy. For the saintly, the destruction of evil can be valued only as an element in the inauguration of a redemptive divine order, not as "some autumn night of delations and noyades when the unrepentant thieves . . . are sequestered and those he hates shall hate themselves instead."[23]

Perhaps it is in order to secure the proper framework for the justice-hungry feelings that satisfaction at the downfall of the wicked must come *after* their menace has been lifted. The major crises of biblical history, the Vilna Gaon

---

Nietzsche (e.g., *Genealogy of Morals*) and Foucault (*Discipline and Punish*, among other texts). A neutral, analytic treatment of revenge, including features not relevant to this note, is developed by Robert Nozick, *Philosophical Explanations* (Harvard, 1981), 366ff.

[23]W. H. Auden, "Vespers," in *Selected Poetry* (New York, 1958), 169–170.

observes, exhibit a two-step structure: first Israel is rescued from Egyptian bondage, but the time for praise is after God avenges Himself on the Egyptians at the sea.[24] However that might be, these aspects of our response to evil go far beyond the issues usually raised in the context of theodicy and deserve more sustained treatment than is possible here.

The Nightmare of History

Our title—*Jewish Perspectives on the Experience of Suffering*—highlights the emphasis on the experiential dimension as contrasted to the speculative. Nowhere is this more the case than in our treatment of the Holocaust: both Polen and Eliach report on the thinking and living that took place within the fiery furnace. Other aspects of Holocaust theology have entered the book only indirectly. Of course this allocation of space reflects the experiential orientation of the book. That the Holocaust precipitates something signifi-

---

[24]Gra, commentary to Prov. 11:10. He also discusses Purim in a similar vein. Yitzchak Blau has brought to my attention a discourse of R. Yehezkel Levenstein, *mashgiach ruhani* at Mir and Ponivezh, printed in his *Or Yehezkel* vol. 4, *Middot* (Bnei Brak, 5748). R. Yehezkel sharply chastizes Jews, including elements in his own community, for joining uncritically in the jubilation that accompanied the capture and trial of Adolf Eichmann. The gratification, in his opinion, was motivated not by joy at the realization of divine judgment, but by pleasure at the triumph of Jewish power. A genuine desire for the vindication of the divine, he maintains, would not make so much of the distinction between one murder and six million. Nor could it coincide with a routine contempt (*zilzul*) toward non-Jews and with an indifference bordering on satisfaction when non-Jews suffer natural calamities such as earthquakes. Truly religious Jews, hearing of such disasters, naturally would turn to self-examination rather than glee. One wonders how vigorously the yeshiva world inculcates this view of humanity, or even tries to. R. Yehezkel's teaching, in any event, clearly illuminates the gap between prevalent attitudes and the sense of revenge that Judaism would endorse.

cantly new at the purely philosophical level has been contended furiously, though without much success, so far as I can see. But as is commonly the case with philosophical argument, the presuppositions and motives of the participants are more important than the results professed; they deserve lengthier discussion than space limitations permit. What is beyond any doubt, however, is that for most thoughtful Jews and many non-Jews, the memory of these events is a never-ceasing source of horror and anguish and perplexity, and it is these vivid experiences that constitute an essential part of the book.

Having recognized this, it was argued at the conference that awareness of the Holocaust should have pervaded all the papers precisely because of the experiential orientation of the project. For what is more experiential than history? And how can any discussion claim to be rooted in reality when it brackets the greatest catastrophe to affect the Jewish people in our time, a catastrophe that shook and may have shattered the foundations of Western culture? Will it really suffice to say that real life, like academic study, is divided into distinct compartments and that the destruction of European Jewry, though many of us think of it daily, is not—and need not be—omnipresent in our consciousness?

As presented in the last paragraph, the argument presupposes that the only way an historical event can affect the theological awareness is when that event becomes the direct, conscious basis of reflection. This is demonstrably untrue. Significant historical experiences make their most momentous contribution to the shaping of Jewish thought precisely when the response to the event is grafted onto theological grappling with perennial questions. Let us take responses to the destruction of the Temple and the Hadrianic persecutions as a model. The reader of tannaitic literature who has not boned up on dates will miss the context of many statements that have no overt connection to the *hurban* and might well conclude that the most devastating event in Jewish history had little echo in Jewish thought. Yet commentators and scholars have plausibly made the connections and demonstrated the manifold ways in which halakhic analysis and *aggadic* formulations expressed such responses. The greatest testimony to the impact of the *hurban* on our thinking is its presence in the background of seemingly unrelated discussions on perennial topics such as atonement or the status of the Jewish people.[25] It is too early to judge how much the events of our century—the Holocaust, the establishment of a Jewish state, the breakdown of western culture, have permanently affected the shape of our world outlook. This is true even with respect to a thinker like Rav Soloveitchik, whose major pronouncement on theodicy (*Kol Dodi Dofek*) alludes explicitly to the Holocaust.

* * *

Every age has its blindspots, and every thinker is vulnerable to his or her special absurdities. In eighteenth-century Britain, for example, many intellectuals subscribed to the celebrated "great chain of being" doctrine, which they regarded as the primary solution to the problem of evil. According to this view, God necessarily maximizes the varie-

---

[25]See, for example, Urbach, *Hazal*, ch. 15 (on suffering and atonement) and ch. 16 (on the election of Israel). I have not gone into detail because the validity of my point about the interaction of history and theology does not require the endorsement of any particular proposal. Some hypotheses that enjoyed great popularity in their time no longer hold sway: e.g., Scholem's interpretation of Lurianic Kabbala as a reaction to the Spanish expulsion, which Idel has challenged. See the overview by Robert Alter, "Jewish Mysticism in Dispute," *Commentary* (September 1989), 53–59.

ties of being in the world, and the realization of variety justifies the evil that necessarily results.[26] One version of the doctrine, having filled out the chain of being by hypothesizing orders of being superior to man, suggests that human suffering might provide intellectual amusement for these superior beings. In Samuel Johnson's parody of this view:

> As we drown whelps and kittens, they amuse themselves, now and then, with sinking a ship. . . . Some of them, perhaps, are virtuosi, and delight in the operations of an asthma, as a human philosopher in the effects of the air-pump. . . . As they are wiser and more powerful than we, they have more exquisite diversions; for we have no way of procuring any sport so brisk and so lasting, as the paroxysms of the gout and the stone, which, undoubtedly must make high mirth, especially if the play be a little diversified with the blunders and puzzles of the blind and deaf. . .[27]

But Johnson does not stop here, and his next sally makes required reading for anyone dealing with the questions raised in this book:

> One sport the merry malice of these beings has found means of enjoying, to which we have nothing equal or similar. They now and then catch a mortal, proud of his parts, and flattered either by the submission of those who court his kindness, or the notice of those who suffer him to court theirs. A head, thus prepared for the reception of false opinions, and the projection of vain designs, they easily fill with idle notions, till, in time, they make their plaything an author; their first diversion commonly begins with an ode or an epistle, then rises, perhaps, to a political irony, and is, at last, brought to its

---

[26]The classic history of this idea is A. O. Lovejoy, *The Great Chain of Being.* On the eighteenth century, see ch. 6–7 (183–226).

[27]Johnson, 240–1.

height, by a treatise of philosophy. Then begins the poor animal to entangle himself in sophisms, and flounder in absurdity, to talk confidently of the scale of being, and to give solutions which himself confesses impossible to be understood. Sometimes, however, it happens, that their pleasure is without much mischief. The author feels no pain, but while they are pointing him out to one another, as a new example of human folly, he is enjoying his own applause and that of his companions, and, perhaps, is elevated with the hope of standing at the head of a new sect.[28]

In preparing this volume I repeatedly have taken inspiration from this passage. Reality defies our impulse for comfort, not only because wishful thinking and sham sentiment taint that impulse, but also because truth ever will exceed the ambitions of speculation. If simple human honesty invariably detects a note of the ridiculous in the earnest striving to comprehend that which is hidden from learning and from ignorance alike, then it is good that Providence has instilled in us the capacity to be amused at our own folly. This, too, belongs to the humble religion of reality.

---

[28]241–2.

2

The Duties of the Heart and Response to Suffering

Aharon Lichtenstein

Give or take, in Hazal's chronology,[1] a few hours, the history of suffering is coeval with man himself. From the wrenching anguish primordially attendant upon the bitterest of bites to the immediately present distress of millions, human existence has been fraught with pain, sorrow, frustration—with no end, until the millenium, in sight.

That history has borne a dual aspect. Primarily, it is, of course, an existential reality. Secondarily, however, it is a philosophic issue. As such, it has germinated differently in varied traditions. In the world of general thought, it has been, with moral and psychological elements interlaced, a

---

[1]See *Sanhedrin* 38.

21

major crux of ethics. Obviously, however, within the religious orbit, it has assumed additional dimensions. For many, foremost among these has been the attempt to understand and explain suffering as a metaphysical phenomenon—particularly, its reconciliation with faith in omniscient, omnipotent, and beneficent God. This concern has spawned the genre of theodicy, familiarly associated in Western literature with a number of major works—Aeschylus's *Prometheus Bound*, Boethius's *De Consolatione Philosophiae*, Milton's *Paradise Lost*, Leibniz's *Essais de Theodicée*, Pope's *Essay on Man*, and Tennyson's *In Memoriam*, to cite just a few— but it obviously pervades so much else.

Not surprisingly, that concern has found expression within *yahadut*. In the Bible, *kitvei ha-kodesh*, the *locus classicus* is, of course, the Book of Job. But the Ramban[2] also regarded the question as the central topic of *Kohelet*, in his homiletic discourse upon that *sefer*, he listed other relevant scriptural texts. Hazal, for their part, ascribed concern with the issue to Moshe Rabbenu, asserting that this was the thrust of the plea petitioned after the episode of the golden calf:

> "Show me now Thy ways (Shmot 33:13)." Mosheh said before Him: Lord of the Universe, why is it that some righteous men prosper and others are in adversity, some wicked men prosper and others are in adversity.[3]

And Hazal themselves confronted the question in typically scattered anecdotes and epigrams.

Nevertheless, I presume we are inclined to acknowledge the justice of the generalization enunciated by the Rav, zt"l,

---

[2]See his "Sermon on Kohelet," in *Kitvei Ramban*, ed. C. Chavel (Jerusalem, 1963), 1:193–199.

[3]*Berakhot* 7a.

that Judaism has not confronted suffering primarily as a speculative matter. Rather, it has related to it as an existential and experiential reality, to be dealt with pragmatically and normatively. Response, not explanation, is focal. Its message, in sum, is: "Don't waste your passional experiences; utilize them; exploit them; let every passional experience become a point of departure for a higher and nobler life." [4]

It is against this background that the question put to me—"How the classic *hovot ha-levavot*, the duties of the heart (repentance, prayer, fasting, etc.) can/should affect our response to suffering, evil and disaster"—should be considered. It is, in one sense, not a single question but an entire phalanx: the product, crudely stated, of the multiple of the *hovot* by the varieties of calamity, doubled to encompass both the "can" and the "should." And yet there is a specific issue to be discussed, with respect to the full gamut. Read literally, the formulation evidently rests upon an implicit assumption. That *hovot ha-levavot*—presumably, *qua hovot*—indeed can/should have an impact upon our response to calamity is taken for granted. What remains to be analyzed is the modality.

I must confess, however, that I find this proposition far from self-evident. That a Jewish response to suffering both

---

[4] The citation is from a summary remark made at the conclusion of a discussion following his lecture on "Mental Health and Halakha," at a symposium of the NIMH, 1961. In the opening section of Kol Dodi Dofek, the Rav relates this theme to the distinction between the covenant of fate (*goral*) and that of destiny (*yeud*) and their respective responses to suffering. Of the latter, he writes: "His approach is halakhic—moral—and is lacking any metaphysical—speculative—note." (*Divrei Hagut ve-Haarakha*, Jerusalem, 1982, 12). As a summary of the attitude of *Yahadut* in general, however, this strikes me as overly sweeping.

can and ought to include elements such as prayer and fasting goes without saying. But to what extent, if any, is their inclusion grounded upon their normative aspect? Most *rishonim* held that, as an obligation, the mitzvah of *tefilla* (prayer) only has *d'rabbanan* status, probably even in times of distress.[5] *Ta'anit*, likewise, is designated as such by the Rambam: "From Rabbinic tradition one must fast for every calamity that befalls the community till Heaven brings compassion."[6] By contrast, *teshuva* (repentance) is patently mandated *mi'd'oraita*. Should our response to the question confronting us severally, with regard to these mitzvoth therefore be significantly different respectively? Further, none of these is mandatory for a non-Jew. Would we consequently formulate for a Muslim or a Christian inquirer an answer very much at variance with what we develop for ourselves?

I am, of course, fully mindful of the weight Hazal assigned to the normative character of a spiritual datum. We are all familiar with the Gemara which, after initially presenting the popular view that freely willed voluntary action is more meritorious than its required counterpart, concludes by citing Rav Hanina's contrary position that "greater is the reward of those who being enjoined do [good deeds] than of those who without being enjoined [but merely of their own free will] do [good deeds]."[7] This view has unquestionably been accepted as definitive, being cited by *rishonim* and *poskim* in various contexts and multiple applications, ranging from the central mitzvah of Talmud Torah[8] to the minutest *d'rabbanan*.

---

[5] See *Sha'agat Aryeh*, 14; *Mishkenot Yaakov*, 90.

[6] *Ta'anyiot* 1:4.

[7] *Baba Kamma* 87a.

[8] See Rambam, *Talmud Torah* 1:13.

Nevertheless, my reservations about the significance of the normative aspect in our context remain. For one thing, to the best of my knowledge, Hazal nowhere prescribe the degree of the superiority ascribed to the *mezuvveh*, so it is difficult to determine how much weight should be assigned to this factor. Secondly, some *rishonim* apparently assumed that a mandated act was not intrinsically more meritorious *per se*. Rather, it was only deemed greater because it was likely to be accompanied by keener anxiety, growing out of concern that one has discharged one's duty properly, which, in turn, might ensure that the fulfillment meets a higher standard. As Tosafot put it: "It seems that this is the reason: one who is commanded and performs good deeds is preferred since he is more concerned [about his performance] and more cautious lest he violate the commandment, than the one who is not enjoined, who has the freedom to opt out of the performance at will."[9]

The Ritva, for his part, focuses upon the merit deriving from the need of the commanded to overcome greater resistance: "Our teachers explained the reason for this: Satan (evil inclinations) tempt him when he is commanded, but not when he is not, and according to the effort is the reward."[10] Beyond these largely subjective considerations, I believe that the obligatory element with respect to our question, even in light of the interpretation ascribed to the Ramban—"the commandments are not for God's benefit, who commanded them, but rather for our merit, and one who is commanded fulfills the decree of the King; thus his reward is much greater than that of the one who did not fulfill the decree of the King"[11]—is of little moment. The

---

[9]*Kiddushin* 31a, *s.v. gadol.*

[10]*Hiddushei haRitva, Kiddushin* 31a.

[11]*Hiddushei haRamban, Kiddushin* 31a.

impact of *tefilla* or *teshuva* upon our response to suffering derives, overwhelmingly, from their sheer existence as facets of our relation to the *Ribbono shel Olam*, from the bare fact that their respective gates have not been barred, from the access, and all that flows therefrom, to Him, that they represent. The critical element is the interrelation, at some stage and in some form, between human suffering and the presence of God. In this respect, the phenomenon of the capacity of the inner self to engage its Maker is crucial, but its duty to do so, at the level of formal mitzvot, is not.

Turning, then, to our topic in its expanded version, with respect to *havayot* (experiences) rather than *hovot ha-levavot*, I would like to open its analysis by deviating from its formulation in yet another respect. We should, I believe, address ourselves not just to response to suffering but, more extensively, to relation to it. In discriminating between various aspects, we need to discern not only different modes but distinctive phases. Response comes, logically—and, by and large, psychologically and temporally, as well—*post facto*. It constitutes, virtually by definition, an aftermath. The impact of inner religious sensibility upon the experience of suffering, however, also precedes and coincides with that suffering. It significantly might condition not only *how* the sufferer feels but *what* he feels. That sensibility is not merely an instrument of subsequent understanding and emotional response but a prism through which calamity initially is perceived and possibly refracted. Indeed, beyond perception, it is not just an observer of suffering but the epicenter of its victimized object.

Hence, contrary to the impression the itemized list of my assigned topic conveys, the impact of *hovot ha-levavot* upon our relation to suffering is not confined to those that fundamentally are conceived as addressing themselves to it. Rather, it includes more comprehensive elements that are critical to the total development of a spiritual personality and its relation to its Creator. We have been set down in the "vale of soul-making," in Keats's phrase, confronted with the challenge of molding ourselves—and this without reference to its possibly also being a vale of tears. Clearly, however, the extent to which we have discharged our task, conscientiously and creatively, will significantly affect how suffering will be received, if and when it comes. Enthralled by *ahavat Ha-Shem* (love of God), awed by *yir'at Ha-Shem* (fear of God), charged by faith (*emuna*) and suffused with trust (*bittahon*), an individual, steeled and illuminated, faces calamity quite differently from a vacuous colleague—and this, again, anterior to response, at the plane of *ab initio* experience.

The point might be readily exemplified by reference to the apex of *hovot ha-levavot*, at least in Rabbenu Bahye's view. "Whatever has been earlier stated in this work about the duties of the heart, about virtues and spiritual nobility," he writes at the opening of his concluding chapter on *ahavat Ha-Shem*, "are rungs and stages leading to this supreme object."[12] How, then, we ask ourselves, does this loftiest of *hovot* affect our response to suffering? At one plane, of course, it affects it directly. One facet of this mitzvah refers, quite specifically, to disaster—indeed, to ultimate disaster. "With all your soul—*be-khol nafshekha*," we learn from the Mishnah in Berakhot, "Even though He takes your soul [life]. 'With all that is yours [*méodkha*],' that is, whatever measure He metes out to you."[13]

In the ensuing Gemara, Rabbi Akiva is cited as the source of this *drashah*, and he also is presented as its ex-

---

[12] *Sha'ar Ahavat Hashem*, introduction; based on Ibn Tibbon's translation.

[13] *Berakhot* 54a.

emplar—"When R. Akiva was taken out for execution, it was
the hour for the recital of the Shema, and they were comb-
ing his flesh with iron combs, while he was accepting upon
himself the yoke of the kingdom of heaven. His disciples
said to him: Our teacher, even to this point? He said to
them: All my days I have been troubled by this verse, 'with
all your soul', [which I interpret] even if He takes your soul.
I said: When shall I have the opportunity of fulfilling this?
Now that I have the opportunity, shall I not fulfil it?"[14]—
with the self-evident question, "Such is Torah, and such is
its reward!?" being ascribed in the *baraita* to spectator ministering angels (*mal'akhei ha-sharet*) rather than to the
protagonist. Correspondingly, the Sifre, after citing the substance of the Mishnah, expands upon the theme: "So said
David: I will lift up the cup of salvation, and call upon the
name of the Lord. So too said Job: The Lord gave and the
Lord has taken away; Blessed be the name of the Lord." [15]

But is this direct reference the only aspect of *ahava* that
bears upon response to suffering? Halakhically, the commandment of *v'ahavta* is multifaceted. The Netziv, in a
celebrated *teshuva* concerning "rightists" and "leftists" in
yahadut, speaks of two components: "To begin with, one
should be aware that the positive commandment to love
God, which we read each day, includes two meanings and
both of them are clarified in the Rambam's rulings. The
first interpretation is that a person should commit his body,
soul and all his will to the Will of God. . . . The second
interpretation is that one should cleave in his thought and
desire to attain the Holy Spirit at the time when this was
possible, or, in any event, the higher inspiration which is

---

[14]*Ibid.* 61b.
[15]*Va'ethanan*, sec. 7; on Devarim 6:5.

the state of the enlightened [in the vernacular called *die Liebe*]."[16] However, in addition to the imperative to martyrdom and to *amor Dei intellectualis* he discerned, one could readily append at least four other elements: the constant and consuming passion, at once self-sacrificing and possessive, ascribed by the Rambam[17] to the lovesick (*holat ahava*) of Shir Hashirim; the impetus to kiddush hashem, that the Name of Heaven be sanctified because of you[18] enjoined by the Gemara in *Yoma*; contiguously, the charge of *kiruv* prescribed by the *Sifre*: "Make Him beloved to humanity, as did our father Avraham"[19]; finally—and on the Ramban's view, perhaps one should say primarily—the mandate to ground the totality of *avodat Ha-Shem* (the service of God) in love:

> The purport of love [of God] has been explained by our Rabbis, most explicitly in the Sifre: "Perhaps you will say, I will study Torah in order that I be called wise, in order that I lead an academy, in order that I live long, or in order that I merit the World to Come." Therefore Scripture says: "to love the Lord your God etc."[20]

Does anyone imagine that this complex will barely influence response to suffering? Is it conceivable that the thirsting soul, aroused by passion or contemplation, will react to catastrophe no differently from the flaccid and the placid?

---

[16]*Meshiv Davar* 1:44.

[17]See *Teshuva* 10:3.

[18]See *Yoma* 86a

[19]*Ibid.*

[20]Devarim 6:5. Cf. Nedarim 62a, and Rambam, *Teshuva* 10:1–5. The Rambam speaks of both pure moral idealism, "doing what is true because it is true," and the religious idealism grounded in the love of God. The two are not necessarily identical.

Will a loving spirit's beatific joy leave no imprint in anticipation of crisis? Can one's yearning for eternity effect no
change in one's perspective upon the temporal? Shall the
egoist and the altruist, religiously speaking, share the same
response to perhaps divinely inflicted calamity? Has consistent commitment to loving submissiveness no lasting and
pervasive effect? If one has dedicated himself to inculcat-
ing *ahavat Ha-Shem* in others—in the *Sifre*'s phrase, "like
Avraham your father"—will not his emulation of that para-
gon of love extend to how he experiences tribulation?

The answer is self-evident. Moreover, a similar set of rhetorical questions could be composed with respect to other
hovot ha-levavot. Contemplation of the created phenomenal
world, the Rambam tells us, induces not only love but reverential fear: "And when he ponders these very matters, he
will recoil with fear, and realize that he is a small creature,
lowly and obscure, endowed with slight and slender intelligence, standing in the presence of Him who is perfect in
knowledge. And so David said: When I consider Thy heavens, the work of Thy fingers (Ps. 8:4)."[21] Obviously, a sensibility imbued with consciousness of its relative vacuity will
confront disaster—particularly insofar as it is regarded as
divinely ordained—quite differently from one serenely confident of its own worth. The difference between Prometheus
and Job—even in his more rebellious moods—does not
focus upon respective arsenals of instruments specifically
geared to coping with suffering and interpreting it. It derives, rather, from how each has been religiously condi-
tioned by the totality of his spiritual experience. Or again,
the mitzvah of *devekut* (cleaving unto God)—assuming that
it does not refer exclusively to *Talmidei ha-khamim* but
relates, perhaps primarily and in accordance with the lit-

---

[21] *Yesodei haTorah* 2:2.

eral sense of the *pasuk*, to the *Ribbono shel Olam*[22]—will clearly instill, in those who seek to cleave to Him, a total relationship which will impinge upon the full range of their spiritual being.

Ahava and *yir'a* exemplify *hovot ha-levavot* that have an impact upon our response to suffering but are not primarily formulated with reference to it. Other mitzvoth, of course—certainly those that have been singled out for my analysis—*are* so formulated. This group itself might be differentiated, however. Some might be envisioned as being grounded existentially in suffering, but not as being bound with it normatively. Thus, the Torah clearly places *teshuva* within the context of crisis—not only the intrinsic crisis of sin and consequent alienation from God but the external crisis that results therefrom. In the wake of varied calamities—exile, dispersion, and bondage—physical and spiritual repentance is anticipated and demanded: "And you shall seek from there the Lord your God, and you shall find him, if you seek Him with all your heart and with all your soul. When you are in distress, and all these things have come upon you, in the latter days, if you turn to the Lord your God, and are obedient to His voice." (Devarim 4:29–30) Yet obviously the obligation to repent is not conceived halakhically as a mode of responding to tribulation, and it is not confined to the disadvantaged. Sin requires *teshuva*, and affluence or poverty, robust or failing health, are irrelevant. Some, however, might be more closely related.

---

[22]The Rambam, *De'ot* 6:2, in light of the Gemara in *Ketubot* 111b, refers only to the former: "the positive commandment to cleave unto scholars and their disciples in order to learn from their actions. However, Ibn Ezra and the Ramban interpret the *pasuk* with respect to God, with the Ramban linking the mitzvah to *ahavat ha-Shem*, which it amplifies and intensifies.

Tefilla, for instance, conceivably is mandated specifically as a result of *ba-tzar lekha* (when you are distressed) and as a response to it. Thus, the Ramban, while generally inclined to reject the Rambam's inclusion of prayer as one of the biblically mandated *taryag* mitzvoth, concludes his animadversion with the partial concession that such a duty is to be confined, if at all, to moments of crisis: "If perhaps their derivation is biblical, we will count it in the list of the Rav [Rambam], and say that it is a commandment at times of tribulation for one to believe that He, may He be blessed and exalted, hears prayer and it is He who saves us from trouble through prayer and crying out." [23]

The Rav, *zt"l*, contended on occasion that the Rambam, too, at a fundamental level, subscribed to this view. He suggested that although the Rambam posited daily *tefilla* as mandatory *mi'd'oraita*, this was only because he regarded the human condition, *sans* communication with the *Ribbono shel Olam*, as a perpetual crisis to be resolved only by turning to him in prayer. Even if this view is rejected, there is no doubt but that the Rambam, too, acknowledged the category of a mitzvah specifically geared to *ba-tsar lekha*. To this effect, his remarks at the beginning of *Hilkhot Ta'aniyot* are fully explicit. The preliminary caption reads "One positive commandment, which is to cry out before God at any time of great trouble which befalls the community", while the more detailed body of the text proper opens:

> A positive Scriptural commandment prescribes prayer and the
> sounding of an alarm with trumpets whenever trouble befalls
> the community. For when Scripture says, "Against the adver-

---

[23]*Hassagot* on *Sefer haMitzvoth, Assei*, 5. It is noteworthy that the Ramban speaks of a duty to believe that *tefilla* is efficacious rather than of a duty to pray.

sary who oppresses you, then you shall sound an alarm with the trumpets," (Bemidbar 10:9) the meaning is: "Cry out in prayer and sound an alarm against whatsoever is oppressing you, be it famine, pestilence, locusts, or the like."[24]

The apparent qualification limiting the mitzvah to public disaster is significant,[25] but the principle—that there is a mitzvah whose very essence is defined as a response elicited by crisis and reactive to it—is nevertheless clear.

Taken collectively, the *hovot ha-levavot* we surveyed affect our relation to suffering in several ways, perhaps most easily distinguished by reference to the various stages previously cited. At a primary level, they might condition how suffering initially is experienced; at a second, how it is understood and interpreted; at yet a third, what ensues in its wake. With reference to the first, I believe, as already suggested, that the most critical mizvoth are the more general: *ahavat Ha-Shem, devekut, yir'at Ha-Shem.* Broadly speaking, these mitzvoth mold a person's fundamental experiential relation to the *Ribbono shel Olam,* and their influence upon response to suffering is itself multiplanar. In one sense, their ongoing and cumulative effect transforms the individual, independently considered. The vivifying power of cleavage to the *Ribbono shel Olam,* be it even in reverential awe, charges the human soul so that its reinforced spiritual and psychological fiber is better able to sustain adversity, no matter how acutely perceived.

---

[24]1:1. As in parallel instances, the relation of the caption, in which, despite the source in Bemidbar, no mention is made of *hatsotsrot,* to the body of the halakhot bears examination. Presumably, the caption refers to the quintessential *kiyyum,* the text to the mode of fulfillment.

[25]Later, 1:9, the Rambam speaks of fasting and praying with regard to an individual's crisis as well. But this might be only *mi-d'rabbanan.* See also *Kol Dodi Dofek,* 14 n.

Secondly, these *hovot ha-levavot* affect the perception proper. Religious and secular experiences of the same calamity might vary, not because the sufferers are different, but because the respective blows ultimately are not truly identical. *Sub specie aeternitatis*, the scope of suffering, is circumscribed and its significance diminished—not because an opiate has diverted attention from it, but because, living "as ever in my great Taskmaster's eye," perspectives and values are reoriented. Hazal were highly sensitive to human suffering, not hesitating to describe as *yissurim* what are, after all, only disruptive annoyances:

> What is the measure of suffering? R. Eleazer said: if a man had a garment woven for him to wear and it does not fit him. Raba Zeira (others report, R. Samuel b. Nahmani) demurred to this: more than this has been said. Even if he was to be served hot, and it was served cold; or cold, and it was served hot! And you require so much? Mar the son of Ravina said: even if his shirt got turned inside out. Raba (others report, R. Hisda; some, R. Isaac, or, as was taught in a Baraita): even if he put the hand into his pocket to take out three [coins] and he fetched only two.[26]

Nevertheless, the importance attached to a temporal value—and hence, the dismay engendered by its loss—is patently a function of one's total spiritual context. Elaborating upon the prohibition of retributive revenge, the Rambam concludes: "One should rather practice forebearance in all worldly matters. For the intelligent realize that these are vain things and not worth taking vengeance for."[27] From a purely moral standpoint, the explanation is disappointing. The injunction would be more demanding and its obser-

---

[26]*Arakhin* 16b.
[27]*De'ot* 7:7.

vance more heroically imposing if one thought that temporal matters *were* worthy of being avenged. As a religious affirmation, however, the statement expresses a basic tenet, and its implications for evaluating the impact of *hovot ha-levavot* upon response to suffering are self-evident.

The point obviously needs to be examined within the broader context of the question of otherworldliness, a subject that lies well beyond the scope of this paper. A word may be said, however, with respect to our immediate focus, especially as regards *ahavat Ha-Shem*. The relation between the love of God and disdain for His creation may be reciprocal. On the one hand, contempt for the world may draw one to its Maker. Thus, Rabbenu Bahyye explains the sequence of his work, in light of this fact:

> This is why we placed the chapter on abstinence before this one [on love of God], since it is impossible for the love of the Creator to be firmly established in our hearts if love of the world is fixed there. But when the believer's heart has been emptied of love of this world and freed from its lusts, as a result of perception and understanding, the love of God can be established in his heart and fixed in his soul, in accordance with his yearning for God and recognition of Him, as it is written: Even in the path of Your judgements, O Lord, have we hoped for Your name and Your memorial is the soul's desire. (Isa. 26:8)[28]

On the other hand—and this is the more common, and presumably the nobler, mystical route—love of God may lead to denigration of all else. It is this heightened sense of *ein od mi-levado* (there is nothing but He) that, even in

---

[28]*Sha'ar Ahavat Hashem*, introd. Cf. Rambam, *Teshuva* 10:6 and Guide 3:51, where the same point is made, but with a less conative and more intellectual cast.

much milder form, can have some bearing upon response to suffering.

This is not to suggest, of course, that *ahavat Ha-Shem*, properly realized, necessarily does or should lead to the degree of renunciation espoused by the Rambam's son, Hasidei Ashkenaz, or, for that matter, even by the *Mesillat Yesharim*. That stance is not too prevalent in the modern world—not only at the popular level but at the philosophic. Clearly, the two most prominent *ba-alei mahshava* of this century, Rav Kook and the Rav, *zt"l*, rejected it categorically. And, by and large, the contemporary Torah community fully subscribes to the critique of both world-rejection and Stoic apathy the Ramban enunciates in his preface to *Torat ha-Adam*.[29] As that very text illustrates amply, however, some diminution of the dimensions of tragedy not only can but should flow from religious commitment; in this sense, *ahavat Ha-Shem* serves to ameliorate suffering.

This effect is heightened, moreover, by an additional element. Irrespective of how suffering is perceived or evaluated, its impact can be cushioned by the compensatory import of one's relation to the *Ribbono shel Olam*. When Yirmiyahu sang, "God is my strength and my stronghold, and my refuge in the day of affliction (Jer. 16:19), he celebrated not only the succor or even solace he might hope to attain to overcome his troubles, but the sheer offsetting force of the relation proper.

Beyond experience—albeit, in a sense, interwoven with it—we move to the second phase: understanding and interpretation. The literature of the problem of pain is, of course, quite extensive, even within the bounds of our own Jewish world; here, I shall confine myself to its interaction with our specific theme. In this connection, we need to

---

[29]See, especially, the conclusion, in *Kitvei Ramban*, 2:13–14.

distinguish between two aspects: the ascription of suffering to its agent as an efficient cause, and the designation of its motive as a final cause. The first is mandated as a facet of *teshuva* and, in effect, requires—unpalatable as this might be, theologically and philosophically, in other respects—that human suffering be traced to the initiative of the *Ribbono shel Olam*; or, failing that, to the untrammeled operation of other forces, natural or human, in the absence of His protective shield. The theme is familiar from many *pesukim*, but at the normative level is most succinctly set down by the Rambam:

> This is one of the ways of repentance, that when overtaken by trouble, the community cries out in prayer and sounds an alarm, then all must know that evil has come upon them as a consequence of their own evil deeds, and that their repentance will cause the trouble to be removed from them. But if they do not cry out in prayer and do not sound an alarm, but merely say that it is the way of the world for such a thing to happen to them, and that their trouble is a matter of pure chance, they have chosen a cruel way which will cause them to persevere in their evil deeds and thus bring additional troubles upon them. For when Scripture says: If you will walk with Me by happenstance; then I will walk with you in furious happenstance (Vayikra 26:27–28), the meaning is: If, when I bring trouble upon you in order to cause you to repent, you say that the trouble is purely accidental, then I will add to your trouble fury, to lead you to repent.[30]

The statement is made with respect to public calamity, to which it relates particularly; but the basic motif—that disaster be attributed to divine intervention rather than to "natural" extremes, causal law, or indeterminate chance—applies to personal suffering as well.

---

[30] *Ta'aniyot* 1:2–3.

To what extent the attribution is to be asserted presumably depends upon how the scope of *hashgaha peratit* (particular providence) is defined. The more prevalent view is, of course, the more comprehensive: the notion, however reconciled with human freedom, that whatever befalls each and every individual, for good or for ill, is divinely ordained. Popular provenance aside, this view has apparent support in Hazal: "All is in the hands of Heaven save for the fear of Heaven."[31] The Rambam, to be sure, qualified the statement severely by contending that "all of man's actions are included in *the fear of Heaven*."[32] The general interpretation is presumably quite sweeping, however; *ha-kol* is taken to include all that befalls every person and *yirat Shamayim* to refer to the religious realm, narrowly defined. Rav Hanina's statement, "One does not crook one's finger below unless it is proclaimed above,"[33] thus is understood both literally and comprehensively, with the attribution of misfortune to divine fiat a direct corollary.

Some *rishonim* adopted a far more restrictive view, however, both the Rambam and the Ramban holding that only a select minority benefit from constant providential attention. Their reasons varied, as did the populations they singled out. The Rambam spoke of an intellectual elite that attained personal care by dint of individual effort that raised one's level of spirituality, so that one was now within range, as it were, of providence and attuned to its wavelength. "The divine overflow that exists united to the human species," he postulates, "I mean the human intellect, is merely what exists as individual intellects ... Now if this is so, it follows necessarily according to what I have mentioned in

---

[31] *Berakhot* 33b.
[32] *Teshuvot HaRambam*, ed. J. Blau, 714.
[33] *Hullin* 7b.

the preceding chapter that when any human individual has obtained, because of the disposition of his matter and his training, a greater portion of this overflow than others, providence will of necessity watch more carefully over him than over others—if, that is to say, providence is, as I have mentioned, consequent upon the intellect. . . . As for the ignorant and disobedient, their state is despicable proportionately to their lack of this overflow, and they have been relegated to the rank of the individuals of all the other species of animals."[34]

The Ramban, on the other hand, regarded piety and righteousness as the definitive criteria; and he also appears to ascribe the special concern to divine, rather than human, initiative:

> God's knowledge, which is synonymous with His Providence in the lower world, is to preserve the species, and even human beings are subject to accident as long as they live. But He attends to the pious individually, to guard him always, His knowledge and remembrance of him never departs as it says: He withdraws not His eye from the righteous (Job 36:7). There are many verses on this theme, as it is written: Behold, the eye of the Eternal is toward them that fear Him (Ps. 33:18) and other verses besides.[35]

The common denominator, however, is that the concept

---

[34]*Guide*, trans. S. Pines, 3:18, 473. Initially, the Rambam only speaks of a functional ratio, but the concluding statement about "the ignorant and the disobedient" probably leaves, given the Rambam's general orientation, only a minority under any personal providence whatsoever.

[35]Breshit 18:19. I once asked *mori ve-rabbi*, Rav Hutner, zt"l, about this passage, and he categorically refused to take it at face value, arguing that leaving some to the vagaries of accident did not denote an absence of *hashgaha* but rather was a mode of its operation. The suggestion is striking but does not bear upon our discussion.

and the reality of personal Providence, as generally perceived, is significantly circumscribed.

Clearly, the degree of conviction with which a sufferer
will attribute his travails to the *Ribbono shel Olam* will vary
considerably, depending on his views with respect to this
controversy. And yet the obligation to do so as a facet of
teshuva need not be linked to this debate. Even with the
latter view, misfortune is not necessarily the hand of God.
Assuredly, however, it might be, and one is fully obligated
to take that possibility into account and to draw the inference. The attribution, of course, cannot partake of the nature of blame and concomitant anger. At that level, various *pesukim* clearly bar any causal link: "The foolishness of
man perverts his way, and his heart frets against the Lord."
(Mishle 3:19) Or, even more explicitly, in Eikha: "Out of
the mouth of the most High do not both good and evil
come. Why then does a living man complain, a man for the
punishment of his sins?" (3:38–39) At the level of interpretive reflection, however, the need to assume that one may
have received a divine retributive message is clear, and, as
the subsequent *pesukim* amplify, so is the recipient's need
to repent: "Let us search and try our ways, and turn back
to the Lord. Let us lift up our heart with our hands to God
in the heavens." (3:40–41)

That one should regard personal suffering within the
context of one's relation to the *Ribbono shel Olam* Hazal
took as a matter of course. But as to conjecture concerning its substantive significance, they acknowledged considerable latitude. On one level, they encouraged responses
that would question whether suffering was truly disastrous.
They counseled raising the issue even with respect to the
temporal pragmatic plane. Thus, in the wake of a statement
from the school of Rabbi Akiva that a man should always
accustom himself to say, "Whatever the All-merciful does is

for good,"[36] the Gemara narrates an incident in which Rabbi Akiva himself lost some favored possessions and, as a result, fortuitously was saved from almost certain captivity. More commonly, however, the presumed benefit is projected as being deferred to the world to come. As even the most righteous may be liable for the slightest peccadillo, exacting punishment from them here redounds to their advantage, as they then have a clean slate, having paid their penance with mundane currency.

On the other hand, it is conceivable that affliction is undiluted punishment or that it is, however that elusive term is understood, *yissurim shel ahava*. Perhaps that is precisely the point: the range of perception and interpretation. One can rule out neither the chastising rod nor the stroking palm, and hence none of the correlative emotions. Various possibilities are to be entertained and examined—with no assurance, of course, that uncertainty will be resolved. The key, however, remains acceptance. *Ante facto*, the central tradition of *yahadut* has given every license to fight off impending disaster. *Post facto*, it has urged acknowledgment, as expressions of divine will, of the very affliction to which the most heroic resistance previously had been sanctioned. A simple story in the Gemara in *Baba Kamma* makes the point succinctly:

> When R. Samuel b. Judah lost a daughter, the Rabbis said to Ulla: let us go and console him. But he answered them: what have I to do with the consolation of the Babylonians, which is [almost tantamount] to blasphemy? For they say, what could have been done?, which implies that were it possible to do anything, they would have done it."[37]

------

[36] *Berakhot* 60b; see Maharal, *Netivot Olam, Netiv Ahavat Hashem,* ch. 1.

[37] *Baba Kamma* 38a.

The implicit demand is imposing, indeed. Yet it is firmly ensconced in the Shulhan Arukh,[38] incumbent upon the ordinary Jew.

Clearly, both *teshuva* and *tefilla* can, as well as should, affect our response to suffering, but in different ways. To begin with the former, its import is itself dual. As a mitzvah, *teshuva*, as we have seen, demands first that a person initially regard his suffering as divinely imposed and, secondly, that he consequently examine his life and reorient it: "Raba (some report, R. Hisda) says: If a man sees that painful sufferings come upon him, let him examine his conduct. For it says: Let us search and try our ways. (Eikha 3:40) If he examines and finds [something objectionable], let him do *teshuva* as it says: and turn back to the Lord."[39] The *heshbon ha-nefesh* (self-examination) might not uncover grievous sin, in which case one should probe further the possibility that his affliction is due to the failure to maximize spiritual potential: "If he examined and found nothing, let him attribute it to the neglect of Torah study, for it says: Happy is the man whom You, God, chastizes, and teaches him from Your Torah."[40] (Tehillim 94:12) But Hazal regarded this, too, of course, most seriously. Quite apart from any explicit *issur* (prohibition), the failure to seize spiritual opportunity reflects axiological vacuity and is expressive of disdain for ultimate values. Expanding upon Rabbi Nehorai's comment upon the *pasuk*, "For he has scorned the word of God," (Bemidbar 15:27) the Rambam writes: "Similarly, anyone able to occupy himself with To-

---

[38]See Rama, *Yoreh Deah* 376:2.

[39]*Berakhot* 5a.

[40]*Loc. cit.* Rava speaks of *bittul* Torah specifically, but the Ramban—see *Torat Ha'adam*, in *Kitvei Ramban*, 2:270—explains that a far broader range is intended.

rah study who does not, or who has studied and turned away to the vanities of the world, leaving behind his study and ignoring it, is included in the category of those who scorn the word of the Lord."[41]

This awareness, as an initial phase of *teshuva*, is significant in its own right; indeed, the Torah refers to it at one point as an independent phenomenon: "Then my anger will burn against them on that day, and I will forsake them, and I will hide my face from them, and they shall be devoured, and many evils and troubles shall befall them; so that they will say on that day: Is it not because my God is not in my midst that these evils have found me?"[42] Obviously, however, the mitzvah relates primarily to change that ensues from this awareness. In this respect, *teshuva* lends a practical cast to response to suffering, whether at the level of action proper or, as its context, with respect to attitudes and priorities. Presumably, there might—and probably should—be some functional relation between the degree of suffering and prospective change. Radical suffering might raise the possibility of fundamental revision; moderate affliction, only minor alterations. The principle, however—at least, at the theoretical level—is clear.

From another perspective, however, *teshuva* as a phenomenon rather than *qua* mitzvah has a wholly different effect. It bears two primary aspects, recoil *from* and return

---

[41]Talmud Torah 3:13.

[42]Devarim 31:17. Within the context of the *pasuk*, the phrase "God is not in my midst" probably means that "He has deserted me" rather than vice versa. Even with this view, however, the implicit recognition that the desertion is attributable to sin constitutes an aspect of *teshuva*. Thus was it understood by the Ramban, *ad loc.*: "This is not a full confession like 'they shall confess their iniquity (Lev. 26:40)' but it is reflection and regret. They will regret their iniquity and recognize that they are guilty."

to: "return from your evil ways" (Ezek. 33:11) as opposed to "return Israel, unto your God." (Hos. 14:2) The first constitutes the "moral" element, broadly defined: the recognition of sin and its retrospective and prospective renunciation. The second is its "religious" component: the rehabilitation and restoration of one's relation to God. The latter entails not only repentance but redemption. As a process that intensifies and deepens the individual's link to the *Ribbono shel Olam*, it affects the whole of his being, having an impact, derivatively, upon his response to suffering as well. The whole range of *hovot ha-levavot—ahavat Ha-Shem, yir'ah, devekut*, and others—that mold our relation to Him, influence, as previously noted, our reaction to suffering at the primary level. Hence, insofar as *teshuva* enriches a person's total religious personality, it enhances his or her capacity to cope with suffering and points the direction that such coping will take. In its wake, suffused with greater *emuna* and *bittahon* (faith and trust), one is both better able to withstand suffering and more inclined to experience and interpret it within the matrix of religious existence.

I fully recognize the problematic character of this presentation. Preaching the gospel of adversity's uses sounds, at best, idealistically Utopian and, at worst, glibly insensitive; emphasis upon the normative or positive aspects of response to suffering might convey the sense of dispassionately facile dismissal of profound human tragedy. The modern reader, suffused with Dostoevski's perception that the whole literature of theodicy is not worth the searing pain of a single infant, is properly revolted by the faintest resemblance to cavalier insouciance. Moreover, this response is thoroughly Jewish. The significance that *yahadut* has ascribed to physical and psychological experience confers genuine import upon mundane suffering; hence our response to others' pain as a concrete human reality is tempered accordingly. I trust that the point is obvious, if not platitudinous. And yet, the clear fact remains that, without being Pollyannish, and fully mindful of the depths of pain, *yahadut* indeed has pointed to suffering's value and has encouraged the sufferer to recognize that value. Whether as a vehicle of forgiveness—"One should rejoice more in chastisement than in prosperity, for if one is prosperous all his life, no sin of his will be forgiven. What brings him forgiveness of sins? Suffering"—as a means of bonding with the *Ribbono shel Olam*—"Whom the Lord loves He chastizes, even as a father the son in whom he delighteth (Mishle 3:12)—What causes the son to be pleasing to his father? Suffering"—as an expression of divine grace—"And you shall consider in thy heart, that as a man chastens his son, so the Lord, thy God, chastens you" (Mishle 8:5)—or as an instrument for conveying divine bounty—"Precious is suffering, for three good gifts coveted by all the nations of the world were given to Israel solely through suffering, and they are Torah, the Land of Israel, and the world to come"[43]—it is seen as having a potentially positive aspect, if one can respond to it properly.

This is not to suggest, of course, that one should, ascetically or masochistically, seek out some *felix culpa*:

> R. Yudan said in the name of R. Ami: The congregation of Israel said to the Holy One, blessed be He: Lord of the Universe, even though the verse states, "God chastizes those whom He loves," "Do not rebuke me in Your anger." (Tehillim 6:1) Even though the verse states, "Blessed is the man whom God chastises," "Do not chastise me in Your anger."[44]

---

[43]*Sifre, Va'ethannan*, sec. 7.
[44]Midrash *Tehillim* 6:3.

At the personal level, likewise, Hazal recognized that even
the greatest very well might prefer to forego both pain and
its lucrative aftermath. The *sugya* in *Berakhot* that deals with
the value of *yissurim* concludes by citing several *amoraim*
who, when asked "Are your sufferings welcome to you?"
responded "Neither they, nor their reward."[45] And yet the
central message—that if unsought adversity does strike, it
should serve as a stimulus to nobler and purer spiritual
existence—obtains.

This sense is particularly relevant to what Hazal denomi-
nated *yissurim shel ahava* (chastisements of love). According to one view, the term refers to suffering's modality,
defining it as that which does not disrupt one's spiritual
functioning, whether Talmud Torah or *tefilla*.[46] Presumably,
however, the more prevalent view is that it refers to its
impulse. Thus, Rava and/or Rav Hisda state that if, after
introspective self-examination, one finds no failings to which
to ascribe his suffering, "it is known that these are chastisements of love. For it is said: 'For whom God loves, He corrects' "[47] (Mishle 3:12) Just how this is to be perceived
obviously depends on how one resolves the issue of whether
"there is death without sin, or suffering without iniquity."[48]
In either view, however, these pangs are neither purely
punitive nor merely an opportunity for accumulating points
to be credited in the afterlife. They are inherently purga-

---

[45] *Berakhot* 5b.

[46] *Ibid.* 5a.

[47] *Loc. cit.*

[48] *Shabbat* 55a. The Gemara resolves that even the innocent die, but
adduces no proof with regard to *yissurim*. The Rambam—Guide, 3:17
and 3:24—and the Ramban—*Kitvei Ramban*, 1:199 and 2:271–4—cite
the issue as a matter of debate among Hazal, but both are inclined to
accept the view that there is no suffering without sin.

tive, even if occasioned, as the Ramban held, by the need to remit sin and vouchsafe grace: "When the temple no longer stands, He visits upon them suffering to scour them of those unintentional sins, and to atone through suffering so that they may be cleansed for the world to come. It is like the sacrifices which are love and compassion for Israel, bringing them under the wings of the Divine."[49] For this effect to be attained fully, however, the sufferer, great as the pain might be, must perceive it clearly. No doubt the bare fact of privation might ennoble by changing perspectives and priorities and by purifying motivation. Yet the total impact is very much a function of response:

> Raba, in the name of R. Sahora, in the name of R. Huna, said: If the Holy One, blessed be He, is pleased with a man, He crushes him with painful suffering. For it is said: "And God was pleased to crush him by disease." (Isa. 53:10) Is this so even if he did not accept them with love? Therefore it is said: "If his soul would offer itself in expiation." Just as the trespass offering must be brought willingly, so too must the suffering be endured willingly."[50]

In general terms, much the same as has been said of *teshuva* could be said of *tefilla*, but its impact upon response to suffering also bears a distinctive stamp. At least three elements may be singled out. Most obviously, when confronted by crisis or in the midst of suffering, one prays for succor. Whatever idealistic philosophers might think, petition is, halakhically, the heart of prayer; as long as there is hope, one responds to suffering by asking that it be reversed

---

[49] *Kitvei Ramban*, 2:270. Elsewhere, he seems to ascribe a semi-mystical quality to such suffering. Cf. also Maharal, *Netivot Olam, Netiv Hayissurim*, ch. 1–2.

[50] Berakhot 5a.

or at least contained. Moreover, this is not merely an option but a duty. Heroic self-sufficiency is but an arrogant delusion. The awareness of dependence and the consequent cry for aid is—as the Maharal,[51] well before Schleiermacher, emphasized—the essence of *avodat Ha-Shem*:

> A song of ascents to David: Lord, my heart is not haughty, nor my eyes lofty: nor do I exercise myself in great matters, or in things too wondrous for me. For I have been still and silent, like a weaned child beside his mother; like a weaned child is my soul. Let Israel hope in God from now and forever. (Ps. 131)

Secondly, even if calamity already has struck, one looks to the *Ribbono shel Olam* for solace. In one sense, this, too, is petition. He is the ultimate comforter: "I hoped for condolence and there was none, and for consolers and I did not find them" (Ps. 69:21). Said God: "I am your consoler,"[52] and one turns to Him with a plea for spiritual as well as for material sustenance. In another sense, one does not supplicate at all but simply leans upon Him, even while breaking down in tears. He is also the ultimate shoulder.

Finally, the suffering religious soul turns to the *Ribbono shel Olam* not only as *Avinu she-ba-Shamayim* (our heavenly Father) but as an *ah le-tzara* (a brother in need), as *salve reverentia*, a fellow sufferer. There is strength, there is comfort, in sheer commiseration, in the bare knowledge that somehow He, too, has been affected. This element is presumably most relevant to national calamity, inasmuch as that relates to the theme of *Shekhinta be-galuta*—not the self-willed exile of "I am with him in distress" (Ps. 90), but the enforced *galut*, as it were, imposed when the historical

---

[51]See *Netivot Olam, Netiv ha-Avoda*, ch. 2.
[52]*Yalkut Shimoni* 474, on Isa. 51:1.

process goes awry. It also obtains, however, at the personal level:

> R. Meir said: When man suffers, what expression does the Shekhinah use?—My head is too heavy for me; my arm is too heavy for me. And if God is so grieved over the blood of the wicked that is shed, how much more so over the blood of the righteous."[53]

Awareness of that divine anguish serves to ameliorate the human.

Confronting the *Ribbono shel Olam* in prayer, a sufferer thus is engaged in a highly complex relationship. On the one hand, it is presumably God who has smitten. On the other, it is to Him that one turns for help, whether for relief or comfort. And, finally, it is with Him whom one is conjoined in crisis—He participating in ours, and we, as it were, in His: "What of the father who banished his children, woe to the children who were banished from their father's table."[54] *Klal* Israel—and, to a lesser extent, Reb Israel—thus is bound to its Master-Father-Lover in a covenant of suffering. Paradoxically, in our quest for comfort, we draw solace from the knowledge that, *mutatis mutandis*, He, too, is engaged in the quest, and with only partial success: "So long as the seed of Amalek exists it is as if a corner of a garment covers the Face . . . . So long as the seed of Amalek is in the world neither the Name nor the Throne is complete."[55]

In this vein, the Midrash perceives *hurban ha-bayit* and attendant national exile as no less a divine than a human calamity: "And when Judah and Benjamin went into exile,

---

[53]*Sanhedrin* 46a.
[54]*Berakhot* 3a.
[55]Midrash *Tanhuma, Ki Tetse* 11.

it is as though [*kivyakhol*] the Holy One, blessed be He, said: Woe is me for my breach."[56] (Jer. 10:19) Consequently, the *Ribbono shel Olam* is portrayed as bewailing the course of events: "R. Isaac commenced: For a sound of wailing is heard from Zion: How we are ruined! (Jer. 9:19) Now can wood wail, can stones wail, that you should say, a sound of wailing is heard from Zion? Rather it is from the One whose Presence dwells in Zion."[57] Even more audaciously, He is envisioned as seeking assistance from fellow mourners: "And when Judah and Benjamin went into exile, it is as though the Holy One, blessed be He, said: I do not have the strength to lament for them, but 'Summon the dirge-singers, let them come; send for the skilled women, let them come. Let them quickly start a wailing for us.' (Jer. 9:16–17) It does not say *for them* but *for us*."[58] And when well-intentioned *mal'akhei ha-sharet* (ministering angels) proffer consolation, it is spurned, as it evidently stems from failure to grasp the tragedy's scope and depth:

> About the destruction of the Temple it is written: "Therefore, said I, turn away from me, I will weep bitterly, strain not (*al ta'itsu*) to comfort me." (Isa. 22:4) It does not say here "do not gather together," but "strain not." The Holy One, blessed be He, said to the ministering angels, "The words of comfort which you offer to Me are insults (*niutsin*) to Me." Why? "For it is a day of trouble, and of trampling and of perplexity for the Lord God of Hosts" (Isa. 22:5); it is a day of confusion, a day of plunder, a day of weeping.[59]

---

[56]*Eikha Rabbati, Petihta* 2.

[57]*Ibid.* 8.

[58]*Loc. cit.*

[59]*Eikhah Rabbati, Petihta* 24. In the *pesukim* cited from Isa. 22:4–5, the *peshat*, of course, refers to troubles God caused to others, and not to His own.

For us, commiseration with His troubles supports us as we seek to transcend our own anguish. A neighbor of ours, Leib Rochman, who had lived through the Holocaust and written about it, once was asked by a pseudo-philosopher guest where the *Ribbono shel Olam* had been at the time. Looking her straight in the eye, he responded calmly, "*Er iz geven mit unz*" (He was with us). And, as he repeated the story, one sensed how much awareness of that presence had sustained him.

I write these lines with anxious trepidation. The anthropomorphic note is clear, and associative analogues with Christian and even pagan motifs are unquestionably troubling. While the analogy, of course, is limited—there is nothing here even faintly resembling expiatory sacrifice, and both the reality and the experience of presumed suffering are conceived within a wholly different context and in radically different categories—a growing malaise persists. I ask myself, timorously: how would the Rambam have responded to these speculations? I'm afraid the answer to this rhetorical question is clear. And it is, I repeat, troubling.

Evidently, the compiler of *Eikha Rabbati* was not oblivious to these concerns; he took care to parry them. The familiar modifying *kivyakhol* appears in several of the texts cited, and a fuller qualification appears in another. After portraying the responses of resurrected Moshe Rabbenu and the *avot* to the carnage of the *hurban*, the Midrash presents its impact upon the *Ribbono shel Olam* Himself:

> When the Holy One, blessed be He, saw them, forthwith: "And in that day did the Lord, the God of Hosts, call to weeping and to lamentation, and to baldness, and to girding with sackcloth." Had the verse not been written, one could not have stated it. And they went weeping from this gate to that, like a man whose deceased lies before him, and the Holy One,

blessed be He, wept, lamenting, Woe for a king who prospers in his youth and not in his old age.[60]

"Had the verse not been written, one could not have stated it." This formulation encapsulates both ambivalence about the comment and determination—in a sense, under the imprimatur of the *pasuk*, and yet essentially through the initiative of the homilist who has imposed this interpretation upon it—to present it nonetheless.

Still, the chasm between these caveats and the doctrine of negative attributes is wide and deep. Confronted by the polarities of the issue and animated by fealty to a range of sources, we hence find ourselves on the horns of a dilemma; at some point, we need to pitch our tent. After the dialectic between transcendence and immanence has been honed, and our sensitivity to the *va-yered* that stops short at the symbolic plane of ten *tefahim* having been refined,[61] we still must choose—at the philosophic as well as at the literary level—between the graphic vividness of Midrashic theology and the rarefied purity of the Rambam's.[62]

Generally speaking, as the Rav, *zt"l*,[63] once noted in an analogous connection, *Knesset* Israel has chosen: for Midrash and against the *Moreh*. At the popular level, this choice no doubt often has derived from weakness, the result of the inability to scale the heights of theological inquiry and perception and to confront its implications. However, it can be grounded equally in strength: in ten-

---

[60]*Loc. cir.*

[61]See *Sukka* 4b.

[62]With respect to the Rambam, see Simon Rawidowicz, *Iyyunim b'Mahshevet Israel* (Jerusalem, 1969), 171–233.

[63]See, with reference to the controversy over reciting *piyutim*, his comments in *Ish haHalakha* (in *Ish haHalakha, Galuy veNistar, Jerusalem* 5739), 56.

sile religious sensibility and in the conviction that the language of *kitvei ha-kodesh* and Hazal clearly dictates this option. For those who face the dilemma squarely—most, of course, simply are swept along by instinctive inclinations or societal norms—resolution is not easy. It is accompanied by awareness that we are all wide of the mark, doomed to misapprehend and therefore, to some extent, to misserve Him whom to know and serve is the alpha and the omega of our existence. Precisely, however, because a measure of failure is endemic and inevitable, it can be regarded, in the spirit of *lo nittena Torah l'mal'akhei ha-sharet* (the Torah was not given to angels), with a degree of acceptance, if not equanimity. We are charged to transcend crudity and purify religious sensibility, and Heaven forfend that we relax our efforts. But the mandate has its limits—not because at the personal level these might prove counterproductive, but inasmuch as purported purification might falsify reality.

At stake is not just the prospect of desiccated experience or truncated imagination. From the perspective of *baalei ha-midrash* and *hakhmei ha-kabbala*, the exaggeration of transcendence distorts objective truth with respect to the nature of divine revelation and engagement. In perceiving and defining what we understand by immanent Shekhinah, we can err on either side.

This excursus's relevance to the theme of suffering's relation to the *Ribbono shel Olam* should be self-evident. The point is crystallized, however, in a well-known, albeit admittedly enigmatic, Gemara in *Hagiga*. Referring to a *pasuk* in Jeremiah (13:17)—"But if you will not hear it, my soul shall weep in secret for your pride"—the Gemara comments:

> But is there any weeping in the presence of the Holy One, blessed be He? Did not R. Papa say: There is no grief in the presence of the Holy One, blessed be He; for it is written: "Honor and majesty are before Him; strength and beauty are

in His sanctuary!" (Ps. 96:6)? There is no contradiction; the one case [refers to] the inner chambers, the other case [refers to] the outer chambers. But it is written: "And in that day did the Lord, the God of Hosts, call to weeping and to lamentation, and to baldness, and to girding with sackcloth!" (Isa. 22:12) The destruction of the Temple is different, for even the angels of peace wept [over it]; for it is written: "Behold for their altar they cried without; the angels of peace wept bitterly." (Isa. 33:7)[64]

The cryptic responses are obviously open to varied interpretation. But the tenor and thrust of the entire passage are perfectly clear.

The Maharal took note of this and sought both to elucidate and to qualify the Gemara:

> It is puzzling, as in the earlier cases, for there is no weeping with regard to Him. The answer is that before, the discussion was not about God in Himself, only that God's Glory is imperfectly present to the recipients. For when Israel is imperfect and deficient, when they are in exile, so is God present to the world as explained before that God is present to the world according to the recipient.[65]

To this deflection of wail from the Creator to the creature one at some level, of course, can subscribe fully. That His quintessential being is wholly immutable is beyond question, and, at most, we can speak of impact upon His interactive relation to the world. The point is, however, that this impact is no mirage, that the effect upon the *Ribbono shel Olam*'s manifest presence is genuine, and, hence, that the

---

[64]*Hagiga* 5b. In the context of the *pasuk* cited, the call to weeping might refer to the cries of others rather than those of the *Ribbono shel Olam*. As the link to *tivke nafshi* (My soul weeps) amply indicates, however, Hazal here clearly did ascribe it to him.

[65]*Be'er haGola*, ch. 4 (London, 1964), 66–67.

grief Hazal daringly attributed to Him is both real, *per se*, and related to an objective correlative.

Throughout this presentation, I have spoken of response to suffering primarily with respect to its victim. In drawing to a close, I would like to touch, however briefly, upon response at the level of *hovot ha-levavot* to the suffering of others. Broadly speaking, we are doubly engaged. At one level, we react as outsiders, almost as angels are envisioned in numerous midrashim as reacting. This response is itself dual. There is, first, the philosophical and theological issue of the sheer existence of evil and suffering, whatever their locus.

Secondly, we also are engaged emotionally, commiserating—be it as outsiders—with the pain of others. Among *hovot ha-levavot*, this empathy relates at the very least to *tefilla*. In this context, prayer more likely will be almost exclusively a plea for succor; but even as such, its significance is considerable.

The primary impact of *hovot ha-levavot* upon our relation to the suffering of others is felt, however, insofar as it becomes—in some sense and at some level—our own. From a purely moral standpoint, this degree of empathy is desirable, *per se*, as a reflection of the ability to transcend egocentrism and weave an element of fellowship, community, or universality into the fabric of personal identity. Donne's affirmation "No man is an island, entire of itself; every man is a piece of the continent, a part of the main; if a clod be washed away by the sea, Europe is the less, as well as if a promontory were; any man's death diminishes me, because I am involved in mankind"[66] is both a statement of fact and an imperative demand. Possibly, its very scope is self-defeating; so comprehensive an identity is difficult to sustain. At

---

[66]Devotions upon Emergent Occasions, 17.

the national level, however, such a sensibility is both requisite and possible, and readers of *Kol Dodi Dofek*[67] will recall the metaphor of the two-headed Jew, both of whose
heads scream when either is scalded.

This sense bears directly upon response to a fellow Jew's
suffering, and all the more so to response to a calamity that
strikes *knesset* Israel collectively. Between these situations
proper, there might be a significant difference, as in one
case we deal with a parallel, albeit intersecting, entity and
in another with an encompassing context. The element of
enlarged identity is, however, common to both, and we can
deal accordingly with the role of *hovot ha-levavot* in affect-
ing our response to suffering with respect to both.

In this connection, I believe we should distinguish between recourse to *tefilla* and *teshuva*, respectively. As regards the former, all three aspects that were discussed previously with respect to personal suffering—the quest for
help, a shoulder to cry on, and a covenant of anguish—
are here, too, very much in order. Moreover, there exists a
reciprocal relation between prayer for others and interaction with them. On the one hand, one prays not only out
of a religious imperative, inasmuch as "if one is in a position to pray on behalf of his fellow and does not do so, he
is called a sinner,"[68] but out of empathetic identification;
on the other hand, the process of *bakkashat rahamim* itself reinforces that identification.

The situation is somewhat different, however, with regard
to *teshuva*, whether as interpretation or *tikkun*. In one
sense, there ought be no difference. The theoretical assumption that sin and punishment are related functionally
applies to others no less than to oneself and to the ex-

---

[67]See pp. 35–36.
[68]*Berakhot* 12b.

tended self no less than to the limited. And yet the expression of that assumption—or, beyond that, even its specific internalization—can be highly problematic, from both a religious and a moral perspective. We recoil instinctively from assertions regarding the causal nexus between sin and suffering. Such statements are, of course, central to *Nevi'im*, and they abound in Hazal as well. Nevertheless, contemporaneously—even as we do not deny any given possibility, to asseverate with assurance—is out of the question. Such statements constitute the height of arrogance *vis-à-vis* the *Ribbono shel Olam* and invite Hazal's comment concerning Bilaam: "Now, seeing that he did not even know the mind of his donkey, could he know the mind of the most high?"[69] *Vis-à-vis* one's fellow, they are both morally and halakhically reprehensible. Regarding Job's religiosity, Hazal entertained widely divergent views, with some perceiving him as rebellious and blasphemous.[70] None, however, challenged the assertion that his comforters' responses were, in effect, models of proscribed *ona'at devarim* (verbal oppressiveness): "One must not speak [to the sufferer] as his companions spoke to Job: Is not your reverence your confidence, and your hope the integrity of your ways? Remember, who ever perished, being innocent?"[71] (Job 4:6) Consequently, while *yahadut* certainly espouses fundamental faith in the relation of sin and suffering, humility and sensitivity both demand that we desist from specific application; hence, continued adherence to the tenet remains more a facet of *emuna* than of *teshuva*.

The point is perhaps more delicate with respect to communal calamity, inasmuch as here the functional association

---

[69] *Sanhedrin* 105b.

[70] See *Baba Batra* 15b–16b.

[71] *Baba Metzia* 58b.

has deeper roots and the Rambam's emphasis upon proper interpretation as an element of *teshuva* greater imperative force. Here, too, however, the need for balancing humility and sensitivity against the impetus to *teshuva* obtains. If one genuinely counts himself among the guilty, *u-mippenei hatta'enu* ("because of our sins were we exiled") can be a most positive response. However, at the point at which it begins to shade off into *u-mippenei hatta'ekha* ("your sins"), let us beware—all the more so today in the shadow of the most frightful *hester panim* (hiding of the divine face) and the awesome silence it imposes upon us.

The realm of *tikkun*, by contrast, is less problematic—except insofar as it is itself predicated upon the ascription of blame. Truly collective repentance, grounded upon truly collective acknowledgment of sin as a response to collective suffering, lies at the heart of our tradition. It has, moreover, a dual thrust. At one level, it is a means of averting threatened disaster and thus essentially conjoined with that aspect of *tefilla* that strives to nullify *ro'a ha-gezera* (the evil decree). At another, it is a *post facto* response to suffering and serves as the basis for the spiritual regeneration of a chastised community. This takes place, moreover, at both the personal and the communal plane. When Nineveh was threatened with impending doom, its inhabitants responded with public fast and prayer and with personal self-examination: "and let them turn everyone from his evil way, and from the violence that is in their hands." (Jon. 3:8) All the more so in the case of a Jewish community of which a higher standard is demanded, on the one hand, and that—at least, in the Maharal's view—can be defined as more thoroughly organic, on the other. And unlike acknowledgment, with its possibly concomitant finger-pointing, *tikkun* can be approached without self-righteousness and without recrimination in a forward-looking spirit rooted in commitment to both *avodat Ha-Shem* and to *ahavat* Israel.

Nineveh reminds us symbolically of relation to universal suffering, and most of us sorely need a reminder. The ethnic factor is of little moment at the philosophic level. In dealing with theodicy, whether Job was Jewish, Gentile, or fictional is wholly irrelevant. At the practical level, however, it is of considerable import. Up to a point, this is fully understandable humanly and also, from our perspective, morally. There is no gainsaying the fact, belabored by Weber, that Judaism has espoused a double ethic. The Halakha indeed has championed a double standard grounded in recognition of *kedushat* Israel and the perception—of relevance to ideal Gentile morality as well—that intensive ethnocentric *hesed* is preferred to bland universalism. Yet the tendency, prevalent in much of the contemporary Torah world in Israel as well as in the Diaspora, of almost total obliviousness to non-Jewish suffering is shamefully deplorable. Surely Avraham Avinu and Moshe Rabbenu felt and acted otherwise, and intervening *mattan* Torah has not changed our obligation in this respect. Priorities certainly need to be maintained, as regards both practical and emotional engagement; but between that and complacent apathy there lies an enormous moral gap. Relation to enemies is a separate issue, with respect to which many *perakim* in *Tehillim* are highly relevant; but the notion that only Jewish affliction is worthy of Jewish response needs to be excoriated and eradicated. In this respect, the Hafetz Hayyim's remark—that if the Gentiles knew how much we pray for them on Rosh Hashana, they would publish *Mahzorim*—serves as an instructive guide.

In this respect, we need to redouble educational efforts to integrate and inculcate the dual thrust of a most familiar text. In *ashrei*, a "double ethic," in effect, is ascribed to the *Ribbono shel Olam*. At one plane, His mercy and bounty are described as universal: "God is good to all, and His mercy on all His creatures. . . . The eyes of all turn to

You and You give them their nourishment in its time. You open Your hand and satisfy all living beings." At another, priority obtains and they are selective, as He is close to all who "call upon Him in truth," hears the cry and fulfills the desire of those "that fear Him," and securely guards "all them that love Him." Within our community, however, while the parochial element is expounded properly, the universal is often *sotto voce*, if not muted. Where priority turns into apathy, we are witness to a moral and educational failure. Can we confidently assert that we are not at times more affected by the withering of favored ephemeral gourds than by the destruction of a metropolis, "wherein are more than sixscore persons that cannot discern between their right and left hands, and also much cattle?"

In conclusion, I return to the sinking feeling that much of what has been said here might fall upon deaf ears. In a scientific age, any linkage of suffering to sin, even as an instrument of repentance, might seem both hollow and naive; any attempt to cry up the purgative nature of suffering might be viewed, especially after the Holocaust, as trite, platitudinous, and—what is worst—callous. Many now will have no truck with the uses of adversity and brand reference to the crucible of pain as insensitive.

I can understand such a reaction—and indeed, up to a point, share it. But only up to a point. Ultimately, there is no denying the fact that, dissonant as these responses are to many modern ears, they are of the essence of *yahadut*'s traditional reaction to suffering at the speculative, pragmatic, or therapeutic level. That they might sound empty or unpalatable to some brings us back to a central point. Response to suffering cannot be divorced from the totality of religious experience, and the ability to integrate religious solutions is a function of the totality of faith and commitment. But that is precisely the Achilles' heel of modern man and of many a contemporary Jew, to the extent to which he has hitched his wagon to modernity, to a world in which, as Arnold lamented, "the sea of faith" no longer being full, there is "Nor certitude, nor peace, nor help for pain; / And we are here as on a darkling plain / Swept with confused alarms of struggle and flight, / Where ignorant armies clash by night."[72] In such a context, the key to confronting suffering in a Jewish way lies beyond formulae related to the realm of suffering. It entails reaffirmation of one's fundamental *yahadut.*

---

[72]"Dover Beach."

3

Pain: Halakha and Hashkofah

Moshe D. Tendler

OBSERVATIONS ON THE BIOLOGY OF PAIN

Pain is one of nature's earlier signs of morbidity. It is preeminent among the sensory experiences by which we judge the presence of disease within ourselves. When it is acute, it serves as a crucial signal of the disorder's location and nature. When it is chronic and persistent, it challenges the diagnostic skill of the best physician to determine its cause or significance. Unlike most stimuli, which lose their effectiveness when applied continuously (accommodation), pain might persist as long as the pain stimulus is operative and, by establishing a central excitatory state, even might outlast the stimulus itself. Not all pain is a consequence of serious

disease. Seemingly healthy individuals have many pains that
are part of their sensory experience. For example, a sharp,
momentary pain over an eye or in the ear might strike with
suddenness, or a more persistent ache of shoulder or joint,
or even a fleeting discomfort in the chest that arouses the
thought of cardiac disease; all might be of no consequence.
These so-called normal pains occur at all ages and depart
as obscurely as they came. When pain appears to be abnor-
mal because of its intensity, duration, or circumstance of
occurrence, a cause or mechanism must be sought. There
are diagnostic clues to evaluate in order to determine the
significance of the pain sensation. Its location, the factors
that provoke or relieve it, its quality and duration, as well
as its severity and time of occurrence are all factors in determining the pain's significance. Pain is not a purely physical phenomenon, divorced from the individual's mental,
psychological state. The placebo effect clearly illustrates the
intimate association between the perceptive processes that
go on in the higher brain and the ability to experience and
interpret physiological pain. Thirty-five percent of patients
suffering from a variety of pains benefit greatly when given
therapeutically inert substances under the guise of pharma-
cological therapy. It now is believed that this effect, the
attenuation of pain, is mediated by activities within the
body. Indigenous opioid substances called endorphins are
manufactured within the brain and serve to counter the
painful experience.

Is there a theological complementarity to the physiology
of pain? The Talmud in *Shabbot* (55a) teaches: "*Amar Rav
Ami, ein mita be'lo heit ve'ein yissurin be'lo avon.*" ("There
is no death without sin, no pain without iniquity.") Hence,
pain receptors in our body are designed not only to enable
us to experience our environment and differentiate between
the safe and the unsafe, the benign and the dangerous, but

also to experience our relationship with the Creator of the world. Pain stimuli, therefore, are directed to us so that we can differentiate the right and proper activities in our lives from those that are forbidden and evaluate our own relationship with God. Pain is a warning signal that the relationship requires further attention and correction. Are there "ethical endorphins" that attenuate the message of *Ha-Shem*? Does accommodation occur with theologically significant pain even though it does not occur with physiologically induced pain?

On September 13, 1994, in Michigan, lawmakers passed a law requiring pain-management education for physicians and other health-care professionals. It goes into effect in 1995 and requires practitioners to show proof of pain-management education within the previous three years. This measure is the first by a state government to mandate specific pain-management education for such professionals. In approving the measure, the lawmakers noted the need to provide better access to pain relief for dying patients because the medical profession had not shown an ability to address the problem adequately.

This paper is designed to focus on the role of pain in our lives as understood by our Sages and as elucidated in halakhic principles in which pain serves as a significant component of the decision-making process. It is an attempt to add pain education to our Torah education so that we can better understand the many references in our Torah literature to pain as a human experience of theological significance.

I. Pain as a Halakhic Determinant

Pain plays a significant role in determining permissibility of actions on the Sabbath. It can be a reason for a Sabbath prohibition, and it can be a reason for leniency. Pain is a halakhic determinant in prohibiting activities on the Sabbath. The *Shulhan Arukh Orah Hayyim* 328a states:

> *Mi sheeish lo meihush be'alma ve-hu mithhazeik veholeikh kebari*
>> *asur la'asos lo shum refua afilu al yedei akum gezeira mihum shehikat samamanim.*

This is based on the *Gemora* in *Shabbat* 53b:

> *Beheima she-ahazah dam ein ma'amidin otah ba-mayim bishvil shetiztannen*
>> *Adam she'ahazo dam ma'amidin oto ba-mayim bishvil sheyitztannen.*
>> *Amar Ula gezeira mishum shehikat samamanim.*

Rashi explains: if you will permit him to seek medical relief on Shabbat, he possibly will also commit an *Isur D'Oraita* of grinding herbs to make the medicine. The *Gemara* then continues to question if this indeed be a fear, then why do you permit the man to seek relief on the Shabbat by entering the cold water? Why are we not afraid that he, too, for his own comfort, will seek medicine that might require the grinding of herbs and violate the *issur* of *tohain be-Shabbos?* The *Gemora* answered: "No. When you do it to an animal it is clearly a therapeutic measure *adam nir'eh ke-meikar.*" When he immerses himself, it appears that he merely was overheated and entered the water to cool off. It is the Rif who gives the insight into pain's role in Sabbath laws. He explains that the Halakha should be that it is permissible for a man to lead an animal into the cold pool of water to cool him off because there is no danger that he will commit a Sabbath prohibition of grinding herbs for the animal's welfare. The Sages feared he would transgress when his own health is of concern. In this particular case it is permissible for the man to enter the water to cool off because it is not perceived as an overtly therapeutic act. It is like *ma'akhal briyim*, a food substance that is eaten as a dietary component as well as a medicinal one and may be eaten on the Shabbos. However, if it were clearly a medical treatment, we would prohibit it for fear of man's overreaction because *adam bahul al gufo*. When seeking relief from his own pain sensations, there is the danger that if we permit the taking of medication it might lead to transgression of biblical laws on the Sabbath. Minor discomfort, defined in Halakha as *meihush be-alma*, is reason for prohibiting the taking of any medication on the Sabbath. This degree of pain is to be viewed as a normal component of our mortal life. We have no right to expect that *Ha-Shem* will protect us from even the most minor of discomforts: the occasional mild headache or a stab of pain that has no medical significance. Hypochondria has no place in the personality's healthy development. A hypochondriac is subject to panic, which might lead to desecration of the Sabbath. Our sages, therefore, prohibited doing anything for these minor aches and pains. In doing so they taught us a lesson in personality development: we are mortal, and, therefore, we are subject to untoward events. Halakhic restrictions prohibit us from responding to these minor pain sensations lest we magnify and exaggerate them so as to endanger our observance of Sabbath laws.

There is a second aspect of pain on the Sabbath that also leads to prohibition. This is not a prohibition against responding to the pain stimulus; rather, it's against entering a situation where pain and discomfort might interfere with proper observance of the positive commandment on the Sabbath, namely *Oneg Shabbos*. The Rambam in *Hilkhot Shabbat* 21:29 records, as does the *Shulchan Oruch*, the types of waters that may not be used for bathing on the Sabbath. These are waters that cause discomfort to man because of their dissolved salts or the unpleasant contaminants contained therein. It is forbidden to cause oneself discomfort on the Sabbath, for it says: "You shall proclaim the Sabbath a day of joy, a pleasurable day." Here the Rambam is referring to actual pain sensation due to the water's sulfur content or to other irritants that might be therein. In *Hilkhot Shabbat* 30:13, the Rambam lists conditions that impose great psychological stress on the individual and hence, if possible, should be avoided on the Sabbath. Specifically listed are the prohibitions against initiating a military campaign within three days of the Sabbath and leaving on a sea voyage within three days of the Sabbath; fear of the impending battle or the planned sea voyage will prevent the individual from properly fulfilling the mitzvah of *Oneg Shabbos*. Fear and depression are emotions that are the antitheses of joy. It is interesting to note that the Rambam separates physical discomfiture from psychological stress, listing the physical discomfiture that is forbidden because of *Oneg Shabbos* in chapter 21 and the psychological stress in chapter 30.

II. Pain as a Reason for Leniency in Applying Sabbath Prohibitions

The Shulhan Arukh Orah Hayyim 328:17:

Holeh she-nafal me-hamat holyo le-mishkhav ve'ein bo sakana

A patient is not critically ill and his life is not endangered, but he is sufficiently pained to prefer being in bed. He is experiencing discomfort that interferes with his normal daily activities. He has become an invalid temporarily, even though his illness does not cause any concern for his safety. In such a circumstance, our Sages removed their prohibition against seeking medical help on the Sabbath and permitted the use of a non-Jew (*amira le-akum*) to seek any comfort that is available. They even went a step further and removed another rabbinic prohibition not directly related to illness. This is the one against using food that a non-Jew cooked without the actual involvement of a Jew. (Halakha 19) They did not permit a *Jew* to do an *issur de-Rabbanan* but merely exempted the individual from the prohibition of *refuah be-Shabbat,* as well as from the prohibition of eating *bishulei akum.*

The Halakha recognizes that pain might vary in intensity, *meihush, holeh she'ein bo sakhanah,* and *tsa'ar tuvah.* If the patient is experiencing a greater amount of pain, further leniency is to be extended. In a case of significant acute pain, the sages even permitted the individual himself or another Jew to transgress rabbinic prohibitions on the Sabbath; but not those of biblical authority (*de-oraita*). There are two sources for this last ruling. At this third level of pain, the individual may violate rabbinic ordinances, as can any other Jew seeking to help him. This Halakha also is recorded in the *Shulhan Arukh* on *ha-meifis shehin be-Shabbat* Halakha 28. It is permissible for an individual to lance a boil on the Sabbath to relieve the pain caused by the boil's pressure against the nerve endings. Simply to lance the boil—not to do a definitive, curative surgery—in order to release some of the pus and thus relieve the pain is permissible on the Sabbath. Why? It is the application of the principle *be-makom tsa'ar lo gazru Rabbanan* if *"tsa'ar"* is of a significant intensity. The second source is *Ketubot* 60a, where it is recorded that if someone is suffering from a severe, hacking cough that racks his body so that he is greatly discomforted, he is permitted, in accordance with a then-held medical belief, to suckle a goat on the Sabbath, drinking the fresh milk directly from its teat as a *Refuah,* as a treatment for the severe cough. Milking a goat on the Sabbath is a biblical prohibition. Suckling the goat and drinking the milk directly from its teat is looked upon as an unusual way to obtain the milk; hence, in accordance with Sabbath laws, because it is unusual (*al yedei shinui*) it is only a rabbinic prohibition, which may be vacated for the individual to obtain relief from his hacking cough. In both the case of the lancing of the boil and in this treatment for the severe cough, it is the Jew himself who is permitted to transgress rabbinic law. Thus, we see that pain can be a component in the halakhic decision to prohibit taking medication on the Sabbath; if the pain's intensity is greater, then it serves as a reason for leniency in observance of Sabbath laws.

It is interesting to note that both the *Shulhan Arukh* of the *Ba'al Ha-Tanya* and the *Eglei Tal* of the *Avnei Nezer* prohibit the taking of medication even in the case of intermediate intensity of pain *be-holeh she'ein bo sakana.* They permit medical ministrations other than the actual taking of a pharmaceutical substance because they both interpret the Halakha that the actual use of a medication that can be made by the grinding of herbs was not included in the leniency. The use of a non-Jew, indeed, was the main leniency, as well as the exemption of the laws of *bishul akum*, but the taking of medication, which was our Sages' original concern, was not included. The *Eglei Tal* compares this Halakha to the Halakha of shofar on Shabbat where the Sages issued a prohibition against performing a mitzvah *min ha-Torah* for fear it would lead to Sabbath transgression. Likewise, their prohibition against taking medication, which was designed to protect the sanctity of the Sabbath was not revoked even in the case of a more severe pain. They do agree, however, in a case of pain of the higher intensity—one referred to as *tsa'ar tuva*, when the Sages permitted the transgression of rabbinic ordinances—the actual taking of medication also would be permitted.

III. Pain as a Determinant in Deciding when not to Treat a Terminal Patient

There are numerous references in the Talmud and in the Midrash that define quality of life in Halakha. It is a concept that is well-accepted if halakhic parameters are observed carefully. Only the patient can judge quality of life. Those who have suffered slow deterioration due to chronic illness adjust to each level of reduced abilities and, therefore, cannot be judged by any absolute standard. However, one common denominator can be discerned from all the references to be cited: intractable pain is an unacceptable quality of life for a terminal patient. Although it is forbidden to hasten death in order to escape even the most intense pain, it is within Halakha's parameters to withhold life-prolonging or death-postponing therapy if it is not possible to provide the patient with pain relief. The following references serve as the basis for this decision.

A. *Ketubot* 77b

Rabbi Yehoshua ben Levi, recognized in the Talmud as one of the greatest of the tzaddikim in an era of tzaddikim, is involved in a miraculous encounter with the Angel of Death. As recorded, he asked the Angel of Death to show him his place in *Gan Eden*. He then requested that he be permitted to hold the Angel of Death's sword so as to reduce the fright he felt seeing it in the angel's hand. As the tale continues, Rabbi Yehoshua forced his way into Paradise and took an oath that he would not leave. The Angel of Death, therefore, appealed to *Ha-Shem*, who ruled that because Rabbi Yehoshua took an oath and never in his life had occasion to abrogate it even through legal means (*hatarat nedarim*), He would not force Yehoshua to leave Paradise. The angel pleaded for Rabbi Yehoshua to return his sword, but he refused. *Ha-Shem* then called out to Rabbi

Yehoshua: "Return his sword. My mortals have need of it."
The sword, or the scythe of the Grim Reaper in modern
imagery, is often a source of relief when pain makes life
too burdensome.

B. *Ketubot* 104a

The death of Rabbi Judah the Prince, known as Rebbi, the
compiler of the Mishnah, is described in *Ketubot* 104a.
When Rebbi fell mortally ill and was in great pain, the yeshiva students prayed for his continued life. His maidservant saw his anguish and prayed instead that the angels
above receive Rebbi and that the students' prayers be rejected. She decided to disturb them by crashing an urn in
their midst. When their prayer was silenced, Rebbi's soul
rose to Heaven. The Talmud records with praise the
maidservant's wisdom. There is a time for prayer to stop;
there is a time for the soul to return to Heaven. Efforts to
fight for "the last breath" are contrary to the Halakha under these circumstances.

C. *Nedorim* 40a

The Talmud records an incident that occurred in the Academy of the great Rabbi *Akiva*. For reasons, difficult to
fathom, human relations were not maintained at the level
appropriate for great *talmidai chakhomim*. The Talmud, in
Yevomos 62b, attributes the plague that decimated this
Academy during the days of *Sfira* as due to this failure in
human relations. One of the disciples took ill and none of
his fellow students came to visit. Rabbi Akiva who did visit
him and was of great help, actually saving his life, rebuked
the students in the Academy by saying that: "He who does
not visit the sick, is as if he sheds blood". Rabbeinu Nissim,
in his commentary on the Talmud printed alongside the
text of the Talmud, analyzes the statement of Rabbi Akiva

as follows: "You should have come to be of help to him. You could have prayed for his recovery. If you had found him in such a state that he was in great pain without hope of recovery, you could have prayed for his quick death." Rabbeinu Nissim thus establishes in unequivocal terms that there is a time to pray for a person's death. Surely, this is not the time for heroics to prolong life by minutes or days, or to attempt to resuscitate such a patient after his heart has stopped.

D. *Avodah Zorah* 18a

Rabbi Chaninah ben Tradyon was burned at the stake for teaching *Torah* publicly, violating the Roman edict. The executioner, in an act of additional cruelty, wrapped Rabbi Chaninah in a Torah scroll and placed wet wads of wool on his chest to prolong the dying process. When his students called out to him to open his mouth and breathe in the flames in order to hasten his death, Rabbi Chaninah refused. "I cannot do that. Let the one who gave me life take it away, for it is forbidden to injure oneself." The executioner, hearing this exchange between Rabbi Chaninah's students and daughter, realized the greatness of his victim and the heinous nature of his own crime. The executioner, in an act of contrition asked for permission to remove the wads of wool and to be credited with a meritorious act for it. Rabbi Chaninah agreed and even swore that his executioner would have a place in the world to come.

Distinction between opening one's mouth to inhale the flames and removing the wads of wool is quite obvious. Opening the mouth is an act of active euthanasia. Removing the wads of wool is cessation of treatment that is prolonging the dying process. The Talmud records this tale of heroism and devotion, to teach the halakhic facts. When the patient is suffering intense pain, and there is no means of alleviating this pain, certainly not of curing the patient, then prolongation of life is without virtue.

E. *Ta'anis* 23a

The Talmud records the strange tale of *Choni* the Circle Drawer who slept for seventy years. Choni was a great *tzadik* whose relationship with *Ha-Shem* allowed him "as a child dealing with his father" to draw a circle around himself and demanding that *Ha-Shem* send rain to the parched land of Israel or else he will not leave this circle. This great *tzadik* arose from his long sleep and entered the house of study where he was quickly recognized as among the greatest *Talmidei Chakhomim* of that time. He overheard one of the scholars saying: "Not since the time of *Choni Hama'agel* was there one who could explain *Ha-Shem's Torah* so lucidly." All of Choni's effort to convince the people that he was, indeed, that Choni were to no avail. They recognized his great mastery of Torah but assumed that he was somewhat unbalanced in identifying himself as the Choni who had disappeared some seventy years earlier.

Choni felt himself an outcast from his society and prayed to *Ha-Shem* for death. The maxim "Give me friendship or give me death" was pronounced by one of the sages to explain *Choni's* plea to *Ha-Shem*. Choni was not suffering from any terminal illness, but suffered severe mental anguish, psychological pain. The Talmud does not look askance at Choni's refusal to continue his life of anguish. Indeed, in halakhah, psychological trauma is fully equated with physiological pain.

F. *Sotah* 46b

The Talmud records the dramatic case in which loss of quality of life was a determinant for refusal to prolong that life. The town of Luz was inhabited by great *tzaddikim* whose main activity was making *tekhailes* for the *tzitzis.* Because of their meritorious behavior, no person ever died in that town; the Angel of Death had no permission to enter. When these elderly righteous men of Luz determined that life had lost its savor, that life had become burdensome to them, they would leave the town to await natural death. The Talmud records this without negative comment, as if fully to concur that loss of quality of life, as defined by the patient, is adequate justification for removing the impediments to death.

G. *Bava Metzia* 84a

The death of Rabbi Yohanan is recorded here. As the story unfolds, Rabbi Yohanan felt that he caused the death of his great student and brother-in-law, Reish Lakish. This feeling of guilt so plagued him as to make him mentally unbalanced. The Talmud records that the sages, therefore, decided to pray for his death. Surely they first must have tried to pray for his recovery. But when these prayers went unanswered, they then decided that this life—that of an individual whom insanity had overtaken—was one without quality and that returning his soul to Heaven would be preferred.

H. Midrash *Tehillim* 8

An elderly woman came to Rabbi Yossi ben Halafta, complaining that she was so old that life had lost its meaning. She complained of loss of appetite and lack of desire to live, and asked to be taken from this world. Rabbi Yossi asked her: "How did you reach such an old age?" She replied: "I attend synagogue services every morning to pray, and nothing is ever allowed to interfere with this obligation." Rabbi Yossi's response to her was: "Absent yourself from the synagogue for three consecutive days." She complied with this suggestion. On the third day she took ill and died. The Midrash, which is a proper source for halakhic directives when unopposed by talmudic sources, thus clearly teaches that mental anguish—when so interpreted by the sufferer—is to be viewed as an unacceptable quality of life. It was, therefore, permissible to pray to *Ha-Shem* to end this life. If one may pray for the life of no quality to end, certainly no one is obligated to initiate heroic measures to prolong it.

The Talmud in *Baitza* 32b sums it up in one succinct phrase: there are three whose lives are meaningless. Among them is listed "one whose body is wracked with pain." These talmudic references serve as the source for the Responsa of Rav Moshe Feinstein, *Igrot Moshe Choshen Mishpot* 3, 73-75, as well as for the opinion recorded in the name of Rav Shlomo Zalman Auerbach, in the fourth volume of the *Encyclopedia of Halakha and Medicine*, edited by Dr. Abraham Steinberg of Jerusalem (pp. 402-411).

The Talmud records an incident that occurred in the academy of the great Rabbi Akiva. For reasons difficult to fathom, human relations were not maintained at the level appropriate for great *Talmidai chakhomim.* The Talmud, in *Yevomos* 62b, attributes the plague that decimated this academy during the days of *Sfira* to be a result of this failure in human relations. One of the disciples took ill, and none of his fellow students came to visit. Rabbi Akiva, who did visit him and was of great help actually saving his life, rebuked the academy students by saying that "He who does not visit the sick, is as if he sheds blood." Rabbenu Nissim, in his commentary on the Talmud printed alongside the text of the Talmud, analyzes Rabbi Akiva's statement as follows: "You should have come to be of help to him. You could have prayed for his recovery. If you had found him in such a state that he was in great pain without hope of recovery, you could have prayed for his quick death."

Rabbenu Nissim thus establishes in unequivocal terms that there is a time to pray for a person's death. Surely this is not the time for heroics to prolong life by minutes or days, or to attempt to resuscitate such a patient after his heart has stopped.

IV. Pain as a Measure to Quantify the Prohibition of Eating on Yom Kippur

The Talmud in *Yuma* 73b quantifies the prohibition of eating and drinking on Yom Kippur, aside from the standard used for forbidden foods. Rather than the *shi'ur ke-zayis* and for fluids *revi'is*, the *shiur* given is a large *koseves* and the quantity of liquid that can fill one cheek. The explanatory note in the *Mishnah Brura, Shulhan Arukh* (612:1) focuses attention on the role of pain or discomfort with reference to this law. I quote: "Even though in all *issurei Torah* we measure the quantity of forbidden food as a *ke-zayis*, that is because the prohibition is recorded as *issur akhila*. The quantity of *akhila*, or eating, always is defined as a *ke-zayit*. However, with reference to eating on Yom Kippur, the language used is that of *innuy*, as it is written: And the individual who will not discomfort himself *ha-nefesh asher lo teunneh*. Our sages established that less than the quantity of a *kotevet* does not provide *yisuv da'at*, or comfort, at all, and the individual is as hungry and as discomforted as before he ate. This is the elaboration offered in the Talmud *Yuma* 79a."

Although eating is measured now with a new yardstick—that of providing solace or contentment—eating less than the quantity that brings contentment nevertheless is also forbidden, as in all other *issurim, hatzi shi'ur asur min ha-Torah*. Indeed, it is difficult to understand what "half of contentment" means. Half a *zayit* might not be a full nutritional contribution, but it surely is a partial contribution. How do

we define half a contentment, except with the understanding that the Talmud gives us that *hatzi shi'ur asur min ha-
Torah* because *hazi le'itztrufi?* Indeed, in the present it
makes little contribution, but it is possible to add to it to
fulfill the goal of eating: namely, removing the hunger
pangs and providing contentment. The Torah prohibited
eating not only as a final act but as a process that begins
with *hatzi shi'ur* and ends with the full *shi'ur*, be it nutritional or contentment and solace. With this analysis it is
possible to understand what many have believed to be an
inexplicable ruling of the Hinukh in Mitzvah 313. The
Hinukh to whom we are so indebted for a deeper understanding of all the mitzvoth issues a ruling that with one
who is ill, even though there is no *sakanah* and he is not
critically ill, it is proper to feed him and offer him drink—
as long as you do so in small quantities, less than the
amount considered a violation of a biblical prohibition and
punishable by *karet* or requiring a *korban hattat*. He should
be fed these small quantities separated by proper units of
time (the time it takes to eat three eggs, which we consider
today to be approximately nine minutes), and he may drink
less than the proscribed quantity of liquid. The *Minchat
Hinukh* objects (313:5): "Nowhere have I seen this permission that someone who is not critically ill be allowed to eat
small quantities on Yom Kippur since half a *shi'ur* is also a
biblical prohibition. Why should we permit the abrogation
of a biblical prohibition for an individual who is classified
as *holeh she'ein bo sakana*? Indeed, the Tur clearly states
when there is no danger to health, the patient is not critically ill; just as he is forbidden to eat full quantities on Yom
Kippur, he is not permitted to eat the smaller quantities
either."

Applying the principle of *yituvei daat*, or psychological
solace, to analyze the Hinukh's decision shines a light

of understanding on his opinion. When a prohibition focuses on caloric intake, then it is possible to understand that *hatzi shi'ur asur min ha-Torah.* However, if the yardstick is solace, *yituvei daata,* then the *hatzi shi'ur* eaten according to halachic orders offer no solace at all. This analysis also provides an answer to the question that the Sha'agat Aryeh, *Siman* 65, poses to the Tur (612), who quotes the Aviezri's opinion that *akal mi-davar she'eino ra'ui le-akhila af isura leika.*

However, in the laws of Pesah, the Tur accepts the ruling of his father, the Rosh, that *hametz* that has been scorched before Pesah so that it is not fit to be eaten nevertheless cannot be eaten on Pesah. The very act of eating restores it to the level of edible food; this is the concept of *ahsheveih.* The Sha'agt Aryeh then poses why is this principle not applicable on Yom Kippur? How would the Aviezri say that it is perfectly permissible to eat things that are not considered to be edible foods, disregarding the principle of *ahsheveih?* The answer to this question is self-evident. When eating is measured with the yardstick of psychological solace and contentment, an individual who is required to eat food that is not considered edible, decides to do so only because of hunger or distress surely has no *yituvei daat.* There is no solace or psychological contentment when one eats food all others consider inedible.

V. The Pain of Circumcision

In 1987, a research paper appeared in the *New England Journal of Medicine* (K.J.S. Anand and P. R. Hickey, November 19, 1987, 1321-1328) that served to focus the medical profession's attention on the pain of the neonate. Indeed, the evaluation of pain in the human fetus and neonate is difficult because pain generally is defined as a subjective phenomenon. Early studies of neurological development had concluded that neonatal response to painful stimuli was not the same as that of adults. It was defined as decorticate in nature, and perception or localization of pain was not present. Furthermore, because neonates might not have memories of painful experiences, they were not considered capable of interpreting pain in a manner similar to that of adults. On a theoretical basis, some postulated that infants have a high pain threshold as an adaptive phenomenon to protect them during birth. These traditional views were widely held; the medical community assumed that fetuses or neonates were not capable of perceiving pain and therefore subjected them to minor surgical procedures without the benefit of analgesia or anesthesia. These authors measured physiological changes associated with pain, including cardio-respiratory, hormonal, and metabolic responses; simple behavioral changes such as basic motor responses, facial expressions, and crying; more complex behavioral changes such as reduced non-rapid eye movement sleep in newborns; wakefulness and irritability after circumcision and an altered arousal level in circumcised male infants, as compared with females and uncircumcised male infants; and an altered sleep-wake state in neonates undergoing heel-stick procedures. These changes persisted for more than twenty-two hours after circumcision. It was postulated that such painful procedures might have a prolonged effect on the neurological and psycho-social development of neonates. In a recent paper by A. Taddio. et. al., published in *Lancet*, February 4, 1995, vol. 344, 291-92, the investigators concluded that neonatal circumcision might affect pain response several months after the event, as evidenced by the fact that neonates who had undergone circumcision respond to subsequent vaccination with longer crying periods and greater behavioral changes than do the uncircumcised group. The 1987 research paper concluded that there were

many lines of evidence to show that cortical as well as sub-
cortical centers necessary for pain perception are well-de-
veloped late in gestation and that the neuro-chemical system now known to be associated with pain transmission and
modulation is fully intact and functional in the neonate.
Physiological responses to painful stimuli were well-docu-
mented in neonates of various gestational ages and reflected
in cardio-respiratory, hormonal, and metabolic changes similar to but greater than those observed in adult subjects.
Other responses in newborn infants are suggestive of inte-
grated emotional and behavioral responses to pain that are
retained in memory long enough to modify subsequent
behavior patterns. What obligation does this put on those
who follow the Halakha? It is forbidden to cause pain to
others. The Torah records a special curse on those who
would cause pain to the defenseless, the widow, and the
orphan. (*Mishpatim* 22:21 and the *Mekhilta* on this verse)
Does this not put an absolute obligation on the mohel to
use whatever means of analgesia is available—within his
competence and without incurring any additional danger
to the infant—in order to reduce the painful experience?
Those who have held a newborn on their lap as *sandek*,
firmly restraining the knees so that the infant's thrashing
does not interfere with the mohel's work, know very well
that there are extreme expressions of pain other than crying. The writhing of a child, the attempt to escape the
painful stimulus, is clearly evident to anyone who is even
minimally perceptive during the performance of this great
mitzvah. Two research papers have appeared relatively recently urging the use of topical anesthetic for neonate
circumcision and confirming the safety and efficacy of this
procedure. The first suggests the use of 30 percent lidocane
in a special base that is applied some time before the circumcision, giving a high degree of pain relief without any

danger to the infant. There was no significant absorption of lidocane, as measured in the infant's blood serum. (K. B. Weatherstone, et. al. *Pediatrics*, vol. 92, no. 5, November 1993). A second paper by F. Benini, et. al., appeared in *JAMA* 1993 (270:850-853) recommending another cream, EMLA, which is a mixture of various anesthetic agents; good success is claimed. I have been *sandek* a number of times when EMLA has been used, and evaluated it as only marginally helpful. However, when 30 percent lidocane was used, there was great pain diminution, as clearly evidenced by the newborn's behavior.

Halakhic literature does contain references to the use of local anesthetic. Rabbi Yehiel Weinberg (*Sridei Esh* 3:96) records the opinion of the Imrei Yosher, who forbids the use of any local anesthesia. He claims that our Sages were aware of the ability to offer local anesthesia, as described in their determination of the payment for pain caused to others, yet did not suggest its use during *milah*. He therefore concludes that pain is an integral part of the circumcision process and brings proof to this opinion from a Midrash. This Midrash, indeed, when analyzed would seem to deny the inference that the Imrei Yosher is drawing from it. Midrash *Rabba* (47:11) records that Avraham experienced the pain of circumcision to increase the reward that Ha-Shem would give him. The theological principle enunciated in that Midrash is the *le-fim tsa'arah agra*. This normally would apply where circumstances not under the individual's control lead to difficulty in performing a mitzvah. The successful surmounting of these obstacles and the successful performance of the mitzvah indeed deserve additional reward from Ha-Shem. The Midrashic application of this concept to a voluntary induction of pain to achieve a greater reward is itself difficult to understand. Surely, to extend this notion to a neonate who is not a conscious participant in the mitzvah's performance would appear to be a misapplication. The fact that pain is looked upon as a basis for additional reward clearly would indicate that the mitzvah itself need not have pain as an accompaniment. The Sridei Esh concludes that whereas total anesthesia indeed should be prohibited, the use of a local analgesic cannot be prohibited, especially because others, such as the Maarkhei Lev, fully approve of such use. Among the *poskim* in Jerusalem, Hagaon Rav Elyashiv, *Shlita*, and Hagaon Rav Shlomo Zalman Auerbach, *zt"l*, permitted it without question. Hagaon Rav Waldenberg and Hagaon Rav Wosner in B'nei Brak prohibited the use of a local anesthetic, claiming that pain was indeed a necessary, integral part of the *milah* mitzvah. The position of these latter two is inexplicable. It should be noted that the use of total anesthesia during a circumcision of an adult convert might present halakhic problems, but surely local anesthesia or analgesia is to be done both for the *ger* and the neonate. It would be, in my opinion, a violation of the Halakha of *lo yosif lehakoto* to fail to do so.

YISSURIM IN HASHKAFAH

A review of Torah literature on the import of pain in our lives reveals five dimensions of pain. Several Talmud passages and Midrash references permit this analysis.

Talmud *Shabbos* 55a:

> *Amar Rav Ami, ein mita be'lo heit ve'ein yissurin be'lo avon. . . .*
>
> *Af Moshe ve'Aharon be-hatai'im metu, shene'emar ya-an lo he'emantem bi.*

The Talmud on that same page questions the justice of the deaths of the *tzaddikim* during the Temple's destruction. Surely there were *tzaddikim* there. The Talmud an-

swers: "No, they should have done more to rebuke and
protest the actions of the *reshaim*, and because they failed
to do so they are held guilty as if they had committed the
transgressions themselves."

The Talmud in *Berakhot* 5a records the statement of
Rava, or Rav Hisda:

> *Im ro'eh adam she-essurin ba'in alav yefashpeish be-ma'asav. . . .*
> *Pishpesh ve'lo matza yitle be-bitul Torah, she-ne'emar.*
> *"Ashrei ha-gever asher te'yasrenu ka u'mi-Toratkha telam-*
> *denu." (Tehillim 94:12)*
> *Ve'im tala ve'lo matza beyadua shey'essurin shel ahava hen*
> *she-ne'emar "Ki et asher yoav Hashem yokhiah." (Mishlei 3:12)*

This passage introduces two additional ways that pain has
an impact on our ethical lives. The first is a function analogous to physiological pain: it is to attract our attention to
some pathology that otherwise would be neglected. People
who because of neurological deficits do not experience pain
are subject to great dangers in our environment. Likewise,
an individual can be so engrossed in his life as to be unaware that he indeed has developed an ethical pathology.
Ha-Shem then sends the stimulus down from Heaven to
make him search his lifestyle, his behavior, so that he can
detect where the pathology is, localize it, and thus focus
curative attention on it. The second component in this
passage in *Berakhot* is best understood as rigorous training.
An athlete or a member of special armed forces will undergo rigorous, physically demanding training far in excess
of what he most likely will encounter in his life as an athlete or military man. It is an exercise regimen in which the
principle "no pain, no gain" is acknowledged. This, I believe, is the true intent of *yissurim shel ahava*, which seems
to have little rationale. Not so. If careful investigation does
not reveal a pathology, then our omniscient God, whose
watchful eye controls the daily fate of man, surely has a plan

for the individual. The sign of affection in these *yissurim* is analogous to a teacher's decision to set higher standards for a particularly apt student, requiring him to devote far more time and effort than others in the class. If careful investigation and introspection do not reveal any defect in an individual's moral and ethical behavior, then the interpretation that the Talmud insists upon is that *Ha-Shem* has asked him to move to a higher plane, to establish greater goals yet to be obtained. The *yissurim* visited upon him, as defined by our sages, are *yissurim sh-ein bahem bitul Torah*. They do not interfere with his ability to study. The study of Torah is the only means of climbing to a new plateau in response to *Ha-Shem*'s stimulus.

The Midrash this educative force that pain exerts explains why *Ha-Shem* decided that only through enslavement in Egypt would the Jewish nation be able to fulfill its role as a "light and prophet" to all nations. Midrash *Shemos Rabbah* 1:1 associates the very first verse, which tells of the families of Yaakov's descendants entering Egypt, with a verse in Proverbs (13:24): *Hosekh shivto sonei be'no ve'ohavo shiharo musar."* ("A father who spares the rod will ultimately hate his son, and one who loves his son rebukes him daily.") The Midrash records the tragedy of failure to discipline a son properly. Avraham had a Yishma'el, Yitzhak had his Eisav, David had Avshalom and Adoniyahu because they failed to rebuke or punish their sons properly when it was necessary. The Midrash then offers this explanation for our *galut* in Egypt: *Ve'ohavo shiharo musar she-zeh ha-Kadosh Barukh Hu al she-ahav et Yisroel*, as it is written: "*Ahavti etkhem amar Ha-Shem.*" Therefore, he subjugates them with *yissurim*. God gave the Jewish people three wonderful gifts, but all require the experience of *yissurim*. They are: Torah, the land of Israel, and the World to Come. None of these can be attained without the stimulus of *yissurim* to drive the Jew to greater heights. What is required is someone who can reach above the average to earn *Ha-Shem*'s respect and love. It is as if *Ha-Shem,* because of his promise to Avraham, Yitzchok, and Yaakov, is indebted or obligated to see that their descendants succeed in their mission to be a light unto the nations. This often requires that *Ha-Shem* use the stimulus of *yissurim* to drive us upward and forward.

Braishit Rabbah 34:2 analyzes a verse in *Tehillim* (11:5): *"Ha-Shem tzadik yivhan ve-rasha ve-ohev hamas san'a nafsho."* ("God tests the *tzadik,* the evil one God despises.") Two parables then are recorded. The first, in the name of Rav Yonata: the manufacturer of ceramic barrels does not check the broken barrels for soundness, but only the good ones. If the barrel is constructed properly, it can be hit many times and will not break. So it is that God tests only the *tzaddikim,* not the *reshoim.* The second is that of one who makes flax. After the retting operation, he checks his flax. Those that survived the complex process are subjected to further processing, for he is confident that the fibers will only be stronger and more uniform because of this additional stress placed upon them. Those fibers that clearly show damage during the retting operation are not subjected to further complex processing because they never will be able to serve to produce a quality garment. These two images present two reasons for subjecting individuals to the test of *yissurim.* The first speaks of the need for the individual to know himself, to know that he has been tested and not found wanting. It is not that *Ha-Shem* needs this proof but that the individual requires the recognition that life's minor discomfitures have not interfered with his relationship with *Ha-Shem.* The second simile speaks not of differentiating between the wheat and the chaff, the good and the bad, but rather *yissurim*'s influence enabling the individual to climb to greater heights, to attain greater perfection in his ethical and moral behavior. The Kloizenberger Rav, *zt"l*, in one of his magnificent *Humash Shiurim* on the verse in *Bamidbar* (1:49) instructing Moshe not to count the tribe of Levi, noted Rashi's comment: "Because they are the legions of the King." They are the palace guard and should not be counted with the regular army. The Kloizenberger Rav, with great pathos, made the observation that he would prefer another reason why the *shevet* Levi should not be counted. They never had suffered the enslavement in Egypt. They are untested. They might break and run at the first sign of battle. *Ha-Shem* wants to know who are his veteran soldiers on whom He can count. He concluded: "If someone would ask me how many Jews there are in the world, I would answer how many were in the camps, the work camps, the annihilation camps, who survived as God-fearing, Torah-observing Jews? That's all *Ha-Shem* has for certain. All others are untested, untried. Who knows how they will respond in time of great personal stress." They are the clay barrels that never have been subjected to the hammer blow to check their soundness. The second parable concerning the flax is really an issue that is best understood as an attempt to live up to a full potential. Many attain great perfection in their lives, fine reputations for integrity and honesty and cooperativeness; yet if measured by their potential, they must be viewed as failures. A parent in the yeshiva once asked my great father-in-law, *zt"l*, what he should do. The parent has no excuse to chastise his son. He is the best in his class. He is a pleasure to have at home. He is most obedient and respectful. Yet the verse says: "He who spareth the rod, will learn to hate his son." Rav Moshe answered without hesitation: "Raise your standards for him; you'll then have reason to rebuke him."

The Talmud (*Bava Batra* 10b) records a near-death experience that Rav Yosef's son had. Upon the son's recovery, convinced that he indeed had crossed over into the
next world, his father asked him: "What did you see there?"
He answered: "I saw a topsy-turvy world. Those of high esteem in this world were considered of low esteem there,
and those of low esteem were treated there as if they were
people of high esteem." His father answered: "No, you saw
a true world." The son added a recollection: "Indeed, I
heard them say: 'Fortunate is he who comes to this world
and his studies are in his hand, *talmudo be-yado*.' " Rav
Moshe offers his understanding of this passage by posing
the question: "Surely, everyone knew that the other world,
the World to Come, is *Olam ha-Emet*, the true world. What
the son should have said was: "Our world is a topsy-turvy
world. People who are held in low esteem there in the
Olam ha-Emet are held in high esteem here." The explanation Rav Moshe offers is a fundamental principle in education. *Ha-Shem* has not blessed all equally with intellectual powers. However, those who have been so blessed are
judged by the degree to which they lived up to their full
potential. Because of their great accomplishments, those
held in high esteem here are so recognized in the World
of Truth. Yet they are not given the honor and respect that
is seemingly their due because they failed in their mission.
They failed to live up to their full potential. They could have
been even greater but were not. Those whom we hold in
low esteem here are held in high esteem there because they
did live up to their fullest potential and that's the way they
are judged. They are judged by *talmudo be-yado,* his own
learning ability, his own quantity of learning that he could
have achieved. Those who are seemingly less accomplished
are judged there as if they had achieved greatness. The story
is told of the Hazon Ish, whose custom was to receive many

people on *erev* Rosh Hashana. They came to receive his blessings and to extend their own to this great *gaon*. He would sit at his desk, and the people would enter, shake his hand, say a few words, and leave. One person, who came every year, would be honored by having the Hazon Ish rise and walk him to the door. When his *rebbetzin* asked for an explanation about what was so special about this young man, the Hazon Ish answered: "This young man was born with a reduced potential. He was intellectually challenged, and with great effort he succeeded far beyond everybody's expectation. I view him as the only one who comes to see me who has lived up to his full potential. I honor him because of that."

THE SUBTLE LANGUAGE OF PAIN

A. *Hulin* 7b:

Amar Rav Elazar dam nikuf meratze ke-dam Olah. Amar Rava be'godel yamin uvnikuf sheini; ve'hu deka'azil le'dvar mitzvah. Amru alav al Rav Pinchas ben Ya'ir: miyamav lo batza al prusah she'einah shelo u'miyom she'amad al daato lo nehene miseudat aviv.

Rabbi Elazar taught that the bleeding of a stubbed toe corrects the relationship between man and God as if it were an *Olah* sacrifice. Rava elaborated: this is true if it was the second time the toe was injured before recovering from its first injury and it occurred on the right toe when the individual was on a mission to perform a mitzvah. This enigmatic passage in the Talmud requires much elaboration. The passage continues with a reference to the great Pinhas ben Ya'ir, who never permitted himself to accept an invitation to eat with anyone and from the day he was mature enough would not even eat at his father's table. Taken together, the Rav Elazar's statement, as elaborated by Rava, and the reference to Pinhas ben Ya'ir's seemingly asocial behavior serve to teach a lesson in the language of pain.

The reference to the right big toe brings to mind the anointing of this toe during the ceremony that initiated Aharon and his sons into priestly service. Thus Rava, by this comment, directs the mind away from punitive pain and substitutes the notion of pain that brings man closer to God, emphasizing the educative role that pain can play for those who can hear the language of *Ha-Shem* as he speaks to man. The fact that the toe was stubbed twice is, as in the repeated dream of Pharaoh, a request for immediate attention. The fact that it occurred while going to do a mitzvah removes the thought that this could be a punitive pain. *Ha-Shem* would not choose this time when an individual is going to do a mitzvah to issue a punitive judgment. Maharsha poses the question of *sheluhei* mitzvah *einan nizakin*. Why was it that *Ha-Shem* would allow him to be damaged while going to do a mitzvah? Does not the mitzvah protect from any untoward event? He therefore offers the less-than-satisfactory suggestion that the individual must have had some ulterior motive in going to do the mitzvah, one that diluted the mitzvah's protective power. There is no need for the question or that answer. It is a non-punitive injury. It is *Ha-Shem*'s expression of esteem and love for this individual. This time was chosen so that the message could not possibly be misunderstood. It is *yissurim shel ahava* that allows man to begin that process of introspection that ultimately will allow him to live up to more of the great potential that *Ha-Shem* gave him. The near-mythical figure Rabbi Pinhas ben Ya'ir, who is portrayed in the Talmud as God-infatuated, chose to remember his dependency on *Ha-Shem* by never accepting any food from others, not even his father. In doing so, he was forced to recognize that *Ki im le-yadkha ha-meleia ha-petuha ha-kedosha ve-harehava,* that everything comes only from *Ha-Shem: Poteiah et yadekha umasbi'a le-khol hai ratzon; Notein lehem le-khol basar ki le-olam hasdo.*

B. *Arakhin* 16b, 17a:

> *Ad heikhan takhlit yissurin. Amar Rabbi Elazar kol she'eino lo beged lilbosh ve'ein mitkabel alav. Matkif lah Rav Zeira ve'iteima Rabbi Shmuel Bar Nahmani gedolah mizu amru afilu nitkavnu limzog be-hamin umazgu lo be-tzonen; be-tzonen umazgu lo be-hamin. Ve'at amart kuli hai; Mar brei d'Ravina amar afilu nehepakh lo haluko; Rava ve'iteima Rav Hisda viteima Rabbi Yitzhak ve'amri lah bematnita tana afilu hoshit yado lekhis litol shalosh ve'alu beyado shtayim. Davka shalosh ve'alu beyado shtayim aval shtayim ve'alu beyado shalosh lo, de-lekha tirha lemishdaihu; vkhal kakh lammah detanya Rabbi Yishma'el kol she'avru alav arba'im yom be'lo yissurin kibbel olamo; bema'arava amri puranut mizdamenet lo.*

What is considered pain in Jewish theology? Rabbi Elazar said: the discomfiture of ordering a garment that did not fit well. Rabbi Shmuel said: the annoyance of having his drink prepared at a temperature not to his liking. Mar said: if he begins to dress and finds his garment turned inside out. Indeed: even if he reached into his purse to take out three coins and only grasped two, necessitating a second effort, this, too, must be considered pain.

Why must we know this "least minimal" definition of pain? In the study hall of Rabbi Yishmael, they explained that if forty days go by without experiencing any pain, not even those minor discomfitures listed above, it means that the individual has received his full reward. In the academies of Israel, it was taught such an individual should be aware that a calamity awaits him.

This talmudic passage is almost inexplicable unless we introduce the notion of *Ha-Shem* speaking to man through the medium of pain, not in a punitive mode but an educational one. If someone has perfected his relationship with *Ha-Shem* as *lehavdil*, with a close friend, it is possible to understand that which others would not. The subtle remark, the changed inflection of the voice, is a message in itself. When someone has stubbed his toe while going to do a mitzvah and thus is sensitized to the voice of *ha-Shem*, he then can read these minor untoward events listed above as stimuli, as *Ha-Shem*'s gentle prodding to be *me-fashpeish be-ma'asav*, to review his lifestyle and behavior patterns, and attempt to rise to a higher plane of ethical and moral perfection. Rabbi Yishmael comments that if forty days have passed by and one has not experienced a single untoward event, not even these minor discomfitures mentioned above, it means that *kibeil olamo*. Rashi defines this term *kibbel olamo* as: *Khol menuhato le'atid ve'im avar aleha had mehanakh harei hu yissurim*. He has received all his "peace" (reward) for the future. If, however, one of the untoward events happened to him, then he has suffered *yissurim*. In the academies of Israel, they taught that if he has not had any of these little warnings, it means that a calamity awaits him. I would suggest that *kibbel olamo* and *puranut mizdamenet lo* really say the same thing. What they say is that *Ha-Shem* has given up on this individual; *ha-Shem* does not talk to him anymore. There is no hope of improving, no hope of living up to a fuller potential, no hope of greater perfection. When *Ha-Shem* sees no hope for this individual to fulfill his full mission in life, then calamity indeed awaits him, for there is then no purpose for maintaining him in this world. Those of us who had the good fortune to grow up in a three-generation family and were exposed to the subtle behaviors of our grandparents might be aware that pain's role as an educational prod was fully understood. When an untoward event happened to our grandparents, they would mumble, *"Zal zain a kaparah"*: "Let this be a forgiveness." This was an acceptance of both the punitive and the instructive roles of pain in their lives. If the pain was to remind the individual of some impropriety, then the response meant *"Ha-Shem,* I got the message. You need not increase the intensity of pain." The belief thus expressed is that if you miss *Ha-Shem's* subtle remarks, then He will begin to speak more forcefully by increasing the intensity of the pain experience. It also recognized the instructive role. If *Ha-Shem* meant it as a prod, then it is time to begin the introspection of *me-faspeish be-ma'asav,* to reexamine past behavior in order to improve the relationship with *Ha-Shem.*

SPECIAL INSTRUCTION TO THOSE WHO SIT IN JUDGMENT ON OTHERS

Rabbonim, chaplains, physicians, psychologists, and psychiatrists evaluate other people. It is part of their professional responsibility even though it imposes serious ethical and moral obligations. Who can properly fulfill the mitzvah of *tokhaha,* to rebuke others, in such a way as to fulfill the mitzvah without incurring any personal sin of excess or inadequacy?

A. *Shemos* 22:23

Ve'hara api ve'haragti etkhem beharev ve'hayu nesheikhem almanot uveneikhem yetomim.

Causing pain or anguish to the defenseless, the widow, or the orphan will incur *Ha-Shem's* anger; your women will be *almanos,* and your children *yesomim.* The *Mekhilta* (18:180) records a dialogue between Rabbi Yishma'el and Rabbi Shimon, the two great martyrs. When they were being taken to the execution site, Rabbi Shimon said to Rabbi Yishma'el: "Rebbi, *libi yotzei she'eini yodei'a al mah ani neherag.*" ("I am so perturbed. I have reviewed all my life's actions. I don't see what I have done so terrible as to deserve this punishment.") Punitive pain does not fit this circumstance. Rabbi Yishma'el posed a series of questions to answer Rabbi Shimon. "Do you recall anyone coming to you for a *Din* Torah or to pose a halakhic *she'eilah,* and you kept him waiting while you finished dressing, while you finished drinking your cup of tea? If you did so, then, indeed, this is punitive punishment." Rabbi Shimon responded to Rabbi Yishma'el, *Kohen Gadol:* "Nihamtani Rabbi, you have consoled me. I had a doubt in my mind whether *Ha-Shem* has forgotten me. I realize that, indeed, He has not. There is justice, and I am being led to the execution for iniquities that I committed in the past."

It is forbidden to cause pain to others, and if these others are particularly defenseless, *Ha-Shem* responds with anger. A moral society is one that extends the greatest protection to the most defenseless. The defenseless coming to you for help acutely feel even the most minor slight. Having lost some of their self-esteem, they magnify any breach of etiquette. The *Mekhilta* is to be understood as an instructive warning that to be in the service of *Ha-Shem* also means to be in the service of all his people. And as a servant, one must be most sensitive to all the rules of etiquette and mutual respect.

   B. An individual's reaction to extreme pain or anguish cannot be used to evaluate his personality or moral and ethical perfection. Extreme pain is an experience that surpasses human endurance. The Talmud (*Sanhedrin* 93a) interprets the verse in *Shir ha-Shirim* 7:9 "*Amarti e'eleh ba-tamar ohaza besansinav*" as: "I thought I would be raised high by all of Israel who

are compared to a *tamar*, to a date palm. But now I
must settle for *ohazah besansinav.*" "*Lo ala beyadi ela
sansan ehad shel Hananyah Misha'eil va'Azaryah.*"
(Only one "branch" supports my role on earth, a
branch entitled "*Hananyah Misha'eil va'Azaryah.*")

The Talmud further elaborates by citing the *pasuk* in
Zech. 1:8:

*"Ve'hinei ish rokheiv al sus adom ve'hu omed bein ha-
hadasim"*
    *Ish zeh ha-Kadosh Barukh Hu. . . . Bikkesh lahafokh et ha-
olam kulo ledam kevan shenistakeil be-Hananyah Misha'eil ve-
Azaryah nitkarera da'ato.*

"And I beheld a man riding on a red horse." The Talmud interprets "*Ish*" as *ha-Kadosh Barukh Hu.* Riding on
a red horse is a sign of his anger, of *Midas ha-Din.* *Ha-Shem*
contemplated destroying the world, turning it into a blood
bath. But having seen the greatness of Hananyah, Misha'eil,
and Azaryah, God was placated. The Talmud in *Ta'anis* 18b
states it simply: "*Tzadikim gemurim hayu, Hananya,
Misha'eil, ve-Azaryah.*" They had lived up to their fullest
potential; they were fully righteous. Nevertheless, the Talmud in *Ketubot* 33b—in citing the Rav's statement questioning whether death is indeed worse than torture—refers
to Hananyah, Misha'eil, and Azaryah accepting death rather
than bowing down to the idol (the statue of the king) with
the following observation:
*Ilmalei nagduha le-Chananyah Misha'eil ve-Azaryah palhu
le-tsalma.*
    Had Hananyah, Misha'eil, and Azaryah been tortured,
they certainly would have bowed down to the idol. Severe
acute pain can overpower the wills of even the most perfect, righteous men. When an individual is subjected to
intense intractable pain, his behavior cannot be viewed as

an expression of his personality or ethical nature, rather, his experience is superhuman and does not in any way reflect on his personality. Patients suffering the "war of attrition" of intractable pain often are said to have a change in personality. They often become much more self-centered, much more demanding, much less concerned with the welfare even of the closest family members. This is not the patient talking. Pain has a voice of its own. Indeed, sometimes it is the voice of *Ha-Shem*. Sometimes pain is so powerful that it even drowns out the voice of *Ha-Shem*.

Rava teaches this lesson in analyzing the story of Job (*Bava Basra* 16b):

Mikan she'ein adam nispas be-sha'at tsa'aro

Rambam expands on this succinct phrase:

Ein adam nispas le-hithayev al she-hu medabber kasheh mehamat tsa'ar ve'yissurin deka'amar lo be-da'at yedabber. Lo amar lo be-rasha yedabbeir ela lo be-da'at.

Job is criticized by friends, and by the tradition for his aggressive remarks to *Ha-Shem*. But they are spoken "without wisdom," not with evil intent.

4

"Tell Them I've Had a Good Enough Life"

Shalom Carmy

Heaven forbid to change the name of the sick person, unless it is done by one whose every action is virtually inspired. For surely the name given a person at birth is invariably appointed by God, insofar as it is his name above, and the vitality of the person all the days that he lives on the face of the earth. Now the sick person surely needs sustenance, and sometimes he has none other than that of the name. If that is uprooted, as when they proclaim, "Your name is no longer called Jacob," and the second name may not be of his vitality, then he remains without that which would sustain his vitality.

(Rabbi Yehiel Mikhal of Zlotchow)[1]

---

[1]Cited by his disciple Rabbi Hayyim of Chernowitz, *Be'er Mayim Hayyim* (Genesis, 101).

97

*Tears poured down his face: he was not at the moment
afraid of damnation—even the fear of pain was in the background. He felt only an immense disappointment because
he had to go to God empty-handed, with nothing done at
all. It seemed to him at that moment that it would have
been quite easy to have been a saint. It would only have
needed a little self-restraint and a little courage. He felt like
someone who had missed happiness by seconds at an appointed place. He knew now that at the end there was only
one thing that counted—to be a saint.*

(Graham Greene)[2]

For the saintly person, whole-heartedly devoted to the service of God, "the beginning of wisdom is the fear of God"
(Ps. 111:10). The endeavor to harness all of one's passions
and creative gifts to this end is not suspended in the face
of suffering and adversity. To the contrary, the commanding voice of Halakha determines that misfortune engenders
a specific obligation of self-examination; in time of trouble,
one is instructed to turn to God.[3] This obedient and creative response presupposes a normative belief in God's
concern for man and in the righteousness and integrity of
God's judgment. Beyond these fundamental principles,
practical wisdom need not postulate a particular theory
about God's governance of the world; it need not claim to
know the precise operation of divine justice and mercy; it
does not affect perspicuity as to the respective merit and
corruption of human beings. We are charged with the task
of repenting our sins, not with that of calculating our

---

[2] *The Power and the Glory* (New York: Viking Press, 1962), 284.

[3] Rambam, *Hil. Taaniyot* 1:1 My interpretation of the Halakha, of
course, is indebted to the discussion by *maran ha-Rav* Joseph B.
Soloveitchik, zt"l, in his *Kol Dodi Dofek.*

deserts. We are here to serve God, not to inspect ourselves from the outside, as it were, under the aspect of eternity.

Nevertheless, many God-fearing Jews have reflected deeply on God's providence for the world of His creation and for the creatures to whom He has revealed His will. Some pious people have shunned thinking about these matters. Because "the matter of judgment is hidden, and we must have faith in His righteousness as the true judge, may He be blessed and exalted," Ramban writes, there are those who would dispense with what they regard as fruitless inquiry and wearying discussion, trusting that "in the end, there are before Him neither iniquity nor oblivion." But this, Ramban continues, "is the argument of fools who reject wisdom."[4] When we formulate an account of God's actions toward the world, we are engaged in the quest for *daat Ha-Shem*, the knowledge of God. Insofar as we succeed in situating ourselves in the mysterious economy of the universe, we are better suited, intellectually and morally, to become the individuals that God bids us to be. That is the saintly individual's goal in life.

If the purpose of our investigation, in keeping with Ramban's dictum, is *daat Ha-Shem*, and in particular the existential appropriation of that insight in order to comprehend our place in the divine economy, we have yet to define the nature of our inquiry. Much depends on how we make this move. Traditionally the inquiry has been called *theodicy*, literally meaning "the justification of God."[5] It opens with a problem that cries out for a solution: the

---

[4]Ramban, *Torat haAdam* (in *Kol Kitvei Ramban*, ed. Chavel, Jerusalem 1963), II, 281.

[5]The term originates with Leibniz. See, for example, Donald Rutherford, *Leibniz and the Rational Order of Nature* (Cambridge University Press, 1995), 7–21, specifically 18 n. 1.

apparent contradiction between the benevolence of the Creator and the imperfection of creation. The religious philosopher's efforts aim to show that the contradiction is merely apparent. He does so by deploying a variety of familiar strategies: evil is illusory in the present or becomes illusory from the perspective of a privileged future time; evil is a necessary ingredient in the greater good or the inevitable consequence of human freedom, the exercise of which is itself essential for the *summum bonum*; and so forth. In the end, there always comes an appeal to human ignorance. Lacking as we do the requisite temporal perspective, nescient of the complex logical dependencies correlating causes and events, deficient in a true appreciation of the *telos* appropriate to man and cosmos, we are asked to give God the benefit of the doubt, so to speak. In the meantime, the apologist's tentative explanations will have to serve as a kind of down payment on the real thing.

The usual context for these arguments is the perennial debate over the truth of theism, construed as belief in an omnipotent, omniscient, and benevolent deity. The champion of theism might hope to inculcate or fortify belief of God. More often he is satisfied to demonstrate that the problem of evil is not an overwhelming objection to theism.[6] Whether any of the theories commonly advanced for this purpose (or some combination of them) are satisfactory—whether, in other words, the case for philosophical theism is made more probable when conjoined to the propositions these theories entail—is not the subject of this

---

[6]C. S. Lewis, in *The Problem of Pain,* maintains that theodicy is an attempt to make the best of a difficulty for theism. The strength of the theistic case lies elsewhere; hence the apologist for evil is justified in calling upon stopgap arguments that, in themselves, would not impress anyone not disposed on other grounds to be a theist.

essay. I am more interested in the interaction between theory and theorist: how does the adoption of a particular mode of thinking affect the awareness, before God, of the individual thinker?

In our age, it seems to me, the search for and insistence upon an adequate theoretical theodicy gives rise to experiential manifestations so bizarrely at odds with one another that they are scarcely recognizable as expressions of the same religious spirit. Worthwhile fragments of moral, psychological, and philosophical insight are jumbled together in pleasant, eclectic heaps and signify nothing. Writers and speakers on the subject frequently propagate absurdities bordering on cruelty and/or exhibit confusion with respect to fundamental Jewish tenets. Let us attempt a brief characterization of prevalent types of theodicy in the hope that it will illuminate our contemporary bewilderment. Please note that we are less interested in the particular dicta proposed than in the overall spiritual mentality that animates them:

1. *Rationalist* theodicy offers a set of explanations for evil that the believer is expected to find acceptable. A friend reported an excellent example to me. When his high school lesson on the verse "Thou shalt not curse the deaf" was interrupted by the question "Why does *Ha-Shem* create deaf babies?" he ventured to confess that we really don't know. At this point a sympathetic student cheerfully volunteered that she had learned no fewer than three reasons: one, to punish the parents for their sins; two, to inspire pity; the third reason she (alas!) had forgotten. One hopes that her opportunity to practice speculative philosophy remains limited to the classroom.

2. *Agnostic* doctrines of providence scoff at the very possibility that human beings are to discern a divinely

bestowed significance in their suffering or be sum-
moned by it to the spiritual regeneration that Halakha
mandates. This attitude is exemplified by a high-pow-
ered intellectual, an observant Jew, who has recovered
miraculously from a prolonged coma. Recalled to
health, he looks incredulously at those who thought
that prayer on his behalf, changing his name,[7] or
having a Catholic friend say Mass on his behalf in any
way affected his destiny. He dismisses as hubris the
conviction of less sophisticated Jews that the Almighty
himself might have devised the illness and recovery
as an instrument of education or chastisement.

3. *Pious acceptance* is reflected in the following remarks
of an early twentieth-century Christian statesman bereaved by his eldest son's death:

In his suffering he was asking me to make him well. I could
not.

When he went the power and the glory of the Presidency
went with him.

The ways of Providence are often beyond our understanding. It seemed to me that the world had need of the work that
it was probable he could do.

I do not know why such a price was exacted for occupying
the White House.

Sustained by the great outpouring of sympathy from all
over the nation, my wife and I bowed to the Supreme Will
and with such courage as we had went on in the discharge of
our duties.[8]

Calvin Coolidge eschews the speculative excesses of ratio-
nalism and agnosticism. He does not reel off a glib list of

---

[7]See the recent handbook *Penei Barukh* for details on changing the
name of a sick person.

[8]Calvin Coolidge, *The Autobiography of Calvin Coolidge*, 190–1.

lessons learned from adversity; nor does he imagine specific sins for which he, his wife, or his boy deserved punishment. At the same time, the recollection of his grief leads the mourning father to reflect on the ultimate questions. He considers with humility the awful contrast between the powers that his eminent position conferred upon him and his helplessness in the face of his child's mortal illness. He contemplates the work ethic that governs his life, and molded the education he gave his son, and resolutely continues in its practice. Lastly, and for reasons difficult for an outsider to fathom, the retired president signifies an obscure connection between his political eminence and the loss of Calvin Jr.[9]

Of the outlooks we have surveyed, Coolidge's seems most in consonance with the general tendency of normative Jewish thought, equally removed from the callous confabulations of those who, in the spirit of Job's friends, know too much about God's involvement in daily events, on the one hand, and the arrogant skepticism of those who are too confident of God's indifference to their affairs, on the other hand. If you were to ask Coolidge for a theological justification of his family's tragedy, he would answer simply that God's ways are often incomprehensible to us but that it is nevertheless incumbent upon us to search out the meaning of his acts for our lives and to live accordingly.

What path, if any, offers escape from the disordered thought and feeling evidenced by the rationalistic and agnostic schools? Much of our predicament stems, in my opinion, from a mistaken way of framing the question of suffering. The conventional, forensic approach philoso-

---

[9]One cannot help wondering, in light of these deliberate, laconic comments, whether Coolidge's choice not to run for re-election in 1928 had anything to do with fears for his remaining children.

phizes about suffering from the standpoint of the theodicy problem. Confronted by the conundrum of a benevolent deity who condones evil, logical analysis gravitates toward clean, extreme, egregious solutions: either by peddling reasons, however incredible, to explain what happens or by spiriting God away from the proceedings altogether, effectively eliminating Him from the affairs of the individual. So long as the theodicy problem dominates reflection, it overshadows the work of theological-existential edification, rendering secondary and fortuitous the insight that would yield a realistic awareness of man's relation to the Eternal, confronting us with the grandeur, mystery, and humility of the human condition before God.

It will be impossible for us to experiment with a different way of thinking about suffering unless we succeed in loosening the grip of the conventional position. To this end, I will attempt to uncover and scrutinize some presuppositions of the entrenched forensic approach. I do not intend to refute these ways of thinking—on the contrary, we sedulously will indicate those elements that survive our critique—but to weaken their power to obscure what I regard as more realistic alternatives. The critical section of the essay, however, will prepare us to entertain new ideas about the human experience of evil.

II

Tevye and the Coherence of Optimization

In the musical *Fiddler on the Roof*, Tevye the Milkman strives to understand the inscrutable ways of Providence. He prefers a world in which he would enjoy the status and prerogatives of a rich man; in the actual world he is poor. If his poverty were a necessary condition for the existence of a better world, he would have no grounds for complaint.

The last assumption, however, is to Tevye counterintuitive: it seems to him—and he invites God to dispute him—that no vast divine plan would be upset if he were a wealthy man.

Tevye is hardly alone in embracing that pillar of the standard approach to theodicy, often associated with Leibniz, which maintains that God must create the best of all possible worlds. Given that possible world W_1 is better than possible world W_2, then God cannot bring into being the inferior world without falling short of our conception of Him as benevolent, omnipotent, and so forth. The conventional response is that Tevye's intuition is erroneous and that a world in which he were a rich man in fact would possess features, known to God even if unforeseen by us, that would make it inferior to the real world, in which he is fated to be poor.

Must Tevye's intuition be mistaken? Is religious belief compelled to accept the proposition that God must create the best? What if the very idea of the best possible world turns out to be incoherent? As this last suggestion no doubt strikes many readers as counterintuitive, a brief explanation is in order.

Imagine the following thought-experiment: it is within your power to increase your share of some good—let us say longevity—as much as you wish. You determine your lifespan by standing at a specified distance from the wall and clicking a button: if you stand 1 foot from the wall, you will live another 40 years; 6 inches from the wall, 80 years; 3 inches, 160; and so on. For purposes of the present discussion, we may ignore the downside of a long life; hence, the closer you position yourself to the wall, the better it is for you. Under the terms of this thought-experiment, there are an infinite number of good-enough solutions, guaranteeing a long and satisfactory life, but there is no optimal solution, for no matter how long a life you obtain, you could have done better. In cases like this, the concept of optimization becomes incoherent.[10]

The previous example is, of course, artificial. Yet it accentuates the more complex structure of normal human aspirations. If the very notion of the best possible world is incoherent because, for any world, it is always possible to conceive of a better one, then it is no longer necessary to insist on the error of Tevye's intuition in order to disarm the force of his complaint. We might be living in a good enough world, though not *the* perfect one, because the best of all possible worlds cannot possibly exist.

Before moving on from this rather technical point, it is necessary to acknowledge what we have *not* established. We have shown that ordinary rational people will not expect God to provide them with the best of all possible worlds and that they will be satisfied with some exemplar of a good enough world. However, we have not given any reason to ignore the dissatisfaction of people who find themselves trapped in a world that is not, in their opinion, good enough.[11] To revert for a moment to the longevity example: although there is no optimal solution, there are plenty of choices that would have to be judged irrational—e.g., a person who decides to stand a mile away from the magic wall, thus assuring himself an exceptionally short life.[12] Likewise, an individual experiencing an especially miserable sojourn on earth might not complain that his existence was imperfect, merely that he was stuck in a thoroughly nasty life.

---

[10]This example is derived from Michael Slote, *Beyond Optimizing*.

[11]To utilize economic terminology, we might not demand of God that He optimize, but we still expect Him to satisfice.

[12]Compare II Kings 13:14–19, where each arrow shot by the king of Israel assures one victory over Aram. When he desists after three shots, Elisha becomes angry with him for abandoning the task before completion.

Rambam, Rav Kook, and Ontological Optimism

As we already have noted, the standard philosophical discussion of the problem of suffering proceeds from the
expectation that God will provide a perfect world: any imperfection threatens that expectation and requires explanation. Whether human beings are pleased with their lives
overall is secondary to the justification of specific occur-
rences for which the omnipotent God is held responsible.

Does the above describe the context in which most individuals raise the question of suffering in real life, when
they are not busy imitating professional philosophers? Ordinarily, it seems to me, real people, who are neither philosophers nor saints, do not trouble to justify the ordinary
suffering that accompanies quotidian life: the casual headache, the routine traffic jam, the bewilderment of frustrated
intentions. The crisis of faith generally is provoked by an
experience of acute disaster that overwhelms our ability to
cope and/or by a drastic upheaval that undermines our
sense of life as a worthwhile enterprise. In a word, "normal" human beings seem predisposed to optimism; this is
a fact that our philosophy ought to take into account.

What is the source of man's perennial optimism? One
possibility is that we consider the good of the world to out-
weigh the bad because our survey of the world has demonstrated this to be the case. According to Rambam, the pre-
ponderance of the good is questioned only by the ignorant
populace and by mistaken philosophers such as Ghazzali:
"every fool imagines that all reality is for his sake, as if there
were nothing other than he, and when something happens
contrary to his desire, infers that all reality is bad."[13] The
Maimonidean fool, depicted in this sentence, subscribes to
the standard contemporary approach and believes that ev-

---

[13]*Guide* III, 12.

ery evil (or at least every evil that affects him) constitutes a
challenge to the divine world order. Rambam goes on to
argue that the truly bad things that happen to people are
not God's fault but, in the majority of cases, their own.

A detailed analysis of the Maimonidean fool's pessimism
would reveal additional layers of motivation. One obvious
truth: most of us like to put the blame elsewhere than on
our own shoulders. At a more subtle level, pain and disorder call attention to themselves more urgently than pleasure
and happiness, of which we tend to be oblivious. Consider
for a moment the asymmetry between physical discomfort
and gratification. We define and localize the former with
ease: the temples that throb, the itching nostril, the sharp
pain of an inflamed elbow. By contrast, when I am pleased
with a good meal, I would hardly refer to a pleasure in my
stomach. Although the same spatial localization does not
occur with generalized feelings such as depression, it nevertheless would be safe to assume that an individual who
devotes attention to recording his sensations and moods
most likely would take note of the negative ones. Perhaps
this perception, too, would come under Rambam's censure
of the self-centered, self-conscious mentality.

Imaginative literature, which frequently offers reliable insight into various dimensions of the human condition, is
liable to mislead us here. Not only does it sometimes reflect and encourage the preoccupations just noted, it also
favors pessimistic themes of its own. The riveting story, more
often than not, is the one with the tragic ending; the poi-
gnant lyric sings of unfulfilled love. Sadness bears scars of
authenticity unknown to commonplace happiness—and is
more interesting.[14] What Graham Greene wrote of the pecu-

---

[14]"I sometimes wonder if not having a taste for a dark or tragic view
isn't a mark of superficiality. Yet cannot very different temperaments be
equally valid?" (Robert Nozick, *The Examined Life*, New York, 1989), 24.

liar sensibility he embraced in adolescence and made distinctively his own is symptomatic of much in our century's poetic conception: "religion might later explain it to me in other terms, but the pattern was already there—perfect evil walking the world where perfect good can never walk again, and only the pendulum ensures that after all in the end justice is done."[15]

Greene's mention of religion reminds us that a disposition to make much of the world's evil is not confined to self-preoccupied fools and writers mining reality at its points of least resistance. Among the *rishonim*, Rambam's view is not beyond dispute. Thus, for example, Saadia contends that belief in reward after death is rationally necessary because all good in this world is mingled with bad and the sadness outweighs the joy.[16] Only the prospect of future existence reassures us that "after all in the end justice is done." One plausibly might suggest that it is precisely the religious believer, alive to the Creator's goodness, who is most prone to be unspeakably distressed by the world's imperfection and depravity. This appalling contrast is the basis of Newman's famous apprehension: "If I looked into a mirror, and did not see my face, I should have the sort of feeling which actually comes upon me, when I look into this living busy world, and see no reflexion of its Creator." This statement serves as a prologue to a page-long list of worldly evils that culminates in the affirmation of original sin, a fact about the world "as true as the fact of its existence," for "*if*

---

[15] "The Lost Childhood," in *Collected Essays* (New York, 1969), 18.

[16] *Emunot ve-Deot* 9:1. See also Shubert Spero, "Is Judaism an Optimistic Religion?" (*Tradition* 4:1, Fall 1961), 21–35. Professor Michael A. Shmidman points out that Rambam himself was hardly oblivious to the miseries of this world. See *Hil. Issurei Bi'a* 13; *Iggeret Teiman* (in *Rambam IaAm: Iggerot*, Jerusalem, 1960), 114ff.

there be a God, *since* there is a God, the human race is
implicated in some terrible aboriginal calamity."[17]

At first blush, it would appear that Rambam's sober
cheerfulness and Saadia's somber diagnosis stand in straightforward contradiction and that only a stubborn, harmoniz-
ing piety would undertake to bridge the gap between them.
They disagree overtly about the actual amount of evil in the
world relative to the good. They differ implicitly about
the fundamental principle of theodicy: Rambam points to
the predominance of good in creation as a whole and expects the wise individual to acknowledge the larger perspective; Saadia, working in the Kalam tradition, is concerned
with the justice meted out to each creature. Nonetheless,
the dejection about the state of this world that we encounter in Saadia is not altogether incomprehensible from
Rambam's viewpoint.

The crucial point is that Saadia does not claim that man
looks upon creation and beholds, contrary to the seeming
implication of God's judgment on the sixth day of creation,
that it is more bad than good. The world that Saadia investigates and finds wanting is *this* life, when viewed in isolation from the reality of the world to come. Real life is the
whole, comprising both this world and the other one. From
a dialectical standpoint, our experience of this world, its joys
and discontents, cannot fail to be affected by the perspective of eternity.

In order to forestall possible misunderstanding, let me
clarify what is meant when I say that the standpoint of eternity suffuses our experience of this world. Eternity does not
mean merely a period of time commencing on the date of
postmortem reckoning and extending endlessly into the

---

[17]John Henry Newman, *Apologia Pro Vita Sua* (Longmans, Green
and Co., London and New York, 1895), ch. 5, 241–243.

future. The contribution of eternity is not merely quantitative, a shower bath of reward that dilutes the evils of this world until they no longer signify. Ordinarily, when a religious person deliberates his or her course and asks whether it is justified before the bar of eternity, the issue is not what we will think after we are dead, but rather how the eternal God judges our course here and now. Eternity is our teacher; in its academy we discover new criteria for judging what is valuable, and it transforms the very standard of significance. As when we wish to distinguish the living man from the cadaver we look for signs of respiration, so the world we inhabit emerges from spiritual lifelessness precisely to the degree that the breath of eternity inspires it. The dialogue with eternal values is not only the vocation of the saint intoxicated with the vision of holiness. The ordinary person of worldly horizons, who wants no more than to follow his will—passively defined by the pursuit of pleasure and avoidance of pain—and whose conception of what his will ought to be does not go beyond the routine table of values set by an unreflective secular society, cannot extricate himself from the broader vistas that expand into eternity. God beheld the world as good, and we, for our part, can see it steadily and see it whole, to the extent that we submit our will to His and learn to envision the living busy world in the light of its Creator. In short, the value of this world is contingent on the meaning inculcated by our vision of the world to come.[18]

---

[18]Rabbi Moshe Hayyim Luzzatto (*Mesillat Yesharim*, ch. 1) supplements his Saadia-like skepticism about the benefits of this world with a detailed argument to the effect that this world cannot be all there is because it cannot afford proper scope for the full development of man's spiritual potential. As Asher Friedman has pointed out, this approach goes a long way toward bridging the gap between Rambam's optimism about this world and the perennial, pessimistically tinged conviction that

By now the discussion of the present section has edged away from its original moorings. The Maimonidean thesis about the goodness of the world, from which we started out, purported to be an interpretation-free assessment of the universe. In the course of our analysis, we have arrived at a criterion of goodness dependent on a certain kind of interpretive perspective, namely a religious outlook that bids us transcend transient individual perceptions or constantly bear in mind the dimension of eternity, and so forth. Human beings, in effect, are inclined to trust the goodness of the universe not only, or primarily, because the scales of empirical evidence tilt toward optimism, but also because of a profound—one might say ontological—instinct about reality.

It is difficult, and I hope unnecessary, to present a phenomenological account of the ontological bias in favor of being. A halakhic analogy derived from a lecture by Rav Kook might communicate something of what I mean. We

---

this world is not man's true home. (For a discussion of Luzzatto's theodicy, using *Daat Tevunot* and other systematic works and placing Ramhal in the context of eighteenth-century Leibnitian theories, see Rivka Schatz-Uffenheimer, "Moshe Hayyim Luzzatto's Thought against the Background the Theodicy Literature," in *Justice and Righteousness* [Sheffield Academic Press, 1992], ed. H. Reventlow and Y. Hoffman, 173–199.) In a similar vein, Bernard Stahl notes passages in which Rav Kook exhibits a keen awareness of this world's evils, without which we would not be adequately motivated to transcend the limited good of the present toward the future that redeems it: see, for example, *Afikim baNegev* (originally published in *HaPeles* 1903; now available in Moshe Tsuriel, *Otserot haReiyah* II 733–742). Rav Kook's primary disciple, Rabbi David Cohen (the Nazir) connects Jewish metaphysics, exemplified by second-generation Habad, to "a pessimistic, pure, distilled ethic." The suffering of love (*yissurin shel ahava*) transforms the bitterness and pessimism into a "supreme joy (*hedva elyona*)." See his *Kol haNevua: haHiggayon haIvri haShim'i* (Jerusalem, 1970), 26.

all know that the thirty-nine categories of work (*melakha*) forbidden on Shabbat are defined as creative acts; purely destructive behavior ordinarily is not included. A destructive act counts as *melakha*, however, when it is intended as a prelude to an act of creation. Ripping a garment, for example, is work when the goal is its repair; likewise, erasing in order to write or demolishing a house when one wishes to erect new construction on the site. But there is a suggestive disparity between the examples. Tearing clothing with the intention of sewing it up as it was before (or the corresponding case of erasure and writing) is not an exercise in creativity: the final product is in no way an improvement over the original; hence it does not exhibit the necessary forethought (*melekhet mahashevet*). Razing a building for the sake of future construction constitutes *melakha*, however, even when the new structure merely duplicates the old. Apparently, Rav Kook infers, the act of construction (*binyan*) is deemed valuable in itself, even when it does not produce a more valuable object. Insofar as *binyan* is a rabbinic metaphor for the divine act of creation, the halakhic reality contains the hint of an ontological truth: that the propagation of being bears inherent value, apart from any other consideration of the value of the thing produced.[19]

From the standpoint of forensic theodicy, the ontological intuition we just have sketched might well be inferior to the calculus of good and evil with which we began. Facts are

---

[19]Rav Abraham Isaac Kook, *"Seder Hosen*—the Ruined Home as the Foundation of a New Home" (*Tehumin* 2), 239–241. Yehuda Gellman, in "Evil and Its Justification in the Thought of Rabbi A. I. Kook" (*Daat* 19, Summer 1987, 145–156), distinguishes two primary directions in Rav Kook's thought. One regards evil as the absence of good; the other justifies evil teleologically. The text examined here appears to transcend both categories.

facts; one man's profound ontological intuition is another's deep-seated, treacherous delusion. It is easy to imagine Schopenhauer—or one of his sociobiological heirs—conceding the power of Rav Kook's halakhic analogy, hailing enthusiastically his conviction that *binyan* as an ontological category is revealed especially in the operation of the procreative instinct yet refusing any inference from our feelings about being to the objective truth about reality. According to these views, the irrational, absurd will to life, in all its boundless power, might well be the ruse by which a natural or metaphysical force, indifferent to our welfare or even malignant, perpetuates the cycle of existence and succeeds in fooling the religious optimists, along with everyone else.[20] My present purpose, however, is not to formulate an argument for theodicy, but rather to describe the source of our convictions as we actually hold them on a day-to-day basis.[21]

---

[20]Schopenhauer's pessimism is presented most fully in his *World as Will and Representation*. It is analyzed, as a philosophical position, in John Atwell, *Schopenhauer: The Human Character* (Temple University Press, Philadelphia, 1990), 143–210, who discusses the secondary literature, and, more recently, in Mark Migotte, "Schopenhauer's Pessimism and the Unconditioned Good" (*Journal of the History of Philosophy* 33:4). Rav Kook found certain elements in Schopenhauer congenial: see *Orot haKodesh* II (Jerusalem, 5724), 482–484; Shalom Rosenberg, "Rav Kook and the Blind Sea Monster" (in *B'Oro*, ed. H. Hamiel, Jerusalem 1986), 317–352. Rabbi David Cohen (*op. cit.* n. 18 above, 26–31) delineates broader affinities between Jewish philosophy and Schopenhauer. The decisive difference is that Schopenhauer's will is passive, while Hebrew philosophy grasps the will as active. Note the similarity to Rav Soloveitchik's stress on the crucial role of human creativity, which will dominate much of our discussion below.

[21]William James' lecture on "The Religion of Healthy-Mindedness," in *The Varieties of Religious Experience*, offers a vigorous account of the psychological sources underlying natural optimism, which is valid independent of the pantheistic, proto-New Age examples that fill the last pages of the chapter. Here, and in the following lecture on "The

"God in the Dock" [22]

Inherent in the very enterprise of forensic theodicy is the idea that God stands accused of failing to govern the world rightly. The apologetic philosopher is, so to speak, the attorney for the defense. A successful theodicy is one that exonerates God. In this scenario someone must play the judge. That would have to be man, meaning you and I. All this follows from the logic of the theodicy-problem.

So we are to sit in judgment on the *Ribbono shel Olam!* But shouldn't it be the other way around? Not only is it supposed to be God who judges man, but any depiction of man's relation to God that omits this essential element of religious consciousness distorts reality beyond recognizability.

The conflict between forensic theodicy's audacious questioning of God and man's humble state as a creature judged by Him engenders explosive and irresolvable agony in the breast of the suffering *homo religiosus*, who knows in his own flesh the contradiction between the abject, guilty truth of the human condition and the grandeur of God, on the one hand, and the accusatory stance toward the Creator, on the other hand: "There is not between us an umpire, who would stretch his hand over us both (Job 9:33)."

That such a paradoxical, tormented, and ultimately intolerable contradiction can be a component of authentic religious awareness is illustrated incontrovertibly by the soliloquies of Job. It is a matter of simple human honesty to acknowledge that, at times, man feels estranged and re-

---

Sick Soul," James argues convincingly that both psychological elements can—and indeed must—coexist in the realistic religious consciousness.

[22]The phrase comes from C. S. Lewis, *God in the Dock* (Eerdmans, 1970), 240–244.

jected by God and that we cannot always even begin to make sense of the situation. The accusatory stance forensic theodicy presupposes thus is borne out, it would appear, by human experience, as confirmed in Tanach. Hence we ought not to be surprised that the accusatory position, so convenient to our vanity, often is taken as the paradigm for contemporary theological discussions of human suffering.

Yet however much we are to learn from the Jobian predicament, the notion that it is man's vocation to judge his Maker and that the experience of judging God is a primary constituent of our relationship to him is false and pernicious. It is not a normative occupation that Job himself would care to make fashionable. Job's experience is an extreme one. Although the extreme often illuminates the ordinary, drastically different situations cannot be regarded uncritically as equivalent to one another. Moreover, as already noted, whatever truth is gained by the gesture of honest questioning is offset by the great falsehood consequent upon the bracketing of man's fundamental relation to God: the eternal truth that, before God, we are always to be judged. *Homo religiosus* is very much aware of his anguish and when he is entangled in Job-like suffering, derives from the knowledge that piety turned accusatory undermines itself. It is therefore intellectually unstable and cannot supply the normative ground of inquiry.

Lastly, the putative isomorphism between Job's complaint and the outlook of forensic theodicy breaks down at one crucial point. Job is not an external observer of his troubles; he is thrown into them. He sticks his finger in the substance of his own life and tastes the gall of his existence on his own parched lips. The philosopher of theodicy, by definition, is claiming a normative perspective. First-person insight is often categorically different from that of the third person, and this is nowhere more true than in assessing the nature of experience under extreme conditions. This, too, is a lesson informed by the misunderstanding between Job and his friends. Insofar as forensic approaches to theodicy lead us to look upon our relation to God—and our relation to our own suffering—in a third-person context when a first-person perspective better serves the reality of experience, we have one more reason to seek alternative ways of thinking about the meaning of suffering and misfortune.

III

Identity, Spiritual Parasites, and the Man of God

In real life, not every instance of apparently undeserved misfortune precipitates the conundrum of theodicy. We are not inclined to be affronted by suffering that we view as "normal"—that is, as the necessary or predictable fallout of the human condition. To take a trivial example: a man trapped in a burning building cannot escape by flying out the window; we do not hold God responsible for failing to provide him with wings. We understand that it is the nature of birds to fly but that the human species is not so endowed. When the same man is struck blind, we are not shocked to hear questions about the justice of the universe, not only because the unfortunate effects of blindness are legion, but because being blind is considered a deviation from the norm and therefore requires explanation. What violates our sense of the normal we usually denominate as "unfair," but it seems that we derive our concept of fairness from the order of normality, not the other way around. The death of an aged, beloved father, however sad, usually does not engender the sense of absurd ruin that we experience when a father intones the kaddish for an adored child. One occurrence belongs to the order of "normality"; the other violates that order.

The metaphysical doctrine corresponding to this common-sense insight is the principle of general providence (*hashgaha kelalit*). This approach maintains that the benevolent Creator wisely designed the divine laws governing what happens to various species. If general providence is the only kind there is, which is the view Rambam and other Jewish thinkers attribute to Aristotle, then God cannot be blamed for the evil that results from the natural operation of His laws.

Judaism, of course, does not limit God's involvement in the world to *hashgaha kelalit*. "For certainly the belief in individual providence is a cornerstone of Judaism, both from the perspective of the Halakhah and from the perspective of philosophical inquiry. . . . The protagonist of the religious drama, according to Judaism, is the individual, responsible for his actions and deeds, and there can be no responsibility or accountability without providence."[23] As noted at the outset, all suffering obligates the individual to turn to God, to examine himself, to repent. The halakhically reinforced intuition that we, as individuals, pass before God's watching and concerned eye is expressed metaphysically in the doctrine of individual providence (*hashgaha peratit*).

At a popular level, the idea of *hashgaha peratit* often is inculcated through formulations that completely obliterate our instinctive belief that "the world follows its custom" (*Olam ke-minhago noheg*), that *hashgaha kelalit*, in other words, is a significant factor in the overall economy of divine governance. While the "hothouse *hashgaha*" emphasis aims to instill a salutary sense of responsibility and a habit of perpetual remorse, its mechanical application leads directly to rationalist theories of particular evils and indirectly

---

[23]Rav Joseph B. Soloveitchik, *Halakhic Man*, 123–124.

to the jaded agnosticism that fancies itself the only sophisticated alternative. A real account of divine providence must do justice both to the aweful uniqueness of God's concern for each individual and to the evidence, drawing both on the traditional sources and on human experience, of the extent to which our fate in this world depends upon the laws governing the groups and species to which we belong.

A theoretical understanding of divine providence along the lines advocated here need not be limited to one specific position within Jewish thought.[24] I will employ Rambam's discussion in the *Guide* as my point of reference because it presents a systematic deliberation on the subject and also because academic and popular writers on the *Guide* have created the image of Rambam as an adherent of *hashgaha kelalit* whose more orthodox pronouncements in the direction of *hashgaha peratit,* whether in the *Guide* or in his halakhic works, need not be taken seriously. Following *maran ha-Rav* Joseph Soloveitchik, *zt"l,* I will treat Rambam not as a precursor of agnosticism, but as an important source for a realistic conception of *hashgaha.*

In part 3 of the *Guide* an apparent discrepancy between two successive chapters confronts the careful reader of Rambam's treatment of providence. In chapter 17 Rambam distinguishes between nonhuman species, which are gov-

---

[24]For example, we might have appealed to Ramban as a *rishon* committed to particular providence who, at the same time, acknowledges natural and nonindividual factors in the operations of Providence. See David Berger, "Miracles and the Natural Order in Nahmanides" (in Isadore Twersky, *Rabbi Moses Nahmanides (Ramban): Explorations in His Religious and Literary Virtuosity* [Harvard, 1983], 107–128. Among modern ethical-philosophical treatises, Rabbi Yosef Eliyahu Bloch's *Shiure Daat* (Feldheim, Jerusalem, 1976), vol. 1, pt. 1, ch. 7 exemplifies a balancing of direct and indirect principles in the account of divine governance.

erned by *hashgaha kelalit*, and the human race, whose destiny is determined individually. In the very next chapter, however, Rambam reserves *hashgaha peratit* for the individual engaged in the knowledge of God; other human beings, it would seem, are abandoned to the laws of nature adequate for the species as a whole.[25] Which statement reflects Rambam's true position: is man different from the animals, or is it only the philosopher whom God notices as an individual?

Rav Soloveitchik resolves the apparent contradiction by recognizing two aspects of man. The human being can be "species man," who expresses the universal essence of his species without becoming an individual. As species man, he is no more and no less than a member of a particular biological species:

> Man, at times, exists solely by virtue of the species, by virtue of the fact that he was born a member of that species, and its general form is engraved upon him. He exists solely on account of his participation in the idea of the universal. He is just a member of the species "man," an image of the universal. He is just one more example of the species image in its ongoing morphological process (in the Aristotelian sense of the term). He himself, however, has never done anything that could serve to legitimate his existence as an individual. His soul, his spirit, his entire being, all are grounded in the realm of the universal. His roots lie deep in the soil of faceless mediocrity. He has no stature of his own, no original, indi-

---

[25]The textual situation is complicated by the pious remarks in chapter 51, which promise miraculous providence for those who merit it. The meaning of this chapter and its place in Rambam's theory of providence aroused the curiosity of Rambam's translator and subsequent medieval readers of the *Guide* but need not detain us here. See Zvi Diesendruck, "Samuel and Moses Ibn Tibbon on Maimonides' Theory of Providence" (*HUCA* 11).

vidual, personal profile. He has never created anything, never brought into being anything new, never accomplished anything. He is receptive, passive, a spiritual parasite.[26]

But man is also capable of becoming an individual and, as such, elevating himself or herself to a relationship with God that transcends his general membership in the human race:

> But there is another man, one who does not require the assistance of others, who does not need the support of the species to legitimate his existence. Such a man is no longer the prisoner of time but is his own master. He exists not by virtue of the species, but solely on account of his own individual worth. His life is replete with creation and renewal, cognition and profound understanding. He lives not on account of his having been born but for the sake of life itself and so that he may merit thereby the life in the world to come. He recognizes the destiny that is his, his obligation and task in life. He understands full well the dualism running through his being and that choice which has been entrusted to him.[27]

To the extent that a person is what the Rav calls a "spiritual parasite," he or she remains within the province of *hashgaha kelalit.* To the extent that the person lives a life of spiritual significance and self-creation, he merits individual providence.

The existential theory of providence that the Rav has extracted from Rambam's medieval categories is more than a philosophical formula. It translates into a religious imperative. For insofar as a person does not merely instantiate the species man, he or she cannot interpret the events of life as no more than the impersonal operation of universal

---

[26]*Halakhic Man*, 126–127.
[27]*Ibid.*, 127–128.

forces. And insofar as the person fulfills the halakhic obligation to turn to God in moments of trouble and does not dismiss suffering as a random occurrence, he or she chooses a place among those who are counted as individuals and who are so judged by the Creator:

> The fundamental of providence is here transformed into a concrete commandment, an obligation incumbent upon man. Man is obliged to broaden the scope and strengthen the intensity of the individual providence that watches over him. Everything is dependent on him; it is all in his hands. When a person creates himself, ceases to be a mere species man, and becomes a man of God, then he has fulfilled that commandment which is implicit in the principle of providence.[28]

Limits of Individualism and the Need for Dialectic

The story we have told so far extols the individual (the *ish ha-Elokim*) and reproaches man's identification with the species. Such a reading is faithful to Rambam's approach in chapters 17–18. More importantly, it accurately reflects the moral thrust of Judaism, which calls upon the individual to be worthy of particular providence. To the extent that one refuses to respond to suffering in the halakhically mandated manner, one turns away from the opportunity "to broaden the scope and strengthen the intensity of the individual providence that watches over him." If only the individual dimension of human existence is authentic and man's submersion in the universal is untruth, then the intuition with which we opened this section of our discussion is nothing but a manifestation of bad faith. Easing the pain of misfortune by treating it as the normal way of the world is, from this point of view, an act of spiritual evasion.

---

[28] *Ibid.*, 128.

Our vocation of increasing the degree of individual providence is no reason, however, to ignore the very real role played in our lives by *hashgaha kelalit*. However much we desire to benefit from direct personal providence—and in moments of spiritual *ennui*, that desire cannot be taken for granted; wishing for the right desire might be all we are up to—we delude ourselves no less than others when we fancy ourselves consistently worthy of God's personal concern. Reflection on our distance from God—the sense of being abandoned to the world's vicissitudes—and our unworthiness to be judged as authentic individuals—itself might be an important aspect of self-examination and a spur to repentance.

Metaphysically, the sharp rhetorical either/or separating species man from the man of God in the Rav's formulation breaks down in the face of a thorough analysis of individuality. No individual is an island; he draws his sustenance and creativity, in large part, from his communal identity. When the Rav celebrates "one who does not require the assistance of others, who does not need the support of the species to legitimate his existence," he surely is not positing an abstract, atomic individual who creates himself *ex nihilo*, standing before God in isolation from his fellows. As pertains to ethical creativity, the individual might precede the group; but in terms of ontological identity, he is unimaginable without his social context. The concrete individual, no matter how courageous and shunning of conformity, is constituted significantly by his connection to the larger community, to which ties of commitment and affection bind him.[29]

---

[29]If proof is needed for the Rav's assent to these affirmations, it is amply provided in *The Lonely Man of Faith, U-Bikkashtem miSham,* and many other texts. The Rav's most explicit discussion of theodicy, in *Kol Dodi Dofek,* reaches its climax in the observation that Job is restored only when he finds it in himself to pray on behalf of his friends.

Moreover, there are circumstances in which the courageous, creative, masterly individual is called upon to sacrifice some aspect of his uniqueness and to serve God by identifying with the collective. In a recently published sermon, Rav Kook utilizes an enigmatic talmudic statement as a vehicle for this idea. The Psalmist praises God, who saves "man and beast" (*adam u-behema*), and the Talmud applies the phrase to "men who are intelligent to the utmost (*arumim be-da'at*) yet make themselves like beasts." Rav Kook, following the tradition of the Rambam, regards the acquisition of creative intelligence as the characteristic that makes an individual worthy of individual providence. Hence those who are "*arumim be-da'at* receive providence by virtue of themselves, as a consequence of their individual perfection. Yet they make themselves like beasts because they make themselves subservient (*mevattelim*) to the *kelal*, as if they had no individual *telos* at all. This is the commandment of peace and its principal manifestation."[30]

But recognition and appreciation of the communal component in human identity have implications that go beyond the honesty required for self-knowledge and the ethicalreligious values that sometimes compel the *ish ha-Elokim* to submerge his own providential destiny in that of the group. One-sided attention to individual providence can be psychologically debilitating as well. We already have remarked on Rambam's allegation that fools exaggerate their own importance within the divine economy and consequently are excessively vexed by the evils that befall them. Now some of the fool's irritation no doubt can be attributed to his refusal to consider his own responsibility for his misfortunes. But Rambam clearly is blaming him for expect-

---

[30]*Meorot haReiyah* on Shavuot (Jerusalem 5754), 12–13, citing Ps. 36:7 and *Hullin* 5b. See also Maharal on *Hullin*.

ing too great a measure of *hashgaha peratit*. Elsewhere in the section on evil and providence, Rambam further insults man's self-centeredness by denying that the human race is the goal of creation.[31] Contrary to the pious spirit of "hothouse *hashgaha*" theology, Rambam fears the vanity, spiritual self-indulgence, and sullen self-justification attendant upon its invocation.

Rav Kook is a more teleological thinker than Rambam, yet he is similarly inclined to discern a heuristic advantage in the tension between a strong awareness of divine intervention in human affairs, on the one hand, and an obliviousness to God's involvement, on the other hand. He knows of "the fear of punishment that enters the bones, to the point of pervasive cringing, prevents the spread of the holy light of love and reverence toward the sublime, and this causes spiritual and physical sicknesses, to the community and to the individual." Such emotions can have a debilitating effect on both the individual and the community. The individual soul and the collective soul must be purified of this dross; this purgation is accomplished because "the poison of vulgar heresy (*kefira gassa*), which wrecks the world, was first established as a poison against that dross of punishment fear."[32] In other words, Rav Kook is prepared to grant *kefira gassa* its useful role in the divine historical economy as a providential corrective to the unwholesome manifestations of "hothouse *hashgaha*."

In light of Rambam's discussion, let us review our attempt to integrate the two poles of divine providence. Each

---

[31]*Guide* III, 13. Rambam's position in this chapter assails not only man's self-centeredness as an individual, but that of the species as a whole. From the cosmic perspective the particular species is as insignificant as the individual in relation to the species.

[32]*Orot haKodesh* (Mossad Harav Kook, Jerusalem, 1990), IV, 32–33 (421–422).

of us must view himself as a member of the human race
and other collective identities as one whom God judges not
as a distinct, unique individual, but as an instance of the
general categories to which he belongs. At the same time,
each person is capable of realizing a singular, creative, authentic destiny, which makes him, or her, a species of one,
worthy of individual providence. The truth about each individual is the dialectic between the two poles.

Let us return to an example we brought forward earlier:
a case of blindness. From the viewpoint of *hashgaha kelalit*,
the blind man is regarded as a defective human being;
normal members of the human species enjoy the faculty of
sight.[33] *Hashgaha kelalit* can explain the defect by referring
to the random operation of natural law: from a statistical
outlook, the general providence that enables most people
to see is compatible with the variety of physiological mal-
functions that cause blindness. No particular, personal story
is needed to explain each specific deviation from the universal human norm. The unlucky individual is free to accept his situation as the unfortunate by-product of a world

---

[33]That blind people, or those who enjoy healthy interaction with
them, adopt this point of view is, of course, contrary to my central
theological thesis, according to which the destiny each individual molds
is more significant than his subsumption under collective categories.
How blind people typically experience their handicap is explored in a
valuable exchange of letters between the philosophers Brian Magee and
Martin Milligan, *On Blindness* (Oxford, 1995). While the
correspondence's original focus was the epistemology of perception, the
existential question forces its way into the book, with Milligan, who was
blind from infancy, explaining to the initially incredulous Magee that
many blind people do not feel they are missing anything essential and
that the joys and worries that fill lives usually have little to do with their
blindness. He concedes, however, that people who lose their sight later
in life are liable to suffer much more and that for them blindness indeed might be a catastrophic event.

that ordinarily works well or to resent the mischance that has saddled him with what he cannot help defining as a deficient organism.

Hashgaha peratit has a very different tale to tell. The individual cannot be explained exhaustively by comparison to the universal. He is unique and therefore fulfills a destiny incommensurable with that of any other. Given his own choice, the person might have chosen a different course of life, but not having been consulted about the concrete situation in which he now finds himself, it is his vocation to make the best of it: to act rather than behave, to respond rather than react. Insofar as he becomes a man of God, "[h]e lives not on account of his having been born but for the sake of life itself and so that he may merit thereby the life in the world to come."

We already have encountered the custom of changing a sick person's name, which often is taken to fancy the Angel of Death as if he were a befuddled policeman easily confounded by an alias. But the earnest import of the changed name is the message of renewal and rebirth, the hope that a person can be altered momentously and for the better. When interpreted superficially, this message, too, can be misleading. For if Yosef's destiny can be redeemed by re-naming him Hayyim, then being Yosef is apparently a matter of little importance. The Hasidic dictum with which we prefaced this essay contradicts this false conclusion. To appropriate thoroughly the doctrine of individual providence is to bear perpetually in mind the importance of being this specific Yosef, with a unique potential to pursue a worthwhile life and to actualize the personal providence ordained for him.[34]

---

[34]Rabbenu Bahye (*Kad haKemah, s.v. Avel #1,* in *Kitve Rabbenu Bahye* ed. Chavel [Jerusalem, 1970] IV 47) cites a midrash, according

Whatever our condition of existence, we surely need sustenance. Sometimes we have none other than that of our name, that which makes us unique, sets us off from the crowd, and which the world, which always judges on the basis of the universal, more often than not regards as an affliction. If the "name" is uprooted, as it were, and the person, estranged from his individuality, is condemned to make do with egalitarian categories distributed by the universal, then he might well be without that which would sustain his vitality. This is true of the blind person, stripped of his unique destiny by a society that knows him as a member of a class.[35] Each reader can substitute his, or her, trials and tribulations. Each of us is charged to discover by self-examination, prayer, and study, the true meaning of our "name."[36]

---

to which each individual has three names: the first is given him by his parents; the second he calls himself; the last is inscribed in the book. Of these, the name one bears at the end of life is the most significant. See also Chavel's nn. 98–99 for other versions of this midrash.

[35]The egalitarian euphemisms that recategorize crippled people as "differently abled" and the like miss the mark for several reasons. To begin with, the bureaucratic jargon, in the very comprehensiveness of its condescension, calls attention to and manages to exploit the deficiency it pretends to ignore, arousing a self-admiring self-righteousness in its philanthropic practitioners, matched only by the embarrassment it causes everybody else. The real problem with such language is that it misconstrues an existential, religious choice of self as an issue amenable to superficial social engineering. At the most fundamental level, the blind man's relation to his situation is integral to his being a human self, implicated in the dialectic of providence outlined in the text. To what extent his blindness is essential or accidental to his existence, to what degree it is a challenge or a burden, is an aspect of his spiritual being, not a subject for adjudication and confirmation by social workers.

[36]See my "Destiny, Freedom and the Logic of Petition" (*Tradition* Summer 1989 [*Festschrift* for Rabbi Walter Wurzburger]), 17–37.

Before examining some implications of the dialectic we have sketched, it might be instructive to uncover its traces in the interpretation of God's speeches to Job. Taken as a statement about God's governance of man's affairs, the content of the speeches tilts conspicuously in the direction of *hashgaha kelalit*. Man, whether as a species or as an individual, is virtually absent from these chapters.[37] God portrays many instances of His general providence for a variety of species and natural phenomena, with special attention to those more readily described as sublime or grotesque than beautiful or attractive."[38] Job is given to understand from the opening verses that his inadequacy in the face of these phenomena disqualifies him from judging his Maker: "Where were you (*eifo hayita*) when I established the earth?" (Job 38:4) From the viewpoint of the biblical text, the only element of personal providence is the fact that God has chosen to address Job. There is nothing about Job's individual standing in the universe, and God scrupulously withholds from him the information that we readers have known all along—the dialogue with the Satan that precipitated Job's afflictions—and that presumably would offer him a measure of enigmatic enlightenment. All this, of course, is consonant with Rambam's claim that Job was not a wise

---

[37]The one exception is the beginning of the second speech (40:9–15), where Job sarcastically is invited to humble the wicked. But note that the wicked are treated here, not as members or representatives of the human race, but almost as if they constituted a force of nature. The passage serves as a prelude to the powerful, grotesque beasts Behemoth and Leviathan.

[38]It is impossible to offer a full exegesis, within the scope of this essay, of these wonderful passages. See preliminary remarks in S. Carmy and David Shatz, "The Bible as a Source of Jewish Philosophical Reflection" (in *The Routledge History of Jewish Philosophy*, ed. D. Frank and O. Leaman, London, 1997), 13–37.

man[39] and that God's refusal to render an account of his individual fate was a way of communicating to him God's endorsement of Rambam's hard words about the self-centered fool.

In terms of our approach, God's treatment of Job is one-sided. However effective it might be in conveying the sublimity of creation and thus moving Job toward reconciliation and repentance, God's speeches confirm only one pole of the dialectic. If, as I contend, a complete theory of providence must do justice to both the general and the individual moments of the dialectic, it would not be surprising to find Hazal introducing the individualistic theme in an effort to fill out the dialectical lacuna in the biblical version.

The anticipated completion occurs in a remarkable midrash. It is based on the notion of an ideal primordial man (*Adam Kadmon*): every individual human being has his "place," so to speak, as part of the great human body. Resh Lakish employs this idea to reinterpret God's initial challenge to Job: "Where were you (*eifo hayita*) when I established the earth?" According to Resh Lakish, God is not questioning Job's knowledge of the cosmic order. As we have seen, the effect of such a question would be to accentuate Job's ignorance and his insignificance within the divine economy. In the midrashic interpretation, the word *eifo* is read *eifa*, the measure of a man's individual character:

> You seek to contend with Me. . . . Tell me, Job, in what place did your *eifa* [your existential source[40]] depend? On his head, his forehead, or some other limb? If you know the place of your *eifa* you may contend with Me.[41]

---

[39] *Guide* III, 22–23.

[40] I prefer this phrase to Soncino's "essential source. . . ."

[41] *Shemot Rabba* 40:3 Cf. *Breshit Rabba* 13:8. The Midrash comments on Gen. 2:5, which implies that rain did not fall until the advent of man. The Midrash goes on to reinterpret Job 38:26, which speaks of

Resh Lakish brings Job, as an individual with a unique, mysterious destiny, into the heart of God's speech. Job can achieve reconciliation and repentance only when he is forced to consider his suffering in connection with that destiny and to confess the ineluctable opaqueness of his own incomparable spirit. His ignorance is not limited to the secrets of cosmology, zoology, and the art of taming Leviathan. He is equally in need of enlightenment about his own "name," his own individual place and vocation in the world.

IV

Shadow and Insight—Rabbi Yohanan and Us

In the absence of explicit prophetic revelation, only the fool would feign unambiguous knowledge of his or anyone else's precise standing before God. This is so not only because man's understanding is finite, but also because it is inadequate to comprehend the secrets of the human self. If the account presented in the preceding section is true, then the mystery of man is wrapped up in his dialectical consciousness. The very attempt to fix his position *vis-à-vis* the poles of general and individual providence redefines his spirit; the work of honest self-examination or self-deception itself alters the quality of his repentance. Hence every self-confident, absolute assertion a man makes about the nature of his relationship to God, every complacent repose upon formula, entails the peril of bad faith.[42]

God causing rain to fall upon a land without people. (See traditional commentators on the Midrash and Theodor-Albeck edition, 117; I am inclined to think that the Midrash connects verse 26 with the following verse, bracketing the fact that man is absent from verse 27 as well.)

[42]Rambam, as we have seen, offers a variety of proposals and postulates about the operation of divine providence, including topics such

Therefore, one cannot help asking, would it not be better to abjure entirely any talk about man's status in relation to God, since speculative exuberance is sure to end in delusion? Would it not be healthier and more honest if we stuck to the critical scrutiny of our actions, an enterprise that, however daunting, offers a chance of arriving at some useful truth? The answer is that we need not abstain from investigating those features of our relation to God that go beyond the diagnosis of sin, *provided* that we can work around the problem of self-deception. How can we avoid lying to ourselves and misleading others? Only if we maintain respect for the mystery of the dialectic, if we steer clear of unambiguously naming what hovers indeterminately between the metaphysical poles, if we recognize for what it is the creative mixtures of insight and shadow without imposing upon the latter our rigid illusion of transparency.

Models for this kind of self-knowledge are available in our classical texts. Hazal recognize categories of suffering that are not punishment for sin.[43] When strenuous self-scru-

---

as matter and form, evil as privation, human responsibility for most evil, teleology, species, and the individual. Nonetheless, in his concluding remarks on the question (*Guide* III, end of ch. 23), where his ostensible subject is God's response to Job, he affirms, in typical Maimonidean fashion, that we no more can understand His providence and governance of the world as coming under our human conceptions than we can grasp any other aspect of God in anthropomorphic terms. Consciousness of this truth enables afflicted man to devote himself to his proper task: not the cultivation of skepticism but the enhancement of love. The significance of this passage, and its confluence with our present discussion, was brought to my attention by Uri Etigson.

[43]Nonpunitive explanations for suffering in rabbinic literature have been most thoroughly investigated from literary, historical, and theological perspectives in a series of articles by Yaakov Elman, up to and including his paper for this book. See also David Kraemer, *Responses to Suffering in Classical Rabbinic Literature* (Oxford University Press, 1995).

tiny fails to discern the act responsible for the suffering, the Amoraim propose the possibility that it is *yissurin shel ahava* (afflictions of love), whose goal is to increase the individual's spiritual level in a manner that presumably could not have been attained by other means. It is beyond the scope of this essay to probe the depths of this theme in rabbinic literature and its medieval and modern inter-pretations.[44] Here I would like to focus on the application of the *yissurin shel ahava* model to individual events. How do the Amoraim, in the course of their own self-examina-tion, keep the *yissurin shel ahava* formula from turning into a cliché?

Most obviously, the talmudic discussion preserves the authenticity of *yissurin shel ahava* by means of theoretical limitations that guarantee its sparing application. *Yissurin shel ahava* can be invoked only when rigorous self-search-ing has failed to yield a more conventional cause; accord-ing to some views, suffering that prevents prayer and/or Torah study cannot qualify as *yissurin shel ahava*. But there is a more subtle and far-reaching safeguard against its mis-use as an explanatory resolution.

Consider the death of Rabbi Yohanan's children. In try-ing to determine the rabbi's view on whether the loss of children can be ascribed to *yissurin shel ahava*, the Talmud observes that he was in the habit of comforting the bereaved by exhibiting a bone of his tenth son. The unstated assump-tion is that Rabbi Yohanan's afflictions must be accounted *yissurin shel ahava*. Why? Rashi posits that the affliction of

---

[44]The talmudic *sugya* on *yissurin shel ahava* (*Berakhot* 5) does not offer a clear explanation of the value assigned to such suffering. I have discussed Rav Kook and his predecessors in an unpublished lecture to the Association for Jewish Studies and have gained much from discus-sions of Rabbi Yitzchak Blau's work in progress on RaN and others. On Rav Soloveitchik and Rabbi Avraham Grodzinski, see below.

an important individual such as Rabbi Yohanan is presumably *yissurin shel ahava*; Tosafot infer from the fact that he used his tenth son's bone to console others that he did not view his suffering as punishment.

But is the Talmud indeed committed to the view that Rabbi Yohanan buried his children because of *yissurin shel ahava*? More important, is there any evidence that Rabbi Yohanan himself subscribed, unambiguously, to the thesis that he was, in this matter, afflicted with *yissurin shel ahava*? The alternative is that Rabbi Yohanan did not hold any settled opinion about the cause of his suffering and that, if he did, he had no reason to communicate it to others. An acquaintance of Rabbi Yohanan's, even a close friend, one who had accompanied him to houses of sorrow on many occasions, might be unable to state with certainty how Rabbi Yohanan regarded his own situation. He knows what Tosafot observe: that had Rabbi Yohanan believed he was being punished for his sins, he would not have displayed his tenth son's bone to other mourners. Hence, Rabbi Yohanan is committed to the *possibility* that his affliction has a nonpunitive explanation, that it constitutes *yissurin shel ahava*, and because he is open to this interpretation, he can present his own life as an example to others. Therefore the Gemara can infer that Rabbi Yohanan accepts the possibility, in principle, that loss of children qualifies as *yissurin shel ahava*. What he thought in his heart, whether as he prayed and studied before God he arrived at any final, constant position, belongs to the intimate world of his soul, over which descends the sacred curtain of eternal silence.[45]

---

[45]In the following section, several Palestinian Amoraim discuss their afflictions. Although the context, the lack of reference to sin, and the implication that the suffering under discussion has value only if accepted willingly suggest *yissurin shel ahava*, it is noteworthy, for the reason we just have given, that the Amoraim refrain from describing their situation

A similar terminological modesty is characteristic of two major discussions of suffering in our own century. We already have noted the thrust of Rav Soloveitchik's *Kol Dodi Dofek*, forcefully shifting our attention from the metaphysics of reward and punishment to the halakhic imperative of self-examination and repentance. Repentance implies that there is something to repent, and the Rav demonstrates that even Job, whose Creator testifies that he is "upright and righteous, God-fearing and shunning evil," must mend his ways. Yet the rhythm and logic of the Rav's position—replacing the imputation of sin as axiom with the quest for moral self-knowledge as imperative—is very much that found in the *sugya* of *yissurin shel ahava*, which likewise begins with the commandment to examine thoroughly one's actions. As a response to the massive destruction of European Jewry, the Rav's Halakha-centered theodicy deliberately sets out to circumvent rationalist explanations of the catastrophe, to rebut the sterile forensic assumption that God's involvement in this horrible part of our history is best interpreted as the infliction of punishment for specific iniquities. Nonetheless, despite the Rav's evident desire to sever the simplistic nexus between suffering as effect and sin as cause, he refrains from appealing to the concept of *yissurin shel ahava*.

Interestingly, the modern clergyman, who generally has shied away from rationalist solutions to the problem of theodicy, has received less solace from the Rav's formulations than one might have expected. The reason, I believe,

---

with this specific theological label. The venue of the *sugya* then shifts to Babylonia with the story of Rabbi Huna's soured wine. When his colleagues summon him to self-examination, his response ("Am I suspect in your eyes?") implies a presumption of innocence, but he does not invoke a theological formula that would close further discussion.

is that the Rav's primary motivation is ethical and dialectical, aiming at an understanding of the human condition and God's demands upon it. He does not evade the reality of human sinfulness, though he does not treat the sin-punishment nexus as the entire story. The modernist, by contrast, is driven by the need to apologize, to exculpate, to flatter his audience at all costs. Where the Rav's dialectic brings man closer to God, the modernist's soothing palaver seeks a conception of God inoffensive to people. The predominance of the therapeutic goal makes it impossible to establish a comprehensive Jewish theology that would appropriate the full range of categories found in the traditional sources. Hence a paradox: the modernist who, in his fear of braving the harsher realities, confines himself to themes of comfort is unable to preach those principles with genuine conviction, either on his part or on the part of his hearers, and thus squanders, as it were, their power to console.

Among examinations of suffering that stem from the Musar movement, far from the modernist mentality's insular preoccupations, the remarkable series of discussions by the saintly martyr Rav Abraham Grodzinski, last *mashgiach* of the Slobodka Yeshiva, stands out.[46] The *Torat Avraham* sought to define those features of *yissurin* that have value over and beyond their punitive function. Contrary to our expectations, however, his texts have nothing—not one word—to say on the subject of *yissurin shel ahava*. The closest he comes is a discussion of accepting suffering with joy.[47] The latter phenomenon, however, is very different from the former: accepting suffering with joy is a subjective mood

---

[46] *Torat Avraham* (2nd Edition, Benei Berak, 5738), 27–56.
[47] *Ibid.* 35, commenting on *Bava Metsia* 84b–85a.

indicating the sufferer's profound reconciliation with his fate and a conviction that it is for the best; *yissurin shel ahava* denotes a hypothesis about the cause and purpose of the suffering. An individual professing to accept suffering with joy might be ridiculously vain to make the claim or might be attesting to the honest psychological truth about himself. An individual who announced that he was experiencing *yissurin shel ahava* would strike us as singularly arrogant.

The dialectical nature of our relationship to God and, for that matter, to ourselves can be a cause of intellectual paralysis. We do not know how to apply properly the conceptual categories bequeathed to us by our sources, and all our labors to construct a dialectical framework for our understanding of divine providence seemed only to underline the foolhardiness of the venture. What we can gain from our teachers, from the talmudic Sages down to the great spirits of our age, is not only a list of arguments and doctrines, but also a practical prototype for their use in making sense of our lives. One lesson we can learn is that sometimes less is more: the self-discipline that enabled the Rav and the *Torat Avraham* to illuminate the experience of suffering without explicitly deploying one of the most attractive and relevant concepts in the rabbinic corpus manifests a greater wisdom than the cleverness that feeds upon its own sparkle.[48]

---

[48]The avoidance of formulaic explanations of suffering already is found in the book of Job. His ordeal never is described as a trial (*nissayon*), though the root *nsh* appears in crucially misleading contexts (e.g., Eliphaz's opening speech at 4:2). The Bible thus prevents us from responding to Job's plight as an instance of a familiar theological phenomenon.

V

The Remorseful Sinner

Many readers will have noticed a curious reticence in an essay devoted to the question of human self-awareness and confrontation with the evils and disappointments of life, and purporting to discuss that question in light of daily experience. For the religious individual, the greatest evil is not physical pain or professional failure, but sin; the greatest unhappiness is to know oneself a sinner, estranged from God. The fear of sin is, or should be, a ubiquitous presence in our daily lives. Within the intellectual discourse of forensic theodicy, the primary issue is God's responsibility for evil. If sin is to be blamed on human beings (and God is *not* saddled with the indirect responsibility for creating sin-prone beings) or if it is a necessary by-product of a greater good (as in the free-will defense), then the evil entailed by sin is less problematic than the existence of natural evil. But if, as I have proposed, our task is to concentrate on the proper response to evil in the light of man's dual nature as species man and man of God, then the dialectic of sin and atonement requires special attention.

I have deferred this reflection until now for considerations theological and psychological. To look in the mirror and see a face estranged from God, to behold this apparition and fully comprehend what it portends, is a terror so overwhelming that it obliterates any other sensation of discomfort or satisfaction. On those occasions when our recitation of *honen ha-daat* ("He who bestows understanding") breaks in and even the bland and spiritually repressed among us is visited by the insight that in the end only one thing counts, we are gripped by so intimidating an apprehension of iniquity that we can hardly look to anything beyond the entreaties of *hashivenu* ("restore us to Your

Torah") and *selah lanu Avinu* ("forgive us our Father"), desperate pleas for repentance and forgiveness. All that remains is to rest one's head between one's knees like Rabbi Elazar ben Durdaya and weep until death redeems with silence the endless footfall of spiritual failure . . .[49]

To many of us, no doubt—particularly those not inclined to amnesia—the experience I just have described is as familiar as their own flesh. Yet Judaism has not recommended Rabbi Elazar ben Durdaya's response as the norm. Our prayers and our lives proceed from the plea for forgiveness to other national, communal, and personal petitions of a more mundane nature. As Rav Kook observed, the strenuous and potentially debilitating penitence of the solemn season culminating in Yom Kippur is followed by prosaic days of preparation for the joyful recuperation of Sukkot.[50] *Homo religiosus* must live with the enormous responsibility that is part of being an individual but must not be crushed by the burden.

The dialectic of expiation and atonement addresses itself to man as an individual. From the perspective of general providence, a sinful individual is simply a spiritually defective human being who falls short of the norm as surely as the blind man fails to meet the normal physical standard. As Rav Soloveitchik has taught us, repentance is a radical creative enterprise in which man remakes himself. Species man cannot undo the actions he already has done; only the individual can rewrite the past so that it can be reread in

---

[49]The allusions in this paragraph are to the fourth, fifth, and sixth benedictions of the weekday prayer. For the story about the repentance of Rabbi Elazar ben Durdaya, see *Avoda Zara* 17a.

[50]*Olat Reiyah* II, 367–368, and *Orot haTeshuva* 9:10. Cf. similar ideas in *Sefat Emet*, Sukkot 5641, and *Pele Yoetz* (cited by Rabbi Zvi Yehuda Kook in his notes to *Olat Reiyah*).

light of the new life he is committed to living.[51] However mortifying the experience of radical guilt might be to the religious individual, it can be comprehended within the same dialectical framework of general and individual providence that we applied to other manifestations of evil.

The movement from species man to man of God is part of the work of becoming a self. As Kierkegaard puts it: "The self is the conscious synthesis of infinitude and finitude which relates itself to itself, whose task is to become itself, a task which can be performed only by means of a relationship to God. But to become oneself is to become concrete. But to become concrete means neither to become finite nor infinite, for that which is to become concrete is a synthesis."[52] One can fail to become concrete in two ways: either by becoming imprisoned in the finite or by becoming volatilized in the infinite. Each expression of bad faith corresponds to a mistaken understanding of the dialectic of providence, inasmuch as it entails a distorted conception of man's responsibility. When man takes the external facts of his situation as an objective definition of his identity and potential, he imprisons himself in the finite: he is what he is, he is what nature has made him, he is what Providence

---

[51]*Halakhic Man*, 110–117. See also Yitzchak Blau, "Creative Repentance: On Rav Soloveitchik's Concept of *Teshuva*" (*Tradition* 28:2, Winter 1994, 11–18). For a congruent analysis of the foreknowledge/free-will conundrum in Rav Kook, see my "On Optimism and Freedom" (in *Essays on the Thought and Philosophy of Rabbi Kook*, ed. Ezra Gellman, Fairleigh Dickinson University 1991), 114–120. Both Hermann Cohen, in his *Religion of Reason,* and Kierkegaard, in *Concept of Anxiety,* require the category of the individual in order to explicate repentance.

[52]S. Kierkegaard, *Sickness Unto Death*, pt. I and III (in *Fear and Trembling and the Sickness Unto Death*, trans. Lowrie, Princeton, 1953), 162.

has ordained—no more and no less. Or, alternatively, dazzled by the imagination of infinite possibilities, he finds it possible to ignore the intimate and undeniable ligatures that bind past and present.

Obviously a one-sided conception of the finite, paralleling the agnostic view of providence, is incompatible with Judaism's commitment to free will and individual providence. Our pious rhetoric is less inured against the siren song of the fantastical, "which so carries a man out into the infinite that it merely carries him away from himself and therewith prevents him from returning to himself."[53] The lack of determination to be a concrete, particular self robs the person both of his identity as a member of the species and of the invitation to become an individual working out his destiny before God. If nothing we do in any way constrains our identity as individuals, then the fantastic self is there to be fashioned and refashioned as if it were no more substantial than the persona of an American politician.

In Chekhov's novella *My Life*, the hero's wife, who quickly has tired of their dream of farming her land and redeeming the peasants, goes to America. In asking for her freedom, she says: "King David had a ring with the inscription 'All things pass.' Whenever I feel sad those words cheer me up, but when I'm cheerful they make me sad." On which the husband reflects: "If I had wanted a ring I would have chosen the following inscription for it: 'Nothing passes.' I believe that nothing actually disappears without trace and that the slightest step we take has some meaning for the present and future."[54] Moral reality endorses the

---

[53]Kierkegaard, 164.

[54]Anton Chekhov, *The Party and Other Stories* (trans. R. Wilks, Penguin Books, 1985), 179 and 186.

husband's view: the road to *hashgaha peratit* runs through repentance, and repentance begins in the dreadful consciousness of remorse, in the irremovable shame and guilt we feel in contemplating what we have done or left undone. Only in the soil of moral realism can the seed of individual providence grow; only when we have recognized that our actions have consequences can we endeavor to wrest creative meaning from the ruins of our iniquities.

VI

Limits of Comprehension

Our analysis has proceeded from certain assumptions about the real psychology of ordinary people, individuals who are predisposed to take an optimistic view of life. What are we to say about people whose calamities are so severe that all talk of dialectic, creativity, and self-transcendence is beside the point?

That such intense physical and psychological pain occurs we have no reason to doubt. Anyone who has spent a long summer afternoon doubled up with a kidney stone; anyone who has shaken with the bone-breaking ague of malaria or undulant fever, aware only that the eventual cycle of respite is followed by one of recurrence; anyone for whom grief has blotted out the sky, who has stood dishevelled at the open grave, all tomorrows murdered at his feet, and leaped blindly into the pit: whoever knows of these matters will not doubt the overwhelming violence of pain and suffering. And however vivid the experience at the time, our recollections invariably take something off the full intensity. The indescribable pain of a winter night's toothache or an urgent asthma attack becomes a distant nightmare by morning. When devastating grief has subsided to the hard, chronic ache of absence, we wonder how we could have lost self-control and all sense of proportion: "For who when healthy can become a foot?"[55] What, then, can our philosophizing say to people for whom such experiences are not passing episodes but the substance of daily life?

It is impossible to say. On the one hand, our inability to enter the state of mind of people in limit situations, or even to recall with precision our own responses to acute illness and grave sorrow, would lead us to dismiss the relevance of any reflection based on ordinary life. On the other hand, the discontinuity between extreme conditions and ordinary situations might not be quite as sharp as we have depicted it.

The discontinuity thesis appears to rest upon the assumption that extreme suffering can be so defined on the basis of objective criteria. Up to a certain level of pain, a headache is an everyday event and can be discussed, in terms of our earlier analysis, as the occasion for an appropriate human response. Beyond that pain threshold, it is impossible for the sufferer to respond as a dignified individual, but only to howl like a wounded animal. Now when it comes to psychological pain, this is certainly *not* the case. The same loss that utterly shatters one person—let us say the destruction of one's family—provides another with the occasion for a dignified religious response (remember Rabbi Yohanan's tragic history). It is possible to imagine comparable possibilities of individual response with respect to physical pain as well. In fact, we do encounter heroic responses to extreme pain and personal distress; even individuals who appear hopelessly submerged beneath their burden of pain, suffering, and vacuity often disclose sud-

---

[55]W. H. Auden, "Surgical Ward" (in *Selected Poetry*), New York, 1958), 46.

den glimpses of an active spiritual life.[56] Although from our
comfortable vantage point it is impossible to bestow upon
those in extreme situations the ample reflective space we
experience as our own, yet we have no right to regard them
as mere victims who cannot benefit from or draw upon the
spiritual reserves available to ordinary people.

Vicarious Resentment

We have examined, as best as we could, the situation of
extreme affliction as it affects the sufferer. Many intellectuals who themselves cannot stake a claim to extreme affliction make the fate of the extreme victim their own. If
Rambam accused the pessimist of self-centeredness, these
individuals would counter that their resentment is founded
upon a resolve to take the part of the unfortunate against
an indifferent Heaven. It is doubtful whether this attitude,
whose most memorable philosophical incarnation is
Dostoevski's Ivan Karamazov, is typical of ordinary human
beings.[57] Should it affect our earlier analysis, and, if so, how?

It seems to me that the kind of strong sympathy that
would cause an individual to identify so zealously with the

---

[56]See, for example, Oliver Sacks' report on Jimmy, "The Lost Mari-
ner" (in *The Man Who Mistook His Wife for a Hat*), who is able to
pray attentively despite the fact that all his memories for the past several decades had been obliterated by Korsakoff's Syndrome. Jimmy has
"a soul," despite the absence of the most rudimentary faculty of short-
term memory.

[57]Ivan's claim that a case of horrible injustice in this world would
justify him in asking God to "return his ticket," even if the evil is fully
reconciled from the perspective of eternity, has a Jewish parallel in one
of the interpretations of the term *olam ha-ba* proposed by Maharal in
Gur Arye, Gen. 18:25. Rashi's commentary on the verse requires further analysis.

victims of divine providence can be understood in terms of two moral impulses or as their combination:

1. One element in sympathy for the unfortunate involves an emotional expansion of the self. It is a common occurrence that people are more affected by the tribulations of those near and dear to them than they are by their own suffering: it would be absurd to wonder at the fact that a healthy adult is liable to be more distraught by a child's serious illness than by her own. By the same token, we might imagine saintly individuals who respond to the sufferings of total strangers as if to those of their own offspring.

2. The sympathetic individual might feel the wrongness of injustice and evil as a spur to rectifying the situation. This kind of response is very much of a piece with that recommended by Halakha, as interpreted by Rav Soloveitchik. The individual who experiences the evil visited upon others with whom he sympathizes will examine himself with the goal of increasing his commitment to the fulfillment of God's will. If the suffering of his fellow man is indeed uppermost in his mind, that response will involve greater dedication to the sufferers' welfare.

Both of these impulses are consonant with the analysis developed throughout this essay. Forensic theodicy, however, entails a different outlook. Here the philosopher, who himself is satisfied with his own lot, is concerned to weigh the good and evil in the universe. His judgment about the evil suffered by certain individuals, or groups of individuals, is so drastic that he returns a negative verdict on God's governance of the world.

From an analytic point of view, this line of debate is like any other attempt to rebut the usual presumption in favor of goodness. Rambam, for example, would have no compunction against accusing his philosophical antagonist of furthering a self-centered conception by assigning to the human race an importance that it does not rate within the divine economy as a whole. But because its champions don the altruistic mantle of attorneys for the doomed, this particular argument carries an atmosphere of its own. At a psychological level, its credibility depends, to a greater degree than is customary, on the authenticity of its proponents. Are they the trouble-making existential tourists they sometimes appear to be, or are they the righteous fighters for truth they present themselves as being?

The attempt to answer this question implicates us in all the mysteries of the human heart, the treacherous business of inferring motivations and generalizing about them. Whatever we said earlier about Job's judgment of God applies to Job's vicarious prosecution lawyers. In particular, let us remember that the adoption of a third-person perspective often falsifies existential realities and that a congealed, philosophical compassion with the victim often bespeaks a cloying condescension toward the object of pity. In the end, we find ourselves in the kind of psychological world on which only a Dostoevski can hope to shed light.

Aesthetic Complacency

We have not repined from posing hard questions about the motivations behind vicarious resentment. Similar concerns can be raised about the general position advanced in this essay. Our entire framework of thought is premised on the idea that we are speaking about ordinary psychological realities, as opposed to the routine professional preoccupations of philosophers. In truth, the very fact that we—you and I—can articulate and debate theories about suffering is a source of comfort, delight, and catharsis and sets us apart from the mass of suffering mankind. It is possible that the insights we have proposed here bear fruit in the souls of those "mute inglorious Miltons" who are incapable of formulating them, but it is also possible that their power and plausibility vanish with the intellectual satisfaction the philosophical occupation provides.

The line of thought pursued in this essay also might give false comfort to readers who misconceive the idea of individuality correlated to the particular providence of the man of God. For Rav Soloveitchik, and most certainly for Rambam, being an individual is connected to having independent worth; it is not a matter of having some characteristic that nobody else possesses. *A*'s mastery of *Bava Batra*, for example, is in no way diminished by the fact that *B* has attained the same grasp. Individual worth is an essential property of the individual's spirit; it pertains to the way he chooses himself before God.

Too many of us are tempted to identify our individuality and uniqueness in the spiritually significant sense with an accidental property. Most often we gain a belief in our importance from some talent with which we are blessed, rather than from the spirit with which we employ the talents we have been given. Having been admired for our skills at reading, writing or politicking, most of us, at some time or other, find enticing the idea that these gifts make us uniquely precious to God and therefore more worthy of *hashgaha peratit* than other mortals. This is to confuse the aesthetic, which glories in the accidental, with the ethical and religious, which are founded on the self's inner integrity. Another odd phenomenon is the competition between individuals and groups who are anxious to demonstrate that they have suffered more than others, as if this confers upon them some ultimate prestige. This undignified race for the crown of thorns becomes a parody of the religious conception of the man of God, as blasphemous as it is vulgar.

VII

What do human beings want out of life? The spiritual orientation that I have presented in this essay is predicated upon a firm belief in the absolute claim of the God relationship, a conviction strong enough to withstand pain and grief, all sorts of failure and disappointment within and without, the terrible moments when God seems unbearably distant from the believer and the impenetrable moments when the divine presence seems intolerably commanding and intrusive. The human being who yearns to stand before God thus is possessed of an unwavering integrity of commitment and an unflinching honesty that can absorb hard truths about the world and oneself. Such an individual longs to make his own the joyous affirmation with which the Psalmist concludes his meditation on the mystery of evil: "As for me, the nearness of God, that is my good."[58]

Where does that leave the rest of us? Does the vision of the nearness of God transfigure our existence? Is the service of God the omnipresent star by which we unalterably fix our compass? For the vast majority of us, the one thing that really matters in life is not paramount, most of the time, in our day-to-day living. Check the contents of your mind at random moments and, among the many preoccupations jostling for your attention, the desire for the nearness of God, although it be ever before our eyes, is rarely the most prominent. When illness threatens, the first worry is for one's physical health and that of one's family. Chronically anxious about our choices for the future, we are equally insecure about our attainments in the present: in

---

[58]Ps. 73:28. This chapter frequently is cited as the quintessence of biblical theodicy. See, for example, Ramban's introduction to the commentary on Job, in *Kitve Ramban*, ed. Chavel (Jerusalem, 1963), vol. I, 20–21, and Rabbi Yosef Albo, *Sefer halkkarim*, vol. IV, 14.

youth, these concerns are often self-directed; later on, we tend to find more and more time to fret vicariously about the situations of persons to whom we are devoted and to lie awake bemoaning our ineffectual help. We hope to be better understood by those we love than we are and wish that we could succeed in understanding them. We might dread the disrespect, humiliation, and failure to which we are subjected on the job, and we might dread the prospect of returning to the misunderstanding and disharmony of an unhappy household. We recall with rage the helplessness, uselessness, loneliness, and pain that marked us in childhood and anticipate with fear and anxiety the helplessness, uselessness, loneliness, and pain that await our old age. Along with all this, we are strangely fixated upon peculiar, undignified longings and vexed with frustrations so petty that we hardly can confess them lest we be exposed to mockery. Even at the verge of committing ourselves to the hand of God, we cling to the safety net of worldly affirmation, to the satisfactions and comforts we fancy ourselves unable to do without. We plead for the purgation of our sins, but "not through suffering and bad sicknesses."[59]

In the course of this essay, we have suggested again and again that ordinary people—those whose dreams are not ones of exceptional saintliness—usually are satisfied with a life that is not perfect, a life that is good enough, as the world measures these things. Except for those rare individuals whose every breath is governed by particular providence, a good enough life is what people hope to get: a life that oscillates between the impersonal, uncaring benevolence of

---

[59]Rav Kook (*Olat Reiyah*, vol. II, 356–358) interprets this entreaty idealistically. We want the type of repentance that love motivates rather than the kind that is extracted from the unwilling penitent. However appealing his approach, it does not, in my opinion, cancel the simple meaning.

general providence and the invitation to transcend one's species identity and be judged according to one's individual worth. Man's ambiguous position, his inability to estimate properly the nature of his relation to God, is a healthy phenomenon. An antidote to self-centeredness, it frees him of the clamminess of "hothouse *hashgaha*" and motivates the spiritual striving that brings him nearer to the pole of individual providence. In this respect, the "good enough *hashgaha*" is not unlike Winnicott's "good enough mother."

The human reality that concerns me is neither that of the obsessive philosopher nor that of the burnished saints. The former, inspired by the categories of forensic theodicy, expects of life nothing less than perfection and cannot endure the shadows and conflicts that plague *homo viator's* journey. The latter, by contrast, having entered the dwelling place of the holy where "the nearness of God, that is my good," happily devote their lives to gratitude and divine service. In addressing again the ordinary individual, this closing part of our discussion shifts the essay's focus from the ambiguity in interpreting God's providence for us as individuals to the ambiguity of the choices that we, as individuals, make for ourselves.

When we look in the mirror, we see neither the unique man of God, "replete with creation and renewal," nor a species man, the "spiritual parasite" subject to general providence, a "faceless mediocrity" excluded from the Psalmist's sacred adventure. We meet a creature mysteriously and sometimes humorously suspended between the categories. The ordinary person I have described does not exhibit the vocation of the saintly individual, but his preoccupations contain the raw material from which we can build bridges from "where all the ladders start"[60] to where all the ladders must lead.

---

[60]W. B. Yeats, "The Circus Animals' Desertion."

Many of the aspirations and aversions that define the ordinary, unheroic, religious believer's spiritual landscape represent legitimate, worthy values. I fear, for example, becoming a dull, embittered old man, in which eventuality my
friends are liable to be less devoted to me than I would like
and than they otherwise would be willing to be. With that
goal in mind, I persist in various enjoyable activities, some
of which, such as Torah study, are religiously mandated,
while others merely fulfill the desire to cultivate one's God-
given talents and to delight one's friends. I hope that these
efforts will make me a cheerful and interesting companion
to them and help ease the misery of old age. Is this mere
worldliness rationalizing the pursuit of pleasure, comfort,
and security, or is it also a passionate manifestation of *ahavat
ha-beriyot*, love of one's fellow man, a fulfillment of the divine call to master the world, and hence part of the quest
that brings one closer to the "nearness of God, that is my
good"? And once having glimpsed the higher, God-oriented
dimension of my motivation, it becomes impossible to remain satisfied with "species man's" torpid, bloodless passivity in the face of the divine summons. Thus a more than
good enough life is not an unreachable elitism to which the
ordinary believer has no attachment, but the proper out-
growth of our natural experience. Our conception of human felicity cannot remain static. There is more to Heaven
and to earth than happiness as the world defines it.

Wittgenstein's dying words: "Tell them I've had a wonderful life."[61] Not a perfect life, nor even a very good one,
for as one of the "them" to whom the cancer-riddled philosopher dedicated his last mysterious utterance observed:
"When I think of his profound pessimism, the intensity of

---

[61]Quoted by Ray Monk, *Ludwig Wittgenstein: The Duty of Genius*
(Free Press, New York, 1990), 579.

his mental and moral suffering, the relentless way in which he drove his intellect, his need for love together with the harshness that repelled love, I am inclined to believe that his life was fiercely unhappy."[62]

In the face of the deep unhappiness that might befall even the blandest among us and in the absence of the perfection to which we have no right, a "good enough" life is not really good enough. The aesthetic personality, at its most clear-eyed and heroic, can look into the abyss, admire its own talent, and summon up the dedication of Nietzsche's Zarathustra: "Am I concerned with *happiness?* I am concerned with my *work.*"[63] The ethical view, having seen through the vacuity at the heart of the brilliant aesthetic kaleidoscope, accepts the universal yoke of Heaven and recites the conclusion of Kohelet: "In the end, when all is heard, fear God, and keep His commandments, for that is all of man." Both of these paths seek to supply the passion and the courage that are absent from species man's outlook. For when all is said and done, our hearts and minds are made for more than a good enough life. Yet beyond aesthetic man's self-dramatizing, self-annihilating vanity and the passive acceptance of the burden of duty that occasionally strips ethical personalities of their unique individuality, we look to the *Ribbono shel Olam*, His rod and His reliance.[64] We ache for eternity, yearn for the purity of

---

[62]Norman Malcolm, *Ludwig Wittgenstein: A Memoir* (Oxford, 1967), 100.

[63]*The Portable Nietzsche*, ed. Walter Kauffmann, 439. Kierkegaard's Judge William provides the crucial distinction between the conception of one's work as a vocation and duty, which defines the ethical stage, and the cultivation of a talent, which belongs to the aesthetic (*Either/ Or* [trans. Walter Lowrie, Princeton, 1971], vol. II, 187ff and 295ff).

[64]See Ps. 23:4, as interpreted by Rashi.

wonder, and know that in the end there is only one thing
that counts. The passionate heart turns from the resigna-
tion of Kohelet to the enigmatic climax of Shir ha-Shirim,
to the love that outstrips ordinary human calculations and
ambitions, to the love as fierce as death.

5

The Contribution of Rabbinic Thought to a Theology of Misfortune

Yaakov Elman

If the foundation of Jewish practice and belief is to be found in the two Torahs, the Oral and the Written, certainly the insights of Hazal incorporated into the latter constitute the ground floor. As we ascend to the upper stories, we encounter apartments, suites, rooms, and closets erected upon the lower ones. To our surprise, however, we find walled-off areas, where rooms opened up by Hazal were left vacant, with little if any new construction laid over the ground floor. We denizens of the upper floor, or perhaps (in Hazal's terms) the attic, all too often lose sight of the lowest floors, fascinated as we are with the contents of the upper stories. Indeed, because of our position and that fascination, we never obtain a complete view of the ground floor at all.

This is all the more the case because we tend to tear down the walls of rooms they constructed, altering dimensions and configurations, reassigning rooms originally intended for one resident to another, or more commonly, leaving the room open to all, as though any Tanna or Amora can be moved from room to room without hesitation, since they are ultimately interchangable.

And, most particularly, we hardly ever consider the "stone which the builders rejected" which may serve as a foundation of a new wing. The purpose of the following is to open a room which has remained mostly neglected, to discover its original designer, and to remove some accretions of lacquer and paint in order to determine its original texture and color.

I

I will begin by examining, for purposes of contrast, a statement that has resounded through the centuries and whose influence still is felt. In one of the chapters of what he himself terms his "conclusion," Maimonides proposes the following rule:[1]

---

[1]By and large, the following remarks will be limited, as far as possible, to the problem of individual providence and individual suffering, though it is impossible to deal with the individual in complete isolation from the community of which he is part.

The same applies to our analysis of Maimonides' view of providence. Note that the chapters of the *Guide of the Perplexed* that deal with the question—III:17–18, 22–23, 51—are devoted almost exclusively to individual providence; the matter of providence over collective Israel, however, is touched upon in some of the lexicographic chapters of part I and in his description of divine governance in II:4–10. On this point, see Charles M. Raffel, "Maimonides' Theory of Providence" (doctoral dissertation, Brandeis University, 1983), 41–60, especially 44–45 and 50–61.

A most extraordinary speculation has occurred to me just now through which doubts may be dispelled and divine secrets revealed. We have already explained in the chapters concerning providence that providence watches over everyone endowed the intellect proportionately to the measure of his intellect. Thus providence always watches over an individual endowed with perfect apprehension, whose intellect never ceases from being occupied with God. On the other hand, an individual endowed with perfect apprehension, whose thought sometimes for a certain time is emptied of God, is watched over by providence only during the time when he thinks of God; providence withdraws from him during the time when he is occupied with something else. . . . Hence it seems to me that all prophets or excellent and perfect men whom one of the evils of the world befell had this evil happen to them during such a time of distraction, the greatness of the calamity being proportionate to the duration of the period of distraction or the vileness of the matter with which he was occupied. If this is so, the great doubt that induced the philosophers to deny that divine providence watches over all human individuals and to assert equality between them and the individuals of the other kinds of animals is dispelled. For their proof for this opinion was the fact that excellent and good men experienced great misfortunes.[2]

In the following discussion, Maimonides buttresses his "most extraordinary speculation" with references to Deut. 31:17–18, from which he concludes that "it is clear that we are the cause of this *hiding of the face*, and we are the agents who produce this separation."

Maimonides' rule derives from his comparison of intel-

---

[2]*Guide of the Perplexed* III:51; see also III:18. The rendering presented is that of Shlomo Pines in his *The Guide of the Perplexed: Moses Maimonides*, translated with an introduction and notes by Shlomo Pines, with an introductory essay by Leo Strauss (Chicago: University of Chicago Press, 1963), 624–625.

lectually or spiritually uncultivated human beings to animals; just as the latter are bereft of individual providence, so, too, are such humans. Because the perfect man can expect greater providential protection, it is a relatively simple matter to relate the amount of providential attention granted each human to his intellectual and spiritual cultivation.[3]

One need not be a Maimonidean to accept this premise. Nahmanides accepts Maimonides' basic premise, though he substitutes *devequt* for Maimonides' "perfect [intellectual] apprehension."[4] Indeed, this rule has been adopted into basically anti-Maimonidean systems of thought, including the Hasidic.

For our purposes it is sufficient to note that Maimonides' position proceeds from the confluence of Aristotelean reasoning and Maimonides' understanding of Jewish tradition. However, it is surprising how few biblical or talmudic texts he actually cites in defense of his central contention;[5] it is an "extraordinary speculation" and not biblical or rabbinic

---

[3]I do not intend to present a full or even balanced review of Maimonides' theory of providence, one of the thornier problems in Maimonidean studies; see, conveniently, Charles M. Raffel, "Providence as Consequent upon the Intellect: Maimonides' Theory of Providence," *AJS Review* 12 (1987), 25–71, and the literature therein cited. For our purposes, Maimonides' approach, as understood and modified by Jewish thinkers over the centuries, serves as a useful contrast against which to view Hazal's position.

[4]See his comments on Job 36:7 in his *Perush le-Sefer Iyyov*, ed. Chavel (H. D. Chavel, *Kitvei Ramban* I, Jerusalem: Mosad Harav Kook, 108–109), and see David Berger, "Miracles and the Natural Order in Nahmanides," in *Rabbi Moses Nahmanides (Ramban): Explorations in His Religious and Literary Virtuosity,* ed. Isadore Twersky, (Cambridge, 1983), 107–128, especially 118–122.

[5]This is not to say that he does not cite texts, but rather that they hardly serve to support his contention. While he cites texts in proving that individual providence is indeed biblical teaching, as he does in III:17, he really cannot prove his central contention from either biblical or rabbinic sources.

teaching.[6] Indeed, his independence from biblical or rabbinic thought on these matters is demonstrated by his rejection of the rabbinic concept of "sufferings of love" and the rabbinic concept of *nissayon*.[7]

Nevertheless, Maimonides' position can be identified with one well-known from the *Bavli*, though he gives it a meaning all his own. According to an anonymous opinion recorded in *Ber* 7a, a righteous person to whom misfortune occurs is imperfect in some respect ("an incomplete *tzaddik*"), while one who is perfect is one who is well-off (*tov lo*). Once we make the necessary alterations in our interpretation of what constitutes a perfectly righteous person, Maimonides' position would seem to become totally congruent with Hazal's.

But is it? By stipulating a condition that is impossible for human beings to meet, Maimonides not only stacks the deck against humanity, but in doing so clearly is engaged less in philosophical speculation than in apologetics. Moreover, the great problem of theodicy relates precisely to those cases where the suffering seems incommensurate with the moral failing, and, as we shall see, Hazal affirm the existence of this possibility. But Maimonides flatly declares this impossible by stipulating that "the greatness of the calamity [is] proportionate to the duration of the period of distraction or the vileness of the matter with which he was occupied."

Maimonides' apologetic intent is clear from his assertion that his proposal would dispell "the great doubt that induced the philosophers to deny that divine providence watches over all human individuals." He thus presents less a theory

---

[6]Raffel already has noted this; see his analysis on p. 47.

[7]Compare *Guide* III:17 and Genesis *Rabba* 55:1–2, for example. For a useful collection of rabbinic texts on the *Aqedah*, see Y. E. Ephrati, *Parashat ha-Aqedah*, Petah Tikvah: Agudat Benei Asher, 1983.

of divine providence than a theodicy—literally a "defense of God." And although the two often are intimately intertwined, we shall see that this connection is not inevitable.

Once we locate the center of gravity of Maimonides' concerns, we can understand why a not inconsiderable number of biblical and rabbinic texts do not fit very well into his system-in-creation. As he himself notes:

> It is a fundamental principle of the Law of Moses our Master, peace be on him, and of all those who follow it, that man has an absolute ability to act.... It is likewise one of the fundamental principles of the law of Moses our Master that it is in no way possible that He, may He be exalted, should be unjust, and that all the calamities that befall men and the good things that come to men, be it a single individual or a group, are all of them determined according to the deserts of the men concerned through equitable judgment in which there is no injustice whatever.[8]

On this matter, as opposed to his extraordinary speculation, he cites *bShab* 55a ("There is no death without sin, and no suffering without transgression"), *mSot* 1:7 ("A man is measured with the measure he uses himself"), and *bB.Q.* 38b or *Pes* 118a ("The Holy One, blessed be He, does not withhold from any creature that which it has deserved.")[9]

---

[8]*Guide* III:17, Pines, 469.

[9]He also cites *bB.Q.* 50a, which vehemently denies God's yielding on His right to punish at some time, and a version of *bQid* 31a, regarding one who performs a mitzvah even when not obligated, different from that in our texts.

We shall return to *bShab* 55a–b, which, in contrast to Maimonides' use of Rabbi Ammi's dictum that opens the *sugya*, concludes with a refutation of that view. Maimonides is hardly alone in citing the opening of the *sugya* and disregarding its conclusion, but this is clearly a partial reading of the passage.

However, as we shall see, Maimonides' use of rabbinic sources is partial in both senses of the word: it is incomplete, and it is skewed in one direction.[10] In the following, we shall examine a number of rabbinic sources that reflect a distinctly un-Maimonidean approach to the matters of divine providence and divine justice.

Less surprising perhaps, but no less noteworthy, is the nearly complete absence of any empirical testing, like that that we find in rabbinic literature, of Maimonides' assertion. The end result is a somewhat circular system; the criticisms Abarbanel raises against Maimonides' levels of prophecy[11] can be raised against Maimonides' theory of providence as well.

It is not my place to argue for the rabbinic view(s) of providence; it is self-evident that an authentic Jewish theology must be based on those views, though we shall see that developing such a theology is hardly a simple matter. In any event, my intention in the following is to lay out a number of alternatives that the Babylonian Talmud, in particular, provides for us and to suggest that traditional Judaism of whatever stripe is not well-served either in ignoring the approaches implicit in rabbinic teaching or in reinterpreting them in accordance with other modes of thought.

---

[10]Raffel already has pointed out the lack of full congruity between Maimonides' "our" position in III:17 and the rabbinic sources he cites; see Raffel, 47, n. 61. However, the incongruity goes far beyond this.

[11]See *Guide* II:45, and Abarbanel "commentary" *ad loc.*, and see Alvin J. Reines, *Maimonides and Abarbanel on Prophecy* (Cincinnati: HUC Press, 1970), 180–232. For the connection between his theories of prophecy and providence, see Raffel, p. 45.

II

In a series of papers, some published and some delivered on various occasions but as yet unpublished,[12] I have argued that Babylonian and *Eretz* Israel rabbinic sources evince different approaches to the problem of theodicy. Sources originating in *Eretz* Israel, chiefly the *Yerushalmi* and Genesis and Leviticus Rabbah, are less inclined to admit that the righteous do suffer, except in extraordinary circumstances. However, the Babylonian Talmud, our primary source for Babylonian rabbinic views, argues in a number of striking *sugyot*, for what might be called an anti-occasionalist philosophy—i.e., that divine providence in the private lives of even the righteous is the exception rather than the rule. In short, the *Bavli* seems willing to admit that in many cases the righteous do not receive just treatment in this world. The merit they accrue, which should protect them against life's vicissitudes, does not influence significant aspects of their lives. These include three factors that make up the greater part of the "human condition": length

---

[12]See "When Permission is Given: Aspects of Divine Providence," *Tradition* 24/4 (Summer 1989), 24–45; "Ha-mal'akh ha-Mashhit bi-Zeman ha-Ge'ulah," *Rinat Yitzchak* (1988–1989), 109–113; "The Suffering of the Righteous in Babylonian and Palestinian Sources," *Jewish Quarterly Review* 80 (1990), 315–39; and "Righteousness as Its Own Reward: An Inquiry into the Theologies of the Stam," *Proceedings of the American Academy for Jewish Research* 57 (1991), 35–67. Two others, " 'Is There Then Anger Before the Holy One?' Aspects of the Theology of the Stam," AJS Twenty-first Annual Conference, Boston, December 19, 1989, and "The Image and Function of Death in Babylonian Rabbinic Sources," AAR/SBL Convention, Kansas City, Mo., November 26, 1991, remain unpublished.

Those who might wish to consult the published papers noted above should be aware that the treatment of these themes in the current discussion differs in one vital respect from that of the others: it is primarily dogmatic and not historical.

of life, viable offspring who will survive the parents, and sustenance.[13] In some circumstances, providential protection might be suspended altogether. Among these are *ᶜidan ritha*,[14] *yissurim shel ahava* ("sufferings of love"),[15] and vicarious atonement.[16] Moreover, as we shall see, even the protection active involvement with mitzvoth affords is limited to the time of involvement[17] and may be overcome by everyday hazards.[18] Indeed, there are occasions when even a righteous person stands in the way of the divine plan for history's fulfillment and must be removed from the stage of human activity.[19]

These suggestions occur in separate discussions in the *Bavli*, and no attempt seems to have been made to construct a comprehensive theology of providence. The situation in this regard is not different from that in other areas of Jewish law and theology. However, in this case, the *rishonim* did not strive to fill the gap; many of these non-"measure-for-measure" mechanisms of divine governance often were ignored or minimized in post-Talmudic times.

The reluctance of sources originating in *Eretz* Israel to admit this concept may be traced in part to the general disinclination to allow the demonic realm the role that Babylonian sources permit.[20] However, this would not account for the reluctance of the *Yerushalmi* and associated

---

[13]*bM.Q.* 28a.

[14]Namely, plague, famine, and war; see *bB.Q.* 60a–b.

[15]See *bBer* 5a–b.

[16]*bM.Q.* 28a. This refers exclusively to the death of the righteous.

[17]See *bSot* 21a.

[18]See *bQid* 39b.

[19]*bTan* 4b.

[20]On the various classes of demons to be found in both Babylonian and Palestinian sources, see Urbach, *Hazal*, 140–151; on the relative distancing of Palestinian sources from the demonic, see L. Ginzberg, *A Commentary on the Palestinian Talmud* (New York, 1941), I: xxiii–xxvi.

midrashim to admit that the innocent do suffer. Alternately, it might be that in this respect *Eretz* Israel *aggadah* is more closely oriented toward homiletical needs—even if the collections of *aggadic* midrashim did not originate as sermons[21]—than is the *Bavli*, which reflects the attitude of rabbinic circles—masters lecturing disciples.[22]

It might be this emphasis on the consolatory that impelled the *Eretz* Israel Amoraim to minimize or avoid altogether the theme of undeserved suffering.

From a dogmatic point of view, however, the particular historical or sociological reason for such a reluctance is irrelevant; we might as well account for the different approaches of the two Talmuds by arguing that divine providence is more active in the Holy Land.

---

[21]See for example, J. Heinemann, "Profile of a Midrash: The Art of Composition in Leviticus Rabba," *JAAR* 39 (1971): 141–50, taken from "Omanut Ha-Qompozitziyah Be-Midrash Vayiqra Rabbah," *Ha-Sifrut* 8 (1969–71), 809–834, and J. Neusner, *Judaism and Scripture: The Evidence of Leviticus Rabba* (Chicago, 1986), 130–136, and, most recently, the discussion in Eliezer Segal, *The Babylonian Esther Midrash: A Critical Commentary*, vol. I (Atlanta: Scholars Press), 1–13, especially 8–9, and my "The Suffering of the Righteous," 338–339.

[22]See B. Z. Wachholder's remarks (in his prologue to a reprint of J. Mann, *The Bible as Read and Preached in the Old Synagogue* (reprint, New York: Ktav, 1971), vol. 1, xxxi) regarding the connection between the *Eretz* Israel seder and *ashlamta*:

> though seemingly strictly verbal, [it] is in addition eschatological. The messianic kingdom, rather than the related contents of the Torah became the dominant theme of the Palestinian haftarot. The Annual [Babylonian] haftara for Gen. 1:1 is Deutero-Isaiah's description of the creation (42:5 ff.); the triennial selection for the same lesson is the prophet's vision of the new creation in the Lord's day, when the account of creation in Genesis would no longer be worth remembering (Isa. 65:17). Thus in Palestine, the haftara seems to have been conceived as a sort of peroration, which as in the later midrashic homilies usually concludes with messianic allusions.

Indeed, Rav Kook suggested an analogous distinction regarding the status of *aggadic* statements in the two Talmuds:

> For the wisdom of prophecy, the foundation of the wisdom of the *aggadah*, which is the inner aspect of the essentials of the Torah, is far more effective in the Land of Israel than in Babylonia, which is unsuitable for prophecy.[23]

The Torah explicitly distinguishes between the Land of Israel and other lands in regard to God's providential concern for the prosperity of the former (see Deut 11:12).

Let us first distinguish between those aspects of life that Hazal consider part of the human condition—and not dependent on merit—on the one hand, and misfortune—which might be atoning—on the other. As noted above, the former includes such aspects of the human condition as length of life, viable offspring who will survive the parents, and sustenance; the latter includes illness, suffering of other types, and death. Note that the first three together go far in determining the quality of an individual's life; it is all the more striking that, according to a number of important *sugyot*, they are beyond the individual's control. As I have demonstrated in my "Righteousness As Its Own Reward,"[24] the various doctrines that coalesce around these points and form a more or less unified approach to the problem of suffering consistently are attributed to Rava:[25]

---

[23]Rav A. Y. Kook, *Iggerot ha-Re'iyah* 1, 124, n. 103. My thanks to Rabbi Yehudah Galinsky, who first called my attention to this source, and to Rabbi Mattis Greenblatt, who suggested that the difference in the views of the two Talmuds might be explained in this way.

See now Simhah Friedman, "*Emunat Hakhamim*: Faith in the Sages," *Tradition* 27 (1993), 10–34; the quote from Rav Kook appears on 23.

[24]See n. 12 above.

[25]Although Rabbi Yosef evinces strong concern for the problem; see *bSot* 21a, *bB.Q.* 60a and *bHag* 4b.

Rava said: [Length of] life, children, and sustenance depend
not on merit but [rather on] *mazzal* [astrological determina-
tion]. For take Rabbah and R. Hisda. Both were absolutely
righteous rabbis; one master prayed for rain and it came, the
other master prayed for rain and it came. R. Hisda lived to
the age of 92; Rabbah only lived to the age of 40.[26] In R.
Hisda's house—60 marriage feasts; in Rabbah's—60 bereave-
ments. At R. Hisda's house there was purest wheat bread for
dogs, and it went to waste; at Rabbah's house there was bar-
ley bread for humans—and that could not be found. This too
Rava said: I requested these three things of Heaven; two were
given me, but the third was not: the scholarship of R. Hisda
and the wealth of R. Hisda were given me, but the modesty
of Rabbah b. R. Huna was not given me.[27]

---

[26]See *Tosafot ad loc.,* b*R.H.* 18a (b*Yev* 105a), and *Tosafot ad loc.*
s.v. *Rava va-Abaye.* The Talmud there explains Rabbah's short lifespan
as stemming from his descent from the high priest Eli (see I Sam. 3:14).
The stam there compares Rabbah and Abaye; the former, who engaged
primarily (or exclusively) in Torah study, lived forty years, while Abaye,
who devoted himself both to Torah study and good works (*gemilut
hasadim*), lived sixty years. According to *Tosafot* in *Yeb,* Rava holds, like
Rabbah, that Torah study alone provides atonement, but this contradicts the information provided by b*Sanh* 98b. *Tosafot* in *R. H.* takes
this problem into account and suggests that while Rabbah did engage
in good works, Abaye did more in this regard.

As to the tradition itself, note that Rabbah and Rabbi Hisda are
classified as "righteous rabbis" because their prayers for rain were immediately effective (*M.Q.* 28a); according to b*Tan* 24a, however, Rabbah
once called for rain unsuccessfully and lamented that he and his generation, though their study of the Mishnah was more extensive, were
not as worthy as the second generation Rabbi Judah [ben Ezekiel], a
statement otherwise attributed to Abaye in *Ber* 20a. It would seem that
the variant Rava (see *Diqduqei Soferim ad loc.,* 144–145 n. *lamed*) is
to be preferred.

[27]b*M.Q.* 28a.

We immediately must note that, despite the astrologically determined nature of *mezonei* (sustenance), Rava prayed for "the wealth of R. Hisda"—and his prayers were answered. Still, he did not rely on *mazzal* alone: he specifically prayed for wealth, even though, as we know from elsewhere, he did not consider himself on a par with Rabbi Hisda, who was a "righteous rabbi," while Rava explicitly refers to himself as a *benoni*.[28] Or perhaps, having sustenance, he felt himself in a position to ask for more.

While we are not informed as to whether Rabbah had prayed for wealth, it is certain that he prayed for sustenance, for such prayer is mandated halakhically. Evidently, his prayer was not granted. Indeed, sustenance classically is considered one of the most "difficult" matters to arrange—more difficult, according to Rabbi Yohanan, than the Redemption itself, and at least as difficult, according to Rabbi Eleazar ben Azariah, as the splitting of the sea.[29] Elsewhere, the provision of sustenance involves the very reordering of Creation,[30] and even Rabbi Eleazar ben Pedath did not press his plea for relief from his grinding poverty.[31] When, in response to his query as to how long he would have to suffer poverty and privation (he had fainted from hunger), God responded, "Eleazar, my son, would you rather I should turn the world back to its beginnings? Perhaps you would then be born in an hour [destined for] sustenance?" Rabbi Eleazar then conceded: "All this, and then only *per aps?*" In the famous *sugya* devoted to "sufferings of love," an anecdote is related that reflects much

---

[28] *bBer* 61b.
[29] *bPes* 118a.
[30] *bShab* 53b.
[31] *bTan* 25a.

the same point of view; indeed, the Maharsha explicitly relates the two:[32]

> R. Eleazar fell ill and R. Yohanan went in to visit him. . . . He noticed that R. Eleazar was weeping, and he said to him: "Why do you weep? Is it because you did not study enough Torah? Did we not learn: One who gives much and one who gives little have the same merit, so long that his heart is directed to Heaven? Is it perhaps lack of sustenance? Not everyone has the privilege of enjoying two tables [learning and wealth]. Is it perhaps because of [the lack] of children? This is the bone of my tenth son!"[33]

The third element, length of life, is more ambiguous, if only because while Rava holds that length of life is determined astrologically, the fact of death generally is considered a penalty. Indeed, suffering and death often are conjoined; halakhically, *malqot* may be a substitute for "death at the hands of Heaven."[34] Let us examine a *sugya*, alluded to by Maimonides in his discussion of providence, that joins the two.

---

[32]Maharsha identifies Torah with "[length of] life" in *M.Q.* 28a, a view that is not without difficulty because Torah knowledge generally is excluded explicitly from matters that are astrologically determined. Moreover, Rabbi Yohanan explicitly is associated with the view that Israel is not under astrological influence (*bShab* 156a). Unfortunately, we lack his *hiddushei aggadah* to the end of *M.Q.*, but from his comments on *bShab* 156a (s.v. *ein mazzal*), it would appear that he does not go beyond the view of *Tosafot* there (s.v. *ein mazzal le-Yisrael*) that great merit (*zekhut gadol*) can overcome one's astrologically determined fate. However, what this illustrates is that both Rabbi Yohanan here in *Ber* 5b and Rava in *M.Q.* 28a agree that, as we might say in Yiddish, "*nachas fun kinder*" and "*parnoso*" constitute the two major sources of good fortune.

[33]*bBer* 5b.

[34]See *bMak* 13a–b; see also *bSanh* 10a–b and 81b for a court-ordained death penalty.

bShab 55a–b opens with Rabbi Ammi's statement, firmly supported by appropriate proof-texts, that suffering and death are the result of sin. Indeed, his *memra* is little more than a restatement of Ezek. 18:20 and Ps. 89:33, the only addition being *perhaps* the assertion that these rules *always* hold. In response, the *sugya* cites two anonymous *baraitot* for which no early parallels exist.[35] The first applies *Koh* 9:2 ("There is one event [death] to the righteous and the wicked") to Moses and Aaron, who, though perfectly righteous, suffered the limitations of human mortality. The *sugya* aligns Rabbi Ammi's view with that of a Tanna who holds that Moses and Aaron died because of their own sin. Note that this is held to be a disputed interpretation, not the plain sense of the biblical text! Moreover, the impression is given that this view of Moses' sin is a minority one.

The second *baraita*[36] lists the four who died only *be-ᶜetyo shel nahash* (because of Adam's sin), which is held to contradict Rabbi Ammi's assertion. The *sugya* then concludes that indeed there is death without sin and suffering without iniquity—*tiyuvta deR. Ammi tiyuvta.*

This is an amazing *sugya*. A recognized authority expounds a doctrine that is at the core of Jewish teaching, clearly based on the plain meaning of two biblical proof-texts—proof-texts that easily could have been multiplied—and is refuted by a *baraita*, where many more could have

---

[35]But see Leviticus *Rabbah* 20:1, ed. Margulies, 442, where the verse is applied to Moses and Aaron. The *memra* is attributed to Rabbi Simeon ben Abaye, otherwise unknown, but a variant gives Rabbi Simeon ben Abba, the *Eretz* Israel Amora who was related to the Babylonian Samuel. If this is correct, the association of *Koh* 9:2 with Moses might go back to the third Amoraic generation. When this teaching would have reached Babylonia, if it did at all, is impossible to say.

[36]It might be that the two *baraitot* are connected because the first opens with the Ministering Angel's disingenuous query as to why death was decreed on Adam in the first place.

been adduced in his support. Again, this *baraita* regarding these four absolutely righteous individuals whose deaths Adam's sin alone caused is found—aside from a parallel in *bB.B.* 17a—nowhere else in the *Bavli, Yerushalmi,* or related literature, so far as I have been able to determine.[37] Indeed, whether this product of (apparently) esoteric speculation ought to be brought into the argument is doubtful. If Rabbi Ammi could accept the possibility of vicarious atonement (see *bM.Q.* 28a) why could these cases not be included under the same rubric?[38] There is another aspect to the matter. As noted, Rabbi Ammi himself holds the doctrine of vicarious atonement. If so, the case of *Cetyo shel nahash* might have been reconciled with his position reported in *bShab 55a* by positing a transgenerational vicarious atonement, somewhat analogous to the case of the golden calf, where future generations suffer for their ancestors' sin (see *bSan* 102a on Exod. 32:34).

Moreover, the *sugya* is constructed in such a manner as to give the impression that Rabbi Ammi holds a *minority*

---

[37]This is characteristic of the *Yerushalmi*'s approach to the problem of theodicy; see my "The Suffering of the Righteous."

[38]E. E. Urbach (*Emunot ve-DeCot*, Jerusalem, 1978, 237 n. 37) interprets this *memra* as a rejection of the doctrine of original sin. He claims that the idea that there is death without sin is not Tannaitic (*ibid.*, 235–37); rather, death is part of the natural order (237). This interpretation unnecessarily detaches the first part of the *memra* from its continuation. The essential point concerns the nexus between sin and suffering and death—"measure for measure" retributive justice, which Rabbi Ammi affirms and the *sugya* denies. Death is merely an extreme form of *yissurim*, and misfortune always is deserved on some level, according to Rabbi Ammi.

Indeed, the statement that "there is no death without sin" can be extended to apply to the concept of vicarious atonement. The death of the righteous atones for the sin of the unrighteous; we need merely enlarge our search for the relevant sin.

opinion, that of Rabbi Simeon ben Eleazar: namely, that Moses and Aaron died through their own sin. But his statement hardly represents a minority view! Moreover, as noted above, Rabbi Simeon ben Eleazar's position is clearly biblical, just as Rabbi Ammi's is.[39]

Yet the ministering angels are supposed to have argued that Moses and Aaron were without sin. Aside from those verses that certainly impute sin to both of them—either in regard to the waters of Meribah or the golden calf—(only Aaron), Rabbi Joshua ben Qorhah and Rabbi Judah ben Bizna pointed to the attack on Moses by the mysterious intruder ("God") of Exod. 4:24–26 as due to Aaron's negligence in regard to circumcision (*Ned* 31b–32a).[40] True, rabbinic exegesis is certainly capable of devising interpretations that contradict the plain-sense verse, or others, on which they are based,[41] but in this case, the sustaining exegesis is lacking and the reference is certainly tendentious. It is asserted as obvious—after all, the ministering angels themselves wonder at Moses' death!—without being proved. Elsewhere in the *Bavli*, Moses' sin is taken as a given (see *Shab* 97a and *Yom* 86b and 87a). Indeed, even the following *sugya*, which quotes *seriatim* Rabbi Jonathan's rejections of the theses that Reuben, David, Solomon, and Josiah ac-

---

[39]For the legerdemain necessary to maintain the position of the ministering angels in the first *baraita*, who are said to oppose that of Rabbi Simeon ben Eleazar in the second, see Maharsha *ad loc.* At any rate, see *tSot* 6:7–8, ed. Lieberman, 186–188, where Rabbi Simeon ben Eleazar defends Moses' righteousness in the matter of Num. 11:23.

[40]Even though Rabbi (or Rabbi Yose) disputes the exact nature of the negligence, he admits that there were grounds for God's anger.

[41]One need do no more than consider "Our Father Jacob did not die" *Tan* 5b), though there the incongruity of the proposed interpretation is pointed out immediately and no far-reaching conclusions are built on it.

tually sinned, does not make the attempt with Moses and Aaron.[42]

In the end, the *sugya* concludes that the existence of four perfectly righteous individuals who died only because of Adam's sin serves to disprove Rabbi Ammi's thesis. All four righteous men—Benjamin, Amram, Jesse, and David's son Kilab—are biblical figures and it is scarcely conceivable in rabbinic terms that their like would appear in historic time. Yet the *sugya* concludes with a resounding *tiyuvta* on the basis of the fate of these four biblical personalities, who probably constitute the only such cases in all of human history![43] It is as if the *sugya* were carrying on a polemic

---

[42]See *tSot* 6:7–8, ed. Lieberman, 186–188 and *Sifrei* Numbers 78 on Num. 11:23, ed. Horovitz, 94–95. In regard to the former, note that Moses' defender is no other than Rabbi Simeon ben Eleazar.

[43]The earliest attestation of Rabbi Ammi's *memra* outside the *Bavli* is *Koh Rabbah* 5:4, which reproduces the *memra* without comment. Although Albeck dates this midrash to early medieval times, the *memra* might have entered *Koh Rabbah* from the *Bavli*. It is worth nothing that it comes after four *memrot* that deal with the effects of the nonfulfillment of vows, based on *Koh* 5:4. The first three threaten collective retribution on the sinner's family or business associates, the last on the sinner himself. Rabbi Ammi's comment follows, which does not relate to vows at all.

Rabbi Ammi is reported to have expressed similar sentiments in regard to retributive justice in other contexts as well. See bTan 7b–8a, where he relates drought to robbery, lack of ethical dealing, or other sins; *B.M.* 105b, which reports that there was famine in his time; and *bSot* 9b, where Samson's reliance on the jawbone of an ass as a weapon is considered "measure for measure" justice. But these are the common coin of rabbinic discourse, and even Rava, who resisted universal application of the principle of retributive justice, makes use of the principle; see *Sot* 11a, 17a, 35a, and 42b.

On the other hand, God's consideration for the exigencies of human existence is stressed in a *memra* attributed to him in *Shab* 63a: if the intention to perform a mitzvah is thwarted by circumstance, the intention is considered as good as the deed.

against Rabbi Ammi and his position—and, by extension, be it noted, that of the prophet Ezekiel.

This *sugya* thus represents an explicit rejection of the normative biblical and rabbinic attitude toward sin, suffering, and death. In the end it must rely on atypical cases; for the argument to work, it must assume that Rabbi Ammi allows for no exceptions whatsoever to his rule. Whether the redactor was aware of the tradition presented in *bM.Q.* 28a, which has Rabbi Ammi accept the doctrine of vicarious atonement by the death of the righteous, cannot be known, but it is clear that for the refutation to be valid, this possibility and others like it must be ignored. Even on its own level, however, the argument does not carry us very far. Rabbi Ammi's view cannot be applied universally because there were four exceptions in all of recorded history. Does such a refutation deserve to be called a *tiyuvta*? Thus, we can see why Maimonides cites the beginning of the *sugya* and ignores its conclusion.

From our point of view, however, it is important to note that this *sugya* illustrates the lengths to which proponents of the view that sin and suffering are not connected ineluctably were prepared to go to argue their case.

Beyond that, the assumption that death and suffering are connected intimately not only on the experiential but also on the theological level underlies this *sugya*. Once Rabbi Ammi has been "refuted" on the matter of the connection of sin and death, no further (dis)proof regarding suffering and iniquity is required. Death and suffering constitute a "package deal."

The question that we face is what to make of this *sugya*. Maimonides—and others[44]—essentially ignore the *sugya* and

---

[44]See section X below, regarding the Maharal, and n. 115 regarding the *Ben Ish Hai*. The Ramban (see my "Ha-Mal'akh ha-Mashhit bi-Zman ha-Ge'ulah," *Rinat Yitzhak* 1988–1989, 109–113) and Maharsha (*ad bShab* 55b and *Qid* 39b) are notable exceptions.

its perplexing conclusion and cite only Rabbi Ammi's initial statement as normative. If this were the only *sugya* propounding this point of view, we safely might do likewise. However, it is far from unique; it represents a sensibility that turns up over and over again in the *Bavli*. But to follow that trail we must examine the *Bavli*'s teachings regarding misfortune (*yissurim*). It also will be useful to distinguish between individual and communal misfortune, for what applies on one level does not necessarily apply to the other. We thus will continue our discussion of rabbinic sources that touch primarily on individual misfortune.

III

bQid 39b is made up of three sections, each with its own generational center of gravity. The first section cites the second- and third-generation masters, Rabbi Yehuda and Rabbi Shemaiah; the second section is dominated by the fourth generation, Abaye and Rava; the third section is anonymous but cites a teaching attributed to the second-generation *Eretz* Israel Amora Rabbi Eleazar but not known from the *Yerushalmi*.[45] This last section has no *Eretz* Israel parallel, a fact of great significance, as we shall see.

The Babylonian *sugya* opens with a problem of Mishnah exegesis, which remains the focus of the first two parts. According to *mQid* 1:10, all mitzvoth are equal as far as the merit that their performance accrues is concerned;[46] accord-

---

[45]At least not in this form and with the attribution. That the sentiment authentically expresses the view of *Eretz* Israel authorities is demonstrated by Mekilta deRashbi, ed. Melamed-Epstein[2], 233, and *yPeah* 3:8 (17d).

[46]S. Safrai argues that this Mishnah reflects Rabbi Akiva's view that even *one* mitzvah properly fulfilled might save one from Gehenna and bring him to the life of the World to Come; see "Ve-ha-Kol le-Fi Rov

ing to *mPeah* 1:1, however, certain mitzvoth count for more than others. Rabbi Yehuda and Rabbi Shemaiah in the *Bavli* understand the Mishnah in *Qid* as referring to one whose merit and debits are balanced; the parallel idea in the *Yerushalmi* appears in the names of Rabbi Yose ben Hanina and Rabbi Eleazar, not as an answer to an exegetical problem, but as part of a theological complex dealing with those whose merit or debit slate predominates and with those whose merits and debits are balanced.

The next section of the *sugya* deals with another aspect of the Mishnah. The Mishnah states that whoever performs even one mitzvah is rewarded. The *Bavli* counterposes a *baraita*, which states that one whose merits outnumber his debits is treated harshly, while one whose debits outnumber his merits is treated well—presumably a paradoxical statement of the doctrine that the righteous are punished for their few sins in this world so as to enable them to enjoy the world to come without let or hindrance, a doctrine that all versions of the *Yerushalmi sugya* parallel. Abaye interprets this *baraita* along these lines. Rava attributes this teaching to Rabbi Jacob, who holds that there is no reward for mitzvoth in this world—i.e., one's merits provide no protection against misfortune.

Thus, though there is no *Yerushalmi sugya* (or unified collection of sources) that strictly parallels *bQid* 39b, the first two-thirds of the *sugya* approaches *mQid* 1:10 in roughly the same way as the *Yerushalmi* does. Significantly, it is the third part of the *sugya*, the anonymous section, that

---

ha-Ma'aseh," *Tarbiz* 53 (1982/3), 31–40, especially 36–39. In his note 27 and the accompanying text, he rightfully points to the difficulty in the interpretations proposed by Rabbi Yehudah and Rabbi Shemaiah when applied to the second half of the Mishnah.

has no *Yerushalmi* or other *Eretz* Israel parallel, though it is based on Rabbi Jacob's *baraita*. Moreover, it is that section that provides the *sugya* with its conclusion.

The *Yerushalmi sugya*, with one exception, concentrates on God's extraordinary mercies, a matter that is emphasized over and over again. Even if one's debits outnumber one's merits 999 to 1, there is hope. The *Bavli's sugya*, by contrast, is much less sanguine in its discussion of God's treatment of humankind. After devoting its first two parts to the matter of one whose merits and debits are balanced or slightly out of balance, the *sugya*, in the anonymous discussion with which it concludes, comes to the question of why those engaged in performing a mitzvah can be harmed or even killed.

Rava's attribution of the aforementioned *baraita* to Rabbi Jacob serves to introduce the famous *baraita* (known from *yHag* 2:1) regarding an incident supposedly witnessed by Aher, Elisha ben Abuya. While the *Yerushalmi* quotes Rabbi Jacob's teaching ("there is no reward for mitzvoth in this world") as emphasizing that the reward for mitzvoth is to be received in the next world, the *Bavli* stresses the lack of reward in this one. While these varying aspects of the matter are not contradictory, the different emphasis in the *Bavli* serves to turn the question into a dour contemplation of the frailty of human life even under the watchful eye of a benevolent Deity.

At any rate, once Rabbi Jacob's *baraita* is introduced into the discussion, the story of Aher's apostasy follows. A father instructs his son to climb up to a loft and bring down some young birds; the son does so, taking care to send away the mother bird before taking the young bird, in accordance with the prescriptions of Deut. 22:6–7. As he climbs down, the son falls and is killed—while in the midst of performing the two mitzvoth for which the Torah promises a long, happy life—filial piety (Deut. 5:16) and *shilluah ha-qen* (Deut. 22:7).[47]

The following dialogue then ensues, and I stress that it has no analogue, either as a whole or in any of its parts, in the *Yerushalmi* parallels:

1. Yet perhaps [it did] not [happen] like this?

   —R. Jacob [actually] saw the incident [take place].

2. Yet perhaps [the son] was considering [committing] a sin?

   —The Holy One, blessed be He, does not combine an evil thought with a [sinful] act.

3. Yet perhaps [the son] was considering [committing] idolatry, as [Scripture] states: "that I may catch the House of Israel in their own heart" (Ezek. 14:5)? [And R. Aha b. Jacob said: this {refers} to the thought of idolatry.][48]

   —That is just what [R. Jacob] thought: Should you think that there is a reward for a mitzva in this world, why did it not protect him from coming to consider [sinning]?[49]

---

[47]The anecdote is substantially the same in *yHag* 2:1 (77b), but the following differences should be noted. There is no hint of *kibbud av;* a man climbs a palm tree on his own and, once he has descended, is bitten by a snake and dies. Aside from the less schematic nature of the situation—the deck has not been "stacked," as in the *Bavli* version— the situation as depicted in the *Yerushalmi* would not have lent itself to so neat a conclusion as the *Bavli* reaches.

[48]Restored from the parallel *sugya* at *Hul* 142a.

[49]The parallel at *Hul* 142a has: If [the doctrine] there is a reward for mitzvot in this world does indeed pertain, let it be effective [to the extent] of protecting him so that he does not come to consider [committing idolatry] and be harmed! [Rather,] there is no reward for mitzvot in this world!

For a discussion of the protective merits of mitzvoth and Torah learning, see *bSot* 21a and see my "When Permission is Given," 32–33.

4. But did R. Eleazar not say that messengers [engaged] on a mitzva are not harmed?

—There, it is different when one is on his way [to performing the mitzvah].[50]

5. But did R. Eleazar not say that messengers [engaged] on a mitzvah are not harmed, either going or coming?

—It was a rickety ladder, and the danger was well-established [qevi^c a hezeqa]; when danger is well-established we do not rely on a miracle, as [Scripture] states: Samuel said, "How can I go [annoint David]? Saul will hear about it and kill me!" (I Sam. 16:2)[51]

---

[50]This apparently unnecessary objection is not found in the parallels at *Pes* 8a, *Yoma* 11a, or *Hul* 142a. It might have been inserted to heighten the suspense and thus prepare the way for the conclusion, a technique noticed by the *rishonim*; see *Tosafot ha-Rosh* on *B.M.* 14b s.v. *qa-tane miha* (ed. M. Hershler and Y. D. Grodzinski, Jerusalem 5719, 49a) and *Tosafot* Rabbenu Peretz *ad loc.,* s.v. *mide-resha'* (ed. H. B. Z. Hershler, Jerusalem, 1969/70, 37a).

Moreover, the following should be noted. Once steps 1–3 dispose of the question of sinful thoughts, it is difficult to understand why the *sugya* continues with steps 4–5. If according to step 3, Rabbi Jacob rejected the possibility of *any* protection from sinful thoughts, why should we assume that messengers engaged on a mitzvah are any different from anyone else engaged in the performance of a mitzvah? It is thus clear that this teaching goes beyond the earlier ones; Rabbi Eleazar holds that even upon returning from his errand the messenger still is protected by the mitzvah from even idolatrous thoughts; see *Etz Yosef* in *Ein Yaakov ad loc.,* and compare the "Rif" (Rabbi Yoshiah Pinto) *ad loc.* The latter suggests that the messenger is in a higher state of grace upon his return because he already has accomplished the mitzvah.

[51]The proof-text never is cited in the *Yerushalmi* or associated literature, nor does the teaching that we not rely on miracles explicitly appear. For the *Bavli*, see *bPes* 8a, *Yoma* 11a, and *Hul* 142a; also, see *Pes* 64b, and compare 50b and *Meg* 7b, *Naz* 66a.

This conclusion is entirely unanticipated. Such a doctrine does not appear in any of the *Yerushalmi* parallels, nor in the *Yerushalmi* itself. Nevertheless, the passage clearly is structured so as to introduce the essential point the redactor wished to stress.

Note that Rabbi Eleazar's rule ("messengers [engaged] on a mitzvah are not harmed") stands at the heart of the dialogue, even though it is introduced explicitly as late as step 4. Considered in this light, the dialogue is carefully constructed to pave the way for the desired conclusion. The following possibilities are considered and rejected as explaining the case at hand:

1. Contemplation of a sin while involved in a mitzvah vitiates the protection the mitzvah affords.
2. Contemplation of idolatry while involved in a mitzvah will vitiate such protection.
3. Rabbi Eleazar's rule applies only to setting out on a meritorious errand.

Clearly these are intended to clear the way for accepting the conclusion, which constitutes the climax of the final third of the *sugya*: Rabbi Eleazar's rule does not apply to a situation of *qevi^{c}a hezeqa*. The proof-text is I Sam. 16:2, where Samuel resists God's direct instruction because of the danger involved in carrying it out. Certainly a direct command from God should suffice to ensure protection, yet Samuel considers himself in danger of death by Saul's order if he were to carry out God's command![52]

---

[52]This understanding of I Sam. 16:2 does not appear in the *Yerushalmi* or its associated midrashim. In this connection, note Judg. 20:23–25, where the Urim Ve-Tumim's instructions led to disaster. To my knowledge, the *Bavli* does not attempt to explain this paradox.

But beyond its proof-text (I Sam. 16:2), *qevi^ca hezeqa* is supported by the *Bavli*'s version of the Elisha ben Abuya anecdote. First, the *Bavli* insists that the story is not parabolic but actually had occurred and, second, that the ladder was rickety. In essence, then, this is an appeal to historical experience.[53]

What then becomes of the Mishnah? In the end, the *sugya* concludes, with Rava, that *mQid* 1:10 was taught in accordance with the position of Rabbi Jacob's opponents. But according to the final analysis, Rabbi Jacob's view is based in reality, while application of the Mishnah's teaching is reduced to those cases, presumably few in number, in which credits and debits are nearly in balance. Note that Abaye's suggestion is ignored when it comes to analyzing the ladder incident.[54] Thus, though formally Rabbi Jacob's view implicitly is rejected as not in consonance with the Mishnah, the point has been made. In contemplating the vicissitudes of everyday life, *qevi^ca hezeqa* is a reality that must be taken into account.

If we look at this *sugya* within a wider context, a number of other solutions, based on other Babylonian *sugyot*, come to mind. For example, it might have been argued that *mazzaleh garam leh*, as in *bM.Q.* 28a, though this would

---

[53]Recently, D. Novak has argued that Rava's halakhic-legislative preference was for the use of reason over scriptural exegesis; see D. Novak, "Maimonides and the Science of the Law," *Jewish Law Association Studies IV: The Boston Conference Volume*, ed. B. S. Jackson (Atlanta, 1990), 99–134, especially 111–122.

[54]In any event, this incident constitutes an extreme instance of "there is no reward for mitzvoth in this world"; because the son died in the performance of his mitzvoth, there was simply no time for him to receive any reward in this world! ·

In truth, the Amoraic part of the *sugya* does not hold together well; see *Tosafot ad loc.* s.v. *matnitin*.

have contradicted *Sota* 21a, which asserts the efficacy of
mitzvoth performance at least during the time of the action (see below); but our *sugya* is seemingly oblivious of
Sota 21a in any case. On the other hand, this *baraita* would
have served admirably as an additional objection in *Shab*
55a–b—indeed, rather better than the *baraitot* that were included. Each of these *sugyot* stands alone, however, content to make one important point regarding the inconstancy
of divine providence. The common denominator of both
is that undeserved misfortune, suffering, and death can and
do occur.

There is another common denominator: Rava's views
play an important role in all of them.

IV

Sot 21a is the *locus classicus* for the question of the this-
worldly protection mitzvoth afford, an issue that is touched
upon in *Qid* 39b. The issue in *Sot* is to what extent Torah
and mitzvoth serve to protect the one engaged in either
studying Torah or performing mitzvoth.

The *sugya* begins with Rabbi Menahem ben Rabbi Yose's
view that performing mitzvoth protects one only temporarily, while studying Torah provides permanent protection.
It continues with Rabbi Joseph's view that a mitzvah only
protects during the time one actively is engaged in it, while
Torah study does so at all times. In part, this is a slightly
more concrete formulation of the previous statement, but
Rabbi Joseph also introduces another distinction. Torah
study not only protects the scholar from suffering, but also
"rescues" him from the evil inclination. Thus, this *sugya*'s
essential premise implicitly rejects Rabbi Jacob's statement
(in *bQid* 39b, introduced by Rava) that "there is no reward
for mitzvoth in this world" (see below).

Modifying Rabbi Joseph's formulation, Rava points to the cases of Doeg and Ahitophel,[55] the classic rabbinic instances of scholars come to a bad end. He proposes that

> Torah protects [one from misfortune] and rescues [one from the evil inclination] when one is occupied in its study; when one is not occupied with it, it protects but does not rescue.[56] Mitzvot protect one [from misfortune] whether he is actively occupied with them or not, but they certainly do not rescue him [from the evil intention].

The protection provided is hardly unbreachable, however, if only because it is not humanly possible to engage in Torah study without stopping and despite Rava's assertion elsewhere that one occupied with Torah study has no need

---

[55]Note that Rabbi Ammi is supposed to have noted that Ahitophel did not die before he had lost all his knowledge of Torah (*bB.B.* 106b).

[56]According to *bBer* 5a, "whoever engages in Torah study—sufferings are kept from him." This dictum, attributed to Resh Laqish, is reworked by his colleague Rabbi Yohanan as follows: "If one has the opportunity to study Torah and does not study it, the Holy One, blessed be He, brings disfiguring diseases upon him to stir him up." It is significant that Rabbi Yohanan is quoted (*ibid.*) as asserting that even sufferings that interfere with Torah study and prayer yet might be considered "sufferings of love" (sufferings that are not occasioned by sin but demonstrate God's concern for the sufferer's spiritual well-being; see E. E. Urbach, *Hazal*, 394), in contrast to the view of others (Rabbi Jacob ben Idi and Rabbi Aha ben Hanina) that chronic or disabling illness cannot be considered "sufferings of love." Note that Rabbi Huna is reported as having stated a generation later: "If the Holy One, blessed be He, is pleased with someone, He crushes him with sufferings."

Nevertheless, it is clear that mainstream rabbinic opinion held that sufferings could be warded off by Torah study, which, indeed, could protect against death itself (see *bShab* 30b and *bKet* 77b). And, on the other hand, the rabbis could not deny the evidence of their senses: even scholars of note fall victim to disease and suffering.

of sacrifices.[57] And, as regards mitzvoth, as we have seen, they cannot protect the doer from danger when *qevi^ca hezeqa* and do not rescue him from evil thoughts in any case, at least according to the third part of *Qid* 39b. If this then represents Rava's view, he must accept Rabbi Jacob's, a matter that is far from clear in *Qid* because there he associates Rabbi Jacob with a *baraita* (one whose merits outnumber his debits is treated harshly) that runs counter to *mQid* 1:10, thus relegating his opinion to a nonofficial status. Here in *Sotah*, however, he is associated with at least one aspect of Rabbi Jacob's view: that mitzvoth do not protect one from the evil inclination. On the other hand, Rava clearly does allow for some reward in this world, though he limits it.

However, it is clear that step 3 in the chain of reasoning in *Qid* 39b suggests, at least as a possibility, that Rabbi Jacob held a view that challenges the one attributed to Rabbi Joseph in *Sot* 21a—that is, that Rabbi Jacob holds that performing mitzvoth does not protect one against the evil inclination. Rava's modification of Rabbi Joseph's *memra* is nowhere in evidence, however, either in the questions propounded in *Qid* 39b or in the answers given. In the end, even Rava's limited view of the protective power of mitzvoth (as expressed in *Sot* 21a) cannot solve the problem Rabbi Jacob's anecdote poses.

We shall return below to the question of the exact relationship of these *sugyot.*

V

Rava's use of an argument from historical experience in *Sot* 21a was noted above; he pointed to Doeg and Ahitophel as cases of scholars gone bad to prove that Torah study does

---

[57]*Men* 110a.

not protect one from the evil inclination, though it serves to protect him from suffering even after he ceases study-ing. Doeg and Ahitophel, however, were not protected against their own evil thoughts and thus came to sin and suffering, Ahitophel committing suicide[58] and Doeg dying at age 37,[59] having lost his share in the World to Come.[60] As noted above, Rabbi Jacob's *baraita* is itself an argument from experience, at least as the *sugya* in *Qid* 39b under-stands it, for the concluding section insists that the incident actually occurred. Another such argument from experience is attested in *M.Q.* 28a, where Rava concludes, based on the lives of Rabbah and Rabbi Hisda, that "[length] of life, children, and sustenance do not depend on [one's] merit, but on *mazzal.*"[61] In essence, then, merit has no part, or perhaps little part, in determining the basic circumstances of one's life, as noted above.

Again, there is a passage that deals with the intersection of communal and individual misfortune (*bB.Q.* 60a–b), which I have dealt with in a study of a *Mekilta* passage Rabbi Joseph cites in *bB.Q.* 60a. This *sugya* establishes the exist-ence of an *ᶜidan ritha*, a time of plague, famine, or other communal misfortune, during which the righteous and wicked suffer alike.[62] Furthermore, the *sugya* contains ad-

---

[58]II Sam. 17:23.

[59]*bSanh* 106b.

[60]*mSanh* 10:2.

[61]See n. 26 above.

[62]See my "When Permission Is Given," 24–55. Rabbi Joseph's espousal of the view of the Mekilta does not contradict his insistence—as inter-preted by the *stama di-gemara*—in *bKet* 30a–b that, though the four modes of execution by a human court have ceased, God carries them out by other natural means. *bB.Q.* 60a refers to communal catastrophe; *bKet* 30a–b to individual sin and punishment.

Finally, it is likely that the protection afforded by Torah study and the performance of *mitzvoth*, in Rabbi Joseph's view (*Sot* 21a), does not apply to cases of *ᶜidan ritha*.

vice, attributed to Rava,[63] to close one's windows in time of plague—not bad advice at all, but not quite in the same category as fasting, prayer, donating to charity, etc.

I suggest therefore that Rava, or more precisely, his view, stands behind the *sugya* in *Shab* 55a–b. This does not mean that Rava rejects a "measure for measure" understanding of divine governance; that is hardly possible for a Jewish thinker. Moreover, we have evidence that he himself applied the principle; see *bShab* 32b, where he applies it to the women of Mahoza, who do no work and thus bring on locusts and famine, or *bA.Z.* 18b, where he begs his students to avoid frivolity so as not to be made to undergo sufferings (*yissurin*).

This principle would seem to operate on the communal level always and sometimes on the individual level. It is Rava—or, according to another tradition, Rabbi Hisda, who was, after all, his father-in-law[64]—who suggests that

> When a person sees afflictions coming upon him, he should examine his deeds; if he does not find [a reason for the afflictions], he should attribute [them to the sin of] *bittul Torah*; if he does not find [the sin of] *bittul Torah*, he should classify them as chastisements of love.[65]

Here Rava carefully coordinates both forms of misfortune: that based on the "measure for measure" principle

---

[63]So in all MSS and attestations but for *Aggadot Ha-Talmud*, which reads Rabbah; see *Diqduqei Soferim ad loc.*, n. *tet.*

[64]There is another tradition preserved in the manuscripts, which attributes this *memra* to the same chain of tradents as current editions do for the following one: Rava in the name of Rabbi Sehorah in the name of Rabbi Huna; see n. 63 below, and *Diqduqei Soferim ad loc.* n. *dalet.*

[65]*Ber* 5a; see *Tan* 8a, where the concept is attributed to Rabbi Shimon ben Laqish.

and that which goes beyond it. *Yissurin shel ahava* ("chastisements of love"), which God brings on the righteous for no reason other than to increase their reward in the World to Come, are a confirmation of merit rather than of the reverse, but they are certainly not an example of "measure for measure."

Finally, we have a small collection of *memrot* in *Hul* 7b, where once again Rava severely limits the operation of divine providence:

1. Again, R. Hanina said: No one bruises his finger[66] Below unless it was so decreed against him Above. [Proof-texts from Ps. 37:23 and Prov. 20:24 follow.]
2. R. Eleazar said: The blood of a bruise atones as [does] the blood of a burnt-offering.[67]
3. Rava added: Only the blood of a second bruising of the right thumb, and only if it happened to one who was about to perform a mitzva.[68]

Rava here seems to limit providential, atoning suffering to those injured while engaged in performing a mitzvah, and only in strictly delimited circumstances. If Rava's comment relates only to number 2, other bruisings must be attributed to causes other than the need for atonement, namely but not exclusively *yissurin shel ahava*. If his comment relates to number 1 as well, he denies even providen-

---

[66]Variant: "leg"; see *Diqduqei Soferim ad loc.*, n. *nun.*

[67]Note that the principle of that "messengers [engaged] on a mitzva are not harmed" is also attributed to Rabbi Eleazar. Maharsha *ad loc.* attempts to connect this with *bQid* 39b and related *sugyot*; he points out that a burnt offering atones for sinful thoughts. Why Rabbi Eleazar compares the atonement to that of a burnt offering and not a sin offering is not clear.

[68]In which case one is a *sheli'ah* mitzvah, as Maharsha points out.

tial status to most bruises, perhaps relegating them to situations of *qeviᶜa hezeqa* or plain carelessness.

In any case, Rava's limitation of providential suffering is clear, no matter what category most bruisings are assigned.

Thus, for Rava, a confluence of natural factors (astrology) and divine judgment determine man's place in the world,[69] while reward is deferred for most until the future world.

Before leaving this subject, it might be worthwhile to examine another aspect of individual suffering that, while not attributed to Rava, sheds light on this aspect of nonprovidential misfortune.

As noted above, that sector of the human condition designated as *yissurim* is the primary venue for providential misfortune, as opposed to length of life, survival of children, and sustenance, which are not dependent on merit. However, even this aspect of the human condition might be subject to illness not dependent on sin. One possibility, attributed either to Rava or his father-in-law Rabbi Hisda, involves *yissurim shel ahava* and already has been mentioned. Another, not attributed to Rava but certainly compatible with his general approach, also limits the providential reach of illness:

> . . . R. Adda b. Ahava objected: How [do you know that] Jacob
> warned his sons [by referring to "harm"] against cold and heat,
> which are by the hands of Heaven; perhaps [he warned them]

---

[69]We already have noted his explicit connection of sin and suffering in *bShab* 32b and *bA.Z.* 18b.; see also his comment in *bHor* 10b, regarding the fate of the righteous in this world, where they are punished for their few sins while the wicked are rewarded for their few good deeds. We therefore must understand Rava's agreement with Rabbi Yaakov (*Qid* 39b) as pertaining to the righteous and the intermediate group (see his comment in *Ber* 61b, where he identifies himself as one of them, to Abaye's dismay), whose reward is deferred until the next world.

against lions and thieves, which are by the hand of man?
[Could it be] that Jacob warned them against this and did not
warn them against that? Jacob warned them against all things
[cold and heat and lions and thieves].

[But] are cold and heat by the hand of Heaven? Is it not
taught: Everything is by the hand of Heaven except cold and
heat, for it is said: "Cold and heat are in the way of the forward; he who keeps his soul holds himself far from them."
(Prov. 22:5) Moreover, are lions and thieves by the hand of
man? Did not R. Yosef say, and R. Hiyya teach: Since the day
of the destruction of the Temple, although the Sanhedrin
ceased [and so too did capital punishment], the four forms
of capital punishment have not ceased?

They have not ceased—but surely they *have* ceased!

Rather: the judgment of the four forms of capital punishment has not ceased:

He who would have been sentenced to stoning, either falls
down from the roof or a wild beast treads him down. He who
would have been sentenced to burning either falls into a fire
or a serpent bites him. He who would have been sentenced
to decapitation is either delivered to the government or rob-
bers come upon him. He who would have been sentenced to
strangulation is either drowned in the river or dies from suf-
focation [croup].

Rather, reverse it: Lions and thieves are by the hands of
Heaven, and cold and heat are by the hands of man [i.e., a
person can keep himself from catching cold].[70]

Thus, there are exceptions even to the general rule of providential suffering.

VI

While additional sources not attributed to Rava can be adduced for this view in the *Bavli*, I think that what has been

---

[70]*bKet* 31a.

surveyed is sufficient to demonstrate that Hazal certainly hold out the possibility of non-"measure for measure" and nonretributory types of divine governance. Of course, as moral individuals we first must assume the nexus of suffering and sin and seek out the sources of our misfortune. Things being what they are, in most cases we will not have to seek much further. But in other cases, especially when we as individuals are caught in communal calamities, other mechanisms of divine governance must be sought.

Moreover, it seems to me we ought not be too literal in our interpretation of "individual" in these cases. While collective retribution might be meted out to family units,[71] a morally random collection of individuals in no way connected with the sin being punished cannot be judged in the same way; they might have run afoul of the Destroyer, who is no respecter of persons, as noted in *bB.Q.* 60a. Likewise, in *Ber* 7a, in a *sugya* devoted to the subject, God's anger is aroused as a response to the existence of idolatry. Once aroused, it becomes a recurrent, almost "natural" phenomenon; one might nearly set one's clock by it. Once aroused, it does not seem to depend on human action at all and might be directed at any convenient target, despite the target's merit or lack of it. Balaam might direct it at the Israelites or Rabbi Joshua ben Levi might direct it at a Christian who was pestering him, without regard to the case's merits. That God's mercy saved both does not change the fact that without that mercy God's anger might wreak havoc. Thus, like the Destroyer or like small-time *shedim* and *mazziqim*, this world's harmful powers express an arbitrary, unfocused aspect of divine anger/judgment.

It is thus likely that Maimonides ignored this large body of Hazal's teaching for the same reason that he rejected the

---

[71]See *bShev* 39b, for example.

existence of demons. Nevertheless, even without these demonic forces, the natural order itself often seems morally
neutral, as in the case of the rickety ladder of *Qid* 39b. How
did Maimonides account for the incidents which these contexts?

We return to the principles he enunciated in III:17 and
that we noted above:

> It is likewise one of the fundamental principles of the law of
> Moses our Master that it is in no way possible that He, may
> He be exalted, should be unjust, and that all the calamities
> that befall men and the good things that come to men, be it
> a single individual or a group, are all of them determined
> according to the deserts of the men concerned through equi-
> table judgment in which there is no injustice whatever.

These principles are not philosophical in origin, but biblical. Moreover, they are principles to which Hazal subscribe,
on the whole. However, Maimonides' understanding of divine justice does not allow for exceptions, even, as noted
above, that of a trial:

> The subject of *trial* is also very difficult; it is one of the great-
> est difficulties of the Law. . . . What is generally accepted
> among people regarding the subject of *trial* is this: God sends
> down calamities upon an individual, without their having been
> preceded by a sin, in order that his reward be increased.
> However, this principle is not at all mentioned in the *Torah*
> in an explicit text. . . . The principle of the Law that runs
> counter to this opinion, is that contained in His dictum, may
> He be exalted: *A God of faithfulness and without iniquity.* Nor
> do all the *Sages* profess this opinion of the multitude, for they
> say sometimes: *There is no death without sin and no suffer-*
> *ings without transgression.* And this is the opinion that ought
> to be believed by every adherent of the Law who is endowed
> with intellect, for he should not ascribe injustice to God, may
> He be exalted above this, so that he believes that Zayd is in-

nocent of sin and is perfect and that he does not deserve what befell him.[72]

It is this absolute conception of divine justice that prevents Maimonides from accepting the ideas of *nissayon* or of *yissurim shel ahava*. Note that he describes Rabbi Ammi's view regarding trials as contradicting that of the multitude and that "sometimes" this is the view of the sages. He then argues that "this is the opinion that ought to be believed by every adherent of the Law who is endowed with intellect," a statement that allows for the possibility that others might differ.

The question thus arises: does Maimonides' own theory of "providence consequent upon intellect" fulfill the requirement of absolute divine justice? Given human limitations both physical and psychic, it is certainly not possible for anyone to commune intellectually with God without any distraction. That itself would seem to impugn the dictates of perfect and absolute divine justice, for God then requires that we maintain a state that is not humanly possible. Moreover, the moment such a person is distracted, the consequences can be catastrophic, proceeding through illness or other misfortune to death. Indeed, even though Maimonides allows for some residue of providential protection for such a person—the perfect man, even when not in communion with God, is still not on the level of one who never has attained such a level[73]—the very existence of the problem of theodicy makes it unlikely that such a residue serves to protect its possessor. Thus, for example, Maimonides might interpret the incident recorded in *Qid* 39b so that *qevi'a hezeqa* is a danger only when the person involved in the mitzvah is distracted from his intellec-

---

[72] *Guide* III:24, Pines, 497–498.
[73] *Guide,* III:51, Pines, 625.

tual communion with God; it hardly matters that he once had been in intellectual communion.

Thus, though the cases that Hazal cite are ones where Maimonides easily could apply his rule of "providence consequent upon the intellect" (or, for that matter, Nahmanides could apply his version of "providence consequent upon *devequt*") without much problem, even when Hazal themselves proffer another explanation this does not mean that these cases conform to an absolutist view of divine justice. Because no one can remain continuously in that state, everyone becomes prone to "accidents." But, for example, the *baraita* cited in *Shab* 55b assumes that Benjamin, Amram, Jesse, and Kilab were absolutely righteous individuals whose mortality was due only to their Adamic descent. That in turn implies that they might have indeed lived forever, despite the inability of human beings to maintain intellectual communion at all times. Maimonides' use of Rabbi Ammi's assertion implies, as noted above, that he did not necessarily take the argument from the "four who died by the advice of the serpent" as seriously compromising his argument; in any case, the longer a person lives, the more likely he is to be distracted at a vital time.

VII

The *Bavli* thus provides us with a number of "mechanisms" of divine governance that in their simple sense violate Maimonides' strict canons of divine justice. These include the astrological sources of the human condition,[74] sufferings of love,[75] *nissayon*, vicarious atonement,[76] situations of neg-

---

[74]*bM.Q.* 28a.

[75]*bBer* 5a–b.

[76]*bM.Q.* 28a (top).

ligence in the face of hazard (*qevi'a hezeqa*),[77] or the workings of a hereditary curse.[78] We may add to these mechanisms certain rules that might not violate Maimonides' assumptions, such as the "sliding scale" of judgment applied to persons depending on their righteousness, the judgment of the righteous to a "hair's-breadth,"[79] either because of their responsibilities as moral leaders of their generation, to whatever (geographical or social) extent their influence carries,[80] or the inordinately severe punishment meted out for certain sins, as noted above, though here he well might have interpreted these assertions as overstatements intended to impress the hearers.[81] We might add to these rules the consequences of being a member of a community or of the community of Israel: the danger of the Destroyer, who, be it noted, could have harmed the very Israelites whose exodus from Egypt he was sent to facilitate;[82] God's hiding of His face during Israel's exile;[83] or the necessities of God's plan for history, which at times sweeps away those who resist it, as when Samuel resisted the command to anoint David.[84]

---

[77]*bQid* 39b.

[78]As in *R.H.* 18a (*Yeb* 105a), where Rabbah's short lifespan is attributed to his descent from the high priest Eli, rejecting the assertion that Torah study alone atones for this hereditary punishment; see n. 26 above.

[79]*bYeb* 121b.

[80]*bShab* 33b, *bShev* 39b.

[81]Similar perhaps to the use of divine anger as an educative tool.

[82]*bB.Q.* 60a. See my "When Permission is Given: Aspects of Divine Providence," *Tradition* 24 (1989), 24–45, especially 26–27, and associated notes, especially n. 25.

[83]*bHag* 5a; see Norman Lamm, *The Face of God: Thoughts on the Holocaust* (New York: Department of Holocaust Studies, Yeshiva University), n.d.

[84]*bTan* 5b.

To some extent, the elements in this list of non-"measure for measure" misfortune do not overlap; some apply to individuals, some to the community, some to individuals who are in a particular position of responsibility, etc. But the demarcation of the various elements that apply to individuals of the intermediate class—*benonim* in Rava's terminology,[85] such as *qevi'a hezeqa*, or *mazzal*, or the workings of a hereditary curse. However, we might assume in most cases that whatever the intermediate source (astrology, hereditary curse, etc.), the actual *mechanism* for its fulfillment is to be found in the hazards of everyday life.

This brings us to another question. Given the availability of various types of *yissurim*—nonspecific pain, wounds, illness, loss of minor children,[86] various forms of court-mandated death or their "informal" analogues,[87] and, at the other extreme, minor inconvenience[88]—on what basis is the selection made?

To some extent, what applies to one applies to the others. For example, note that though Rabbi Ammi's statement in *Shab* 55a applies both to death and *yissurim*, the *sugya* in the end refutes only the linkage of the former with sin, but not the latter's connection to iniquity. Nevertheless, the *sugya* concludes that both assertions have been refuted, as

---

[85] As noted above, in *bBer* 61b.

[86] E.g., *bShab* 32b.

[87] See *bKet* 30b, quoted above, section V, end; the relevant passage is quoted below.

[88] *bAr* 16b–17a, where from among the various possibilities offered, I will quote the one in which Rava had a hand: "Rava—according to others: R. Hisda and according to others: R. Yitzhak, and some report it as a tannaitic teaching: Even if he put his hand into his pocket to take out three [coins] and he takes out two. Now this is only in a case [where he intended to take out] three, and [took out] two, but not if [he meant to take] two and three came into his hand, because it is no trouble to throw it back."

Tosafot notes.[89] The two thus are alike in that what is posited of one applies to the other.

However, that does not mean they are of equal weight. Thus, the four modes of capital punishment are ranked in order of severity, though the exact order is a matter of dispute.[90] Likewise, Rava himself equated stripes with the death penalty,[91] thus providing yet another level below the least of the four, generally held to be strangulation. In this category we ought to include *karet* and death at the hands of Heaven as well.

Because the informal analogies may act as substitutes for the four formal, court-appointed modes of execution, we then might factor in many fatal accidents within the category of retributory justice:

> He who would have been sentenced to stoning, either falls down from the roof, or a wild beast treads him down. He who would have been sentenced to burning either falls into a fire or a serpent bites him. He who would have been sentenced to decapitation is either delivered to the government or robbers come upon him. He who would have been sentenced to strangulation is either drowned in the river or dies from suffocation [croup].[92]

We might note in passing that the equation of stoning and falling from a roof would have served to explain the fate of the one who fell from the ladder in *Qid* 39b; clearly, the primary issue there is the mitzvoth's protective nature.[93]

---

[89] *bShab* 55b s.v. *u-shema minah*.

[90] See *bSanh* 49–51a.

[91] *bSanh* 10a.

[92] *bKet* 30b.

[93] See in sharp contrast the development of this theme in *Sot* 21a, and see my "Righteousness As Its Own Reward," 63–64.

To complicate matters still further, there might not be any one-to-one correspondence between the sin and the suffering to which it gives rise. Just as the sin of the golden calf is being paid out, as it were, on the installment plan, and so any calamity that befalls the Jewish people has some element of that sin in it,[94] so, too, we need not be too literal in our understanding of even "measure for measure." A combination of ingredients might yield a particular result, as in the matter of "its measure is filled."[95] This factor might operate on an individual level as well, for Rabbi Yehudah notes that "one who performs one mitzva *in addition to his [equally balanced] merits* is well rewarded, and he is as though he had fulfilled the entire Torah,"[96] indicating that a variety of merits might be tallied to produce sums that are comparable, despite their differing weight.[97]

To whom, then, is the *baraita* regarding the minimum amount of misfortune for which an atoning function might be discerned directed? One might think that only the righteous have committed sins of so slight a magnitude that they are punished with the inconvenience of reaching into a pocket for an extra coin. There is no indication of that, however. And indeed, if this world is primarily one of judgment and not reward, it might be expected that all of daily life's irritations, all the more serious pain and anguish that are mankind's common heritage, even excluding more spec-

---

[94]*bSanh* 102a.

[95]See *bShab* 10b, though the phrase comes from Rashi on Gen. 19:20.

[96]*bQid* 39b.

[97]As the famous Mishnah in *Peah* 1:1 indicates, "These are the things the fruit of which man eats in this world, while the principal remains for him in the world to come: Honoring one's father and mother, the practice of loving deeds, hospitality to guests, and peace making between a man and his neighbor; [but] Torah study is equal to all of them."

tacular tragedies and calamities, would combine to balance the ultimate reckoning. In the same way, the differentiation of atoning sacrifices bespeaks a complex discrimination of levels and categories of guilt.

Against this background, Rava's advice that one afflicted with *yissurim* examine his deeds must not be seen as an attempt to nail down the misfortune's cause. Rather, the onset of misfortune is to be seen as Ezekiel's watchman calling his charges to repent of whatever misdeeds are to be found. However, the very fact that Rava proposes a three-step process culminating, in the absence of guilt, with *yissurim shel ahava* indicates that some attempt at searching out[98] the misfortune's cause is indicated. It might be that *yissurim shel ahava* served Rava as a catchall for any non-"measure for measure" explanation—for example, the possibility (depending on the person's status) that elements of vicarious atonement are involved.[99]

Again, how are we to understand Rava's advice in light of the minimal *yissurim* of *Ar* 16b–17a? Are we meant to

---

[98]It is noteworthy that the use of the verb *pishpesh* by Rava (or Rabbi Hisda) here is rare or unique in the *Bavli* (see on), though the verb is known from *Tosefta* (*tNeg* 6:7) in its figurative sense and from *Tosefta* and *Sifre* in its concrete sense. The only other possible occurrence in the *Bavli* is in *bEruv* 13b, where the Houses suggest that because humankind has been created for good or ill, one should examine one's deeds. The *Bavli* itself, however, records differing variants, *yefashfesh* or *yemashmesh*. Could this be another indication of Rava's interest in *Eretz* Israel sources? See Z. M. Dor, *Torat Eretz Yisrael be-Vavel* (Tel Aviv: Devir, 1971).

[99]Although vicarious atonement is clearly the subject of Isa. 53, Rava might have assumed that no one in his time was of sufficient spiritual stature to serve as an atonement. Or he might have assumed that death alone served as an atonement, and not suffering or misfortune; however, given his equation of capital punishment and stripes (see above), that is unlikely.

examine our deeds whenever minor inconveniences occur? Or, in the way of the *baalei musar,* if we are to review our behavior during the day before retiring, why wait for *yissurim* at all? Clearly, the latter cannot be what Rava intends, for that regimen continues, whether *yissurim* occur or not. Nor is the former all that likely—but for the fact that Rava himself is reported to have taken part in that debate as well! Nevertheless, the fact that Rava felt the need to define the lower limit of *yissurim* does not mean that limit activated the requirement of introspection. Perhaps he distinguished between *"yissurim ba'in alav"* and *"takhlit yissurim."* [100]

And yet, despite the general *midah kenegged midah* context in which these discussions occur, we must distinguish sharply "measure for measure," as Hazal employ the concept, from the general relation between sin and suffering.

From the many examples of *midah kenegged midah* analyses found in the *Bavli* and midrashim, it is clear that the relationship of the sin to the punishment is not one of degree, except in the roughest sort of way; rather, it is one of theme. For example, one impious act, such as Asa's drafting of scholars, can lead to years of suffering,[101] as did the rabbi's momentary insensitivity to an animal's anxiety.[102] Likewise, while the concept of vicarious atonement maintains the nexus of sin and suffering or death, it hardly re-

---

[100]One interpretive option not open to us is to assume that the author of the dictum regarding introspection was Rabbi Hisda, and not Rava; no rabbinic authority possibly could reject Rabbi Hisda/Rava's advice. The question is one of definition only.

Likewise, we cannot assume that the amount of introspection required is proportional to the inconvenience suffered, and only a moment's thought would suffice in minor cases. The combinatory character of *yissurim,* as noted above, rules that out.

[101]*bSot* 10a; note that Rava is the author of this statement.

[102]*bB.M.* 85a.

tains the proportionality of "measure for measure," even when the righteous person has the ability to reprove and/ or improve his generation.[103]

Are we then to take these statements as homiletical, intended to discourage certain types of behavior, and not as actual insights into divine providence's workings? Are they then not to be included in a rabbinic theology of misfortune? And if we do so, are we not taking the Maimonidean road?

It should be noted that "measure for measure" is not just a rule for punishment; it applies to reward as well. Marriage provides the spouses not only with the benefits of wholeness and purpose, it also initiates a new era of potential sinlessness because it serves to atone for sin.[104] Are we to take these at face value as well? Indeed, there is the possibility of distinguishing between these two types of "measure for measure" retribution, for God's *midat ha-rahamim* is so much greater than His *midat ha-din*; perhaps disproportionate rewards are the norm, while statements involving seemingly disproportionate punishments are to be taken as exaggerations.

I do not think that this matter can be decided in any certain way; I am also skeptical of attempts to reconcile "measure for measure" with Rava's general theory. It might be that God's providence is not caught so easily in the toils of the human propensity for generalization. We must remember that while cause and effect might seem disproportionate, the rule of "measure for measure" in its very disportionality *conforms to human experience*. In its own way, it contributes to our understanding of the world, if not of providence. We now can understand why Rava could assert

---

[103]See *bShab* 33b and *bSanh* 39a.
[104]*bYeb* 63b; see *yBik* 3:3.

that much of the human condition is beyond reach while also at times employing the principle of "measure for measure."[105]

X

In this matter as in others, Maimonides' method involves weighing talmudic sources and judging among them. It also involves a freer stance in rejecting *aggadic* sources than most later authorities are willing to grant. Nevertheless, Maimonides' principle of "providence consequent upon intellect," suitably modified by Nahmanides, has exercised a tremendous influence on later thought, continuing down to our own time in Hasidic texts.[106]

In truth, however, the fact that the *Bavli* contains conflicting views on the matter must be addressed in some way. Maimonides chose to cite some texts and ignore others, though, as we have seen, he well might have reinterpreted most of the rabbinic statements that conflicted with his views.[107] On the other hand, Nahmanides, aside from sub-

---

[105]As in *bShab* 32b in his remarks on the women of Mehoza, or on why David was punished (*bSot* 35a).

[106]See Y. Dienstag, *"Ha-Moreh Nevukhim ve-Sefer ha-Madda be-Sifrut ha-Hasidut,"* in *Abraham Weiss Jubilee Volume* (New York, 1964), 310–330.

[107]In this regard, his famous disquisition on rejecting Aristotle's view of an eternal universe in II:25 is apropos; if "the texts [of the Torah] indicating that the world has been produced in time are not more numerous than those indicating that the deity is a body, nor are the gates of figurative interpretation shut in our faces or impossible of access to us regarding the subject of the creation of the world in time. For we could interpret them as figurative, as we have done when denying His corporeality." (Pines, 327–328) Needless to say, some reconciliation was possible for contrary rabbinic texts, despite his son's dark remarks in his introduction to *aggadah* printed in the introduction to standard editions of *Ein Yaakov.*

stituting mystical for intellectual communion, also allowed for exceptions, as in the case of the Destroyer.[108]

Before attempting to reach some conclusions of our own in this regard, it might be useful to examine the Maharal's approach to this problem. His method is the path of reconciliation, as we shall see. The drawback is that while Maimonides follows some *aggadot* more or less according to their contextual meaning and ignores others, Maharal's reconciliation of conflicting texts can prevent either text from being heard in its original sense or with its original force. Moreover, the logical construct required to do justice to each contradictory element might become so complex that the essential principles of God's governance become obscured. However, the latter is not necessarily a drawback, for all we know of natural processes indicates that they are the result of a complex interaction of conflicting principles. Why should divine providence, which interacts with the complexities of human motivation and action, be simpler? Indeed, this might be the reason that God's justice is obscured so often and why the *Bavli* is full of conflicting *sugyot* whose exact demarcations are not worked out.

Thus, for example, in his attempt to do justice both to Rava's statement regarding *mazzal* and the human condition (*M.Q.* 28a), and to divine justice as well, Maharal concludes, not without hesitation: "but it [length of life] is certainly dependent on merit as well, except that *mazzal* is also a cause."[109]

---

[108]See his comments on Exod. 12:21 and 12:23, and see my "Ha-mal'akh ha-Mashhit bi-Zeman ha-Ge'ulah," *Rinat Yitzchak* (1988–1989), 109–113.

[109]See the multiple versions of his attempt to reconcile the "three books" of *bR.H.* 18a with Rava's statement in *M.Q.* 28a (*Hiddushei Aggadot* I, 108–111, and 132b *ad Yev* 50a). He concludes that merit and astrological determination act in tandem; the quote is from the latter source.

However, despite Maharal's painstaking attempt to incorporate every statement of Hazal into his corpus, some inevitably remain unaccounted for, even when he does deal
with parts of the *aggadic* passage. For example, though he
explains why those embarked on a mitzvah are not harmed
(*Qid* 39b)[110] and discusses other parts of the Talmud's analysis of the son who falls from the ladder and dies, he never
deals with the *sugya*'s conclusion that the ladder was rickety and "the danger was well-established; when danger is
well-established we do not rely on a miracle."[111]

In section 3, I noted the contradiction between *Sot* 21a
and *Qid* 39b as to the protection the performance of a
mitzvah affords. According to *Sot* 21a, we well might have
expected that that protection would have been extended
to the son who fell to his death. Indeed, the *sugya*'s conclusion essentially limits that protection to cases where there
is no established danger, while the whole thrust of *Sot* 21a,
despite Rava's restatement of Rabbi Yosef's rule, is to pro-
mote the protective power of mitzvoth, at least while a
person is occupied with fulfilling them.[112]

---

[110]See *Hiddushei Aggadot* II, 140b s.v. *sheluhei mitzvah*. See also his
extended analysis of *Sot* 21a in *Tiferet Yisrael*, ch. 14, 47–48.

[111]It is interesting to note that the Maharal uses the figure of a ladder to express the hierarchal nature of moral development and rational discourse; he also refers to Jacob's ladder, but never to this fatally
rickety ladder. Indeed, in presenting an example of an accidental death,
in his discussion of *Sot* 21a, he refers not to a rickety ladder but to a
bridge that collapses; see *Tiferet Yisrael*, ch. 14, 47a; see on.

[112]This contradiction it seems to me, is recognized at least implicitly
by Rabbi Yaakov Reisher, author of *Shevut Yaakov*, in his *Iyyun Yaakov* on
Ein Yaakov ad Qid 39b s.v. *sulam*. He wonders why the Talmud does not
proceed directly to its conclusion after concluding that *sheluhei mitzvah*
are not harmed and suggests that the protective power of the mitzvoth
the son performed should have protected him all the more *after* he had
fulfilled them and was on his way down the ladder; thus his tragic end
emphasizes all the more the necessity of not relying on miracles.

Although he makes a number of subtle distinctions between the protective power of Torah versus that of mitzvoth in particular situations, the Maharal does not refer to the case in *Qid* 39b at all:

> The explanation of this matter is that a mitzva is called a "lamp" because the light of the lamp depends on the substance (*guf*) of the oil and the wick, and because of this [the light it produces] is not absolute light (*or gamur*), and so too a mitzva depends on a person's action (*ma^caseh ha-adam*) produced by bodily activity; for this reason, a mitzva is not something which is completely separate [from matter]. But Torah [study] does not depend on the body, but is a separate intelligence alone. Therefore, the Torah is called "light," for the light is totally separate and independent of matter (*geshem*).
>
> It is known that anything which is material is time [dependent], and anything which is not material is not affected by time. [R. Menahem] therefore referred to the mitzva as limited in time (*lefi sha^cah*), that is, [referring to] time—so that the divine light inherent in the mitzva is dependent on the body ['s action], as light is [dependent] on the lamp, which is [in turn] dependent on the body—the oil and the wick, [representing] time.
>
> But just as the Torah which is specifically [compared to] light, which light has no material component, so too the Torah is a separate intelligence, and therefore the Torah protects forever, since something which is separate from material things (*ha-gashmi*) is not time-dependent.[113]

On this basis, the Maharal makes two distinctions. The first is between potential danger, the avoidance of which the mitzvah ensures, and danger that pursues the intended victim, against which only Torah protects. The wild animals

---

[113]*Tiferet Yisrael*, ch. 14, 47a–b. For a parallel, though not identical, explanation of the relationship of Torah to misfortune, see *Netivot Olam*, Netiv ha-Torah, ch. 1, 6–7.

and highwaymen mentioned later in the *sugya* represent the latter.

The second distinction is between accidental and nonaccidental misfortune. A collapsing bridge, which a person can avoid, is an example of accidental misfortune. A mitzvah, represented by the thorns mentioned later in the *sugya*, protects the deer from this type of misfortune. On the other hand, the Maharal classifies illness as nonaccidental misfortune, which requires Torah as protection.

In general, the Maharal defines *yissurim* as anything that impedes a person (*kol davar she-hu' kenegged ha-adam*),[114] but illness is particularly susceptible to the ministrations of Torah learning; because Torah determines the order of the Creation, it is well-suited to combat illness, which is a departure from the normal order of things.[115]

In any event, the Maharal's use of a collapsing bridge to exemplify a misfortune avoidable by the performance of mitzvoth seems contradicted by the ladder's fall in *Qid* 39b. Not only does he not reconcile the two, as noted above, but he seems to go out of his way to intensify the contradiction. It is not without significance that nowhere in his *ouevre*, to my knowledge, does he discuss the category of well-established danger in relation to that incident.[116]

Again, in connection with the Destroyer of *B.Q.* 60a, he specifically limits its application to the Exodus, despite the *sugya*'s linkage of the Destroyer there both to nighttime

---

[114]*Netivot Olam* II, Netiv ha-Yissurim, ch. 3, 179a.

[115]*Netivot Olam*, Netiv ha-Torah, ch. 1, 6–7.

[116]Although he notes that one should not rely on miracles in dealing with *mazzikin* (*Be'er ha-Golah*, ha-Be'er ha-Sheni, 32), he specifically limits that to such matters (*ein somekhin al ha-nes bi-khemo devarim elu kelal*). See, however, *Netivot Olam* II, Netiv ha-Bittahon, ch. 1, 232.

dangers and to *idan ritha*—times of plague, famine, and the like. When he touches on the issue tangentially, he specifically limits the Destroyer's freedom to act against the righteous to instances in which "the decree is made that he should have power over them,"[117] thus converting what is clearly considered a general rule (certainly by Rabbi Yosef and Abaye) to an exception. According to the Maharal, the general rule is that the Destroyer has no power over a righteous person, as he states explicitly.

Likewise, while he adverts several times to the "four who died by the advice of the Serpent" (*Shab* 55b), he ignores the *sugya*'s conclusion entirely.

Thus, despite the Maharal's effort to coordinate all relevant rabbinic statements on this and other issues, his operating assumptions, which are an integral part of his systematization, require him to ignore or reinterpret statements that do not fit his ideas.

In part this is due to the far-reaching range, which in part exacerbates the general tendency to minimize disagreements, though he is far from oblivious to the differing views on essential questions found among Hazal.

In the end, then, despite his sharp disagreement with Maimonides *vis-à-vis* the authority of *aggadic* statements, in the end Maharal's commitment to his system leads him into the same type of partial reading, though to a much smaller degree.[118]

For the proper recognition and utilization of Hazal's contribution to theology, we must take into account *all* their

---

[117]See *Hiddushei Aggadot* I, 30–31 *ad bShab* 55a. He does not deal with the issue in his analysis of *B.Q.* 60a–b.

[118]The same can be said of a more recent exegete, Rabbi Hayyim Yosef of Baghdad, popularly known as the "*Ben Ish Hai*" and author of *Ben Yehoyada* on the *aggadic* portions of *Shas*; see his *Ben Yehoyada* on *Shab* 55a–b, *Ber* 5a–b, and *Qid* 39b, for example.

statements, giving proper attention to the *baal ha-memra*, his time and place, his relations with other sages, and the *sugyot* that seem to follow his general approach. This I have tried to do. The result, in this case, is the discovery of an approach to suffering that can be identified with a prominent Amora: Rava, whose views underlie a number of *sugyot* that express a point of view quite different from that of *Eretz* Israel sources (the *Yerushalmi* and associated midrashim). More than that, the matter-of-fact manner in which Hazal face this problem and their sensitivity to its complexities suit the needs of twentieth-century would-be theologians particularly well. In addition, their insistence that theory fit the realities that we all witness—Rava's argument for experience (Rabbah and Rabbi Hisda, Doeg and Ahitophel, the four who died *be-etyo shel nahash*, the son Rabbi Yaakov witnessed)—provides a salutary lesson for those whose enchantment with theories might cause them to lose sight, if only for a time, of the underlying human realities.

Indeed, the usefulness of *Qid* 39b, whose case study involves not a sage or a biblical figure but an anonymous "everyman," is enhanced by that very anonymity. But it is the *Bavli*'s insistence on his *reality*—Rabbi Yaakov *saw* the incident—that makes the analysis so compelling.

The moral ecology of suffering, like the power of love, delivers up its secrets to theological discourse only with great difficulty, if it all. Thus the prospective theologian must begin with the realization that all his analyses, his root metaphors and categories, his selection and analyses of canonical and noncanonical texts, will not ease the pain of a mild headache one scintilla, though his powers of concentration might blot out awareness of it long enough for it to pass. It therefore behooves him to proceed with great caution. Indeed, the better part of wisdom were to remain silent. It is Hazal's example and teachings that give us the courage to speak.

On the other hand, the inconsistencies that we noted above and Hazal's reluctance to reconcile them indicate their unwillingness to provide an overarching system that, by its very inclusiveness, would be in danger of overlooking painful individual cases. Every rule has a counterrule or an exception. *Middah kenegged middah*, but *yissurin shel ahava* or *hezeqa qevi'a*. We do not rely on miracles, but miracles cannot be ruled out. Torah protects, but not in every circumstance. In the end, we can search out the mechanisms by which providence operates, but not their applications. And in this confession of ignorance, Maimonides, the Maharal, and the Ben Ish Hai ultimately are united, as they are united in their faith in God's ultimate justice. And we, too, must be satisfied with that.

X

While the discussion above does not exhaust the *Bavli's* list of non-"measure for measure" modes of divine retribution, there is one that cannot be ignored, if only because of its extreme difficulty when viewed against the context of our understanding of divine omniscience. I refer to a story regarding the messenger of the Angel of Death:

> When R. Yosef came to the following verse, he cried: "But there is he who is swept away before his time." (Prov. 13:23)
>
> He said: Is there then anyone who passes away before his time? Yes, as in the story [heard] by R. Bibi b. Abaye, who was frequently visited by the Angel of Death. Once the latter said to his messenger: Go, bring me Miriam, the woman's hairdresser! He went and brought him Miriam, the kindergarten teacher.

> Said he to him: I told you Miriam, the woman's hair-
> dresser! He answered: If so, I will take her back.
>
> Said he to him: Since you have brought her, let her be
> added to the number. But how were you able to get
> her?
>
> She was holding a shovel in her hand, heating and rak-
> ing the oven. She took it and [accidentally] put it on
> her foot and burnt herself; thus her luck was impaired
> and I brought her in.
>
> Said R. Bibi b. Abaye to him: Have you permission to
> act in this way?
>
> He answered him: Is it not written: "But there is one who
> is swept away before his time"?
>
> He countered: "One generation passes away and another
> generation comes." (*Koholet* 1:4)
>
> He replied to him: I shepherd them till the generation
> is complete, and then I hand them over to Dumah
> [the angel in charge of the dead].
>
> He then asked him: But what did you do with her [miss-
> ing] years?
>
> He answered: If there is a rabbinic scholar who overlooks
> insults, I will add them to him instead.[119]

Note that once again the *Bavli* provides a report of an actual occurrence. Here, however, the requisite proof-text
precedes the report, so the incident recounted is not explicitly the subject of talmudic analysis. But this hardly ab-
solves us from the task.

There is a talmudic parallel to the idea of mistaken identity in these matters, for Job suggests that he has been
mistaken for another Job. However, that notion indignantly
is rejected;[120] God does not make such mistakes. Here, in

---

[119]*bHag* 4b–5a.
[120]*bB.B.* 16b.

contrast, the heavenly bureaucracy seems to. The Maharsha in *Bava Batra*, responding to *Tosafot*'s juxtaposition of the two sources, makes just that casuistic distinction; the Angel of Death's agent made the mistake, but the angel himself would not have done such a thing, let alone God. Indeed, we might expect that if "the earthly kingdom is like the heavenly kingdom,"[121] the reverse should hold true as well and the heavenly bureaucracy should bear some resemblance to the Persian monarchy, which both errs and covers up its errors.[122]

At any rate, the Maharsha seems to take this story at face value, as does Rabbi Yaakov Pinto in his comments on *Ein Yaakov*. The Maharal ignores the story. Certainly the theme of "impaired luck" is not only found elsewhere,[123] but occasions advice—by Rava!—on how to avoid it, as we might expect.[124] However, while impaired luck provides the mechanism, it does not solve the basic problem of reconciling this story with God's justice.

Indeed, perhaps the most interesting aspect of this story's place within Jewish tradition is precisely the paucity of comment that this problem attracted. Of more interest to exegetes was the implied contradiction to Rabbi Akiva's view that a person's lifespan is set: the fifteen years "added" to

---

[121] *bBer* 58b.

[122] Although *Tosafot* in *Hag* 4b s.v. *hava* dates the occurrence to Second Temple times, identifying Miriam the hairdresser (Miriam *Megaddelah Sa'arei Neshaya*) with Mary Magdalene and identifying the latter as the mother of the Nazarene, there does not seem to be any warrant in viewing this as a special case, given the biblical proof-text and the general tenor of the story.

[123] See *bShab* 53b, *Hor* 12a or *Ker* 6a, and next note.

[124] See *bBer* 55b or *Ned* 40a; note that it is Rava to whom the statement in *Ned* 40a is attributed. However, Rava's advice has perhaps more to do with the effect of the evil eye than astrological influences.

Hezekiah's life were taken "from his own" store. That is, he was threatened with the loss of years originally allocated, and those years were restored to him.[125] *Tosafot ad loc.* note the difficulty and suggest that once years have been allocated to any person's life, as in the case of Miriam the kindergarten teacher, they can be transferred to someone else. This "bookkeeping" problem seems to have occupied the commentators more than the question of the unmerited or unscheduled taking of life.

Thus, despite Maimonides' insistence, the *Bavli's* authority, buttressed by the proof-text quoted, seems to have been sufficient to establish "bureaucratic bumbling" as an occasional reason for death. Can Jewish theology accept a certain randomness in matters of life and death?

The answer might lie in the mechanism the Talmud itself proposes to account for the agent's ability to act contrary to God's justice in the first place. Miriam impaired her luck by carelessly burning herself. In principle this is not much different from the analysis we examined in *Qid* 39b, which established the rule of *qevi^ca hezeqa*.

However, even if we correctly have identified the mechanism by which one Miriam was taken before her time, we are far from solving this report's riddle. Why would God allow such slipshod administration? What of the other Miriam, whose life now has been prolonged mistakenly? As to the second question, Rabbi Yosef's concern was for the injustice of dying before one's time, not the reverse, so the Talmud does not mention the matter. But it seems likely, from the concern the commentators evince for reconciling this report with Rabbi Akiva's view in *Yeb* 50b, that the error was rectified immediately. Generally speaking, the Angel of

---

[125]*bYeb* 50a.

Death "gets his man," whatever difficulties are placed in his path.[126]

The answer to the first question is less straightforward, however. It involves the status of the whole panoply of the divine bureaucracy and associated supernatural creatures, as described in rabbinic sources. Even if we exclude references to the more elaborate angelology of, say, the *Hekhalot* literature and restrict ourselves to the *Bavli*, we have a number of permanent divine messengers, many *ad hoc* agents, and untold numbers of demons.[127]

To what extent is this view of the world normative? Clearly, Maimonides felt free to reinterpret angels as "separate intelligences," and reject the existence of demons altogether, as he did the validity of astrology.[128] Just as clearly, the tendency since has been increasingly to take these de-

---

[126]Among the complement of those who ward off the Angel of Death for a brief time are Rabbah ben Nahmani (*B.M.* 86a) and King David (*Shab* 30b), untouchable while they are engaged in Torah study, and Rabbi Joshua ben Levi, who utilizes his standing with his Creator to foil the angel (*Ket* 77b). In the end, however, Rabbi Joshua does enter Paradise, which in a sense marks a victory for the angel; the troubles the angel faces in bringing in Rabbi Joshua are similar to those that Satan has in inflicting sufferings on Job; see *B.B.* 16a.

[127]Indeed, the Angel of Death is something of a comic figure; he has to work hard to accomplish his mission. See *Ber* 4b (bottom), where he is described as the slowest of the quasi-divine beings—behind Michael, Gabriel, and even Elijah. What the first does in one step Gabriel does in two and Elijah in four. The Angel of Death takes no fewer than eight steps; he is therefore only half as fast as Elijah.

[128]See David Horwitz, "Rashba's Attitude Toward Science and Its Limits," *The Torah U-Madda Journal* 3 (1991–1992), 52–81, especially 53–55, and the up-to-date bibliography on these matters included within Jacob I. Dienstag, "Art, Science and Technology in Maimonidean Thought: A Preliminary Classified Bibliography—Part I," in *Torah U-Madda Journal* 5 (1994), 1–100, especially the sections on astrology and demonology.

scriptions at something approximating face value.[129] Again, the influence of Kabbalah, with its descriptions of the non-material world, encourages such tendencies. Indeed, I daresay that such beliefs are becoming increasingly widespread, both in the Jewish and nonJewish worlds.

This is not the place to question the place of such a world view within Jewish theology. Indeed, because our focus has been on Rava's view of providence, we ought to note that rather little is reported of his "theosophical" views. Certainly God is just and merciful, but this is a world of *din*, which is only the negative side of justice. Torah study and mitzvoth are protective, but only so far. Rava's view of the world, as of man, is direct, unflinching, and empirical[130] rather than metaphysical; he does not reveal the theosophical causes for the state of the world or the human condition. Nor was that my intent here.

Rather, my essential purpose has been to provide a tour of a suite of rooms on the ground floor of Jewish thought that seldom have been examined on their own, to restore some partitions and remove some accumulated lacquer. It is my hope that the result will contribute to a modern theology of misfortune, one that is based on our experience of the world, one that is open to partial solutions and recognizes counterinstances. If what I have presented here conforms with the reader's perceptions of the human condition, I will have attained my goal.

---

[129]See Marc B. Shapiro, "The Last Word in Jewish Theology? Maimonides' Thirteen Principles," in *Torah U-Madda Journal* 4 (1993), 187–242, with further discussion and additional bibliography in the Letters to the Editor section of *Torah U-Madda Journal* 5 (1994), 182–189.

[130]Note that of the various explanations for the origin of the rule of three years habitation for *hazaqah* in *B.B.* 28a–29a, Rava's concentrates on what we might term the "psychology of ownership" rather than providing a biblical warrant for the practice.

6

Metapsychological Dimensions of Religious Suffering: Common Ground between Halakhic Judaism and Psychoanalysis

Moshe Halevi Spero

אדברה וירוח לי
אפתח שפתי ואענה
איוב לב:כ

It is well-known that Sigmund Freud found little value in the comforts of religion, but it is significant that he specifically evaluated these as *illusory* rather than delusional (1927, 31). The key distinction, technically speaking, is that delusions contradict reality, whereas illusions contain wish-fulfillment as a prominent factor in their motivation, making it easier to disregard the relation between an illusional belief and reality. Nevertheless, even according to the most sympathetic interpretation, Freud certainly held that religion's consolations were limited and its illusional approach to suffering short-lived and palliative at best.

Polemics aside, Freud was not altogether wrong about the illusional element of religion. That is, while we might have to concur that his new science granted him no special privilege to make sweeping inferences about the *object* of religious beliefs and feelings, it did, in fact, enable him to sense something very important about the psychological *contents* and *qualities* of religious beliefs and feelings. Freud's scientism, as per the prevailing Zeitgeist, might have urged him toward a sharp contrast between so-called empirical reality and illusion, yet it was precisely the developmentally oriented trend within psychoanalysis that granted pride of place to illusion's role as a vital and necessary component of the normal psyche. Since Freud, illusion has been recast as the cardinal characteristic of the intermediary or transitional spectrum between pure fantasy and so-called objective fact, along which are located in the creative dimensions of aesthetics, play, love, and religious experience. The key milestones of this revised approach began with the work of Winnicott (1951; see Grolnick, Barkin, and Muensterberger 1978) and, specifically in the area of religion, the work of Pruyser (1983), Meissner (1984), Meltzer and Williams (1988), Rizutto (1979), and others.

The benefits, as well as the unresolved dilemmas, of this approach for a full appreciation of religious belief recently have been subjected to vigorous reassessment (see Finn and Gartner 1992; McDargh 1984; Randour 1993; Spero 1992a). One of the undisputed contributions of the contemporary psychoanalytic perspective has been its increased sensitivity to the qualitative nuances of human behavior. Whereas in the past psychoanalysis focused primarily on intrapsychic conflict, the current focus pays special attention to the level and quality of internalization and abstraction that characterize the inner representational states that underwrite human thought, fantasy, and behavior. The study of representational states has provided us with a much better understanding of the ways in which symbol and illusion are part and parcel of everyday life at all stages. Specifically, it has led to a clearer sense that mental health does not reside in the elimination of symbol and illusion, but rather in the maintenance of those conditions that will enable symbol and illusion to achieve developmental maturity. Among the attributes of any "good" object an individual might hope to enjoy a relationship with—be it a human or the divine object—will invariably be that the object enables the individual to capture the relationship within representational structures that guarantee the capacity for mutuality, subjectivity, autonomy, and sacrifice. A "good" object representation will facilitate the objective negotiation of reality and, at the same time, participate in the illusional dimension upon which so much of human-interpersonal and man-God experience depends.

The distinction between mature and pathological *suffering*, the subject of this paper, in many ways is linked to the quality of internal representations that are central or core for a given personality. To some degree, the overall quality of object representations derives from the individual's objective characteristics, his objects, and their relationship. But other factors are relevant as well. Chief among them is intrapsychic, psychosexual conflict in the classical sense. Also enumerated among these other factors are certain prevailing structures that the individual finds "awaiting" him in the environment: deep universal symbolisms, specific cultural beliefs, and the subtle architectonics of language. These factors create a rich bed of preformed or *a priori* representational patterns or dispositions from which all subsequent developments draw. In the present paper, I will be examining some background representational structures inherent in the halakhic reality into which an individual is thrown, pertaining to the mechanisms that might differentiate between mature and pathological suffering.

Let me return to Freud one more time in order to begin our investigation. The ever-pragmatic psychotherapist, he once mentioned that he was satisfied if, through psychoanalysis, he could assist the suffering patient in transforming hysterical misery into common unhappiness (Breuer and Freud 1893–1895, 305). He actually said a lot through this little witticism. Writing in his *Introductory Lectures* in greater detail, Freud took a position that might be regarded as an example of psychoanalytic ethics (1916–1917, 382):

> Indeed there are cases in which even the [psychoanalyst] must admit that for a conflict to end in neurosis is the most harmless and socially tolerable solution. You must not be surprised to hear that even the [psychoanalyst] may occasionally take the side of the illness he is combating. It is not his business to restrict himself in every situation in life to being a fanatic in favor of health. He knows that there is not only neurotic misery in the world, but real, irremovable suffering as well, that necessity may even require a person to sacrifice his health; and he learns that a sacrifice of this kind made by a single person can prevent immeasurable unhappiness for many others.

How, indeed, might we distinguish between "neurotic" or pathological misery that seems to defy comprehension and expose the futility of faith and hope, on the one hand, and "real, irremovable" suffering, the kind that can and must be met with some form of existentially mature and deeply personal ideology and faith, on the other hand?

I: PROBLEMATIZING THE DEFINITION OF SUFFERING

Without the benefit of further introductory comment, share with me for a moment two statements from a suffering individual:

Let me speak for myself: I know that I am perplexed that my fears are irrational, incoherent. At times I am given over to panic; I am afraid of death. At other times I am horrified by the thought of becoming, God forbid, incapacitated during my lifetime. One of my greatest fears is related to the observance of the Day of Atonement: I am fearful that I might be compelled, because of weakness or sickness, to desecrate this holiest of all days.

Or from the same hand:

Eleven years ago my wife lay on her deathbed and I watched her dying, day by day, hour by hour; medically, I could do very little for her, all I could do was pray. However, I could not pray in the hospital; somehow I could not find God in the whitewashed, long corridors among the interns and the nurses. However this need for prayer was great; I could not live without gratifying this need. The moment I returned home I would rush to my room, fall on my knees and pray fervently. God, in those moments, appeared not as an exalted, majestic King, but rather as a humble, close friend, brother, father: in such moments of black despair, He was not far from me; He was right there in the dark room; I felt his warm hand, as it were, on my shoulder, I hugged his knees, as it were. He was with me in the narrow confines of a small room, taking up no space at all.

Here is an arresting, urgent expression of grief emanating from the mind of a psychiatrically intact individual, operating intellectually at the zenith of the human ken. The selections I have quoted, of course, are from two essays by Rabbi Joseph Dov Soloveitchik (1978a, 63; 1978b, 33). Even if the painfulness of the material struck the reader first—and sharply—it is relatively easy to empathize with the writer's thought and existential outcry; the philosopher-poet has the genius for offering us not merely a fragmenting ego wholly in need of immediate psychiatric intervention, but a window made lucid into feelings. His ordeal is personal, but he has rendered his own self permeable so that his feelings could be shared.

Now one must admit that many patients are no less eloquent. Thus we must isolate those factors that more generally distinguish poet from patient: the relatively unimpeded intent to share, the capacity to express symbolically, and—to be further elaborated below—the willingness to capture the reader *and relinquish him,* to capture the object of the written text and relinquish it. Much the same could be said of the works of Kierkegaard, Menaḥem Mendl of Kotẓk, Rabbi Yisroel Salanter, and (with reservation on the psychiatric account) Rilke. This is the world of mature suffering, and only the mature sufferer has sufficient irony and distance to be able to posit meaningfully, as opposed to simply sardonically or neurotically: "*Dolorem ferre ergo sum*—I suffer, therefore I am" (Soloveitchik 1978, 65).

But I will attempt to show that matters are vastly different for those for whom suffering is a way of life or the thesis of a personal myth, different from those for whom suffering's existentially enriching qualities are below perception. The persons Freud accurately termed "criminals from a sense of guilt" (1916) and compulsive "fate neurotics" (1920; cf. Schafer 1970) do not discern the meaning of "the opposite of suffering" and hence perversely must transform suffering and torment into a private, protective, self-alienating credo (Becker 1973). Convention might allow us to say such persons "suffer," but in fact they suffer in a way much different from that amenable to philosophical transformation and, prior to psychotherapy's help, antithetical to what Bakan (1968) terms "the facilitation of awareness." As one of my patients (the victim of near-debilitating family psychopathology) expressed her goal in treatment, "After decades of not being able to imagine myself feeling clean, not mucky, untouched and poked, not exploding inside with unbearable pain and blackness, I'd be quite happy to *simply* suffer!" The individuals who belong to this group first need help in developing the basic psychological structures and inner object representations that will permit the kind of suffering that enables one to achieve meaning.

Judaism-psychology[1] literature includes several essays that deal directly or tangentially with suffering. Many of them possess what one might consider a psychological flavor without qualifying as proper psychological analyses of the topic. In other instances, we have had to settle for the simple itemization and collation of sources extracted from Judaic and psychological-psychiatric literature. Even the more worthy literature (Brayer 1982; Bulka 1977, 1982, and 1987; Rubenstein 1967; Schimmel 1987; Spero 1980a; Wohlgelernter 1981), enlightening as it might be, generally fails to address crucial meta-issues that, in my view (Spero 1980b, and 1986), are central to a more profound Judaism-psychology dialogue on any subject, including suffering. Fox (1987) and Meier (1987) do somewhat better on this account, and I will return to them in the final discussion.

Broadly speaking, the important meta-issues (at least in the current phase of the Judaism-psychology dialogue) are those that help one respond to the following question: *what*

---

[1]When I use the convention "Judaism-psychology" throughout the present essay, I mean by the term "psychology" *psychological processes, functions, and concepts* in general, crossing boundaries between psychology proper, psychiatry, neurology, social work, and counseling. By virtue of training, interest, and focus, most of the time I will have in mind *psychoanalytic* psychology in particular, unless otherwise specified. By the term "Judaism," I mean *Orthodox* Judaism, though my essential preconception here is that the ideas and source material I refer to belong to or are inherent components of what Judaism is all about, regardless of the extent to which one practices it.

is the key unit of analysis that best represents the synthesis
of psychological and halakhic language, and the potential
for a unique moment of human-divine relationship, along
the psychotherapy-repentance spectrum? In the present
case, one is interested in the unit of analysis that applies
to the halakhic/psychological approach to suffering. Many
midrashic, talmudic, and practical halakhic statements and
aphorisms apply to and amplify modern psychological statements and aphorisms regarding suffering, and vice versa. I
am suggesting, however, that we temporarily put aside this
welter of data and focus instead upon discrete halakhic
doctrines that bear upon the operation of suffering, define
its mechanisms, and unfold underlying dynamic processes
by which it is created and perhaps can be ameliorated.

In this paper, I will propose a meta-link between the cornerstone psychoanalytic notion of the repetition-compulsion (Freud 1920) and the Judaic concept of *äveilut*
ye'shänäh. Leaving aside this phrase's literal translation as
"old mourning"—in the specific context of mourning on
Tish'äh be-Av—our proposal will emphasize the connota-
tions of "congealed" or "archaic" mourning.

There exists, in addition, what could be called a second
Judaism-psychology literature that is exceedingly wealthy in
data pertaining to suffering. I am referring, of course, to the
reams of clinical psychotherapy journals of all persuasions
whose pages are a veritable biography of Jewish anxiety,
depression, crisis, exigency, trauma, guilt, shame, doubt, and
other forms of psychic pain. To be sure, the Jewish element
in these clinical or research studies is sometimes peripheral
or even accidental. Most of the time it is highly focal (e.g.,
family crises indigenous to the particular structure of the
Jewish family and larger cultural or biological tendencies that
influence mental health/unhealth). And still other times the
Jewish element is central and all-encompassing (e.g., the aftermath of the Holocaust or the Yom Kippur War; conflicts

about religious belief; and plurivalent religious or halakhic motifs brought to a treatment hour).

While the first kind of Judaism-psychology literature is a heuristic necessity, it is from the second Judaism-psychology literature that suffering and anguish flow; it is in the second literature that angst finds its phenomenological home. The realities reflected in this second literature, as opposed to customary biblical heroes such as Job or the legendary protagonists of well-known talmudic anecdotes, will inform my analysis. That is, my definition of suffering has to do with chronic and intensive pain that is generally way beyond the reach of education, counseling, and mere pastoral intervention. It is the world of the anguished crying, pathetic self-pity, inconsolable bereavement, chaotic fright, aggravated and passive-aggressive apathy, and frighteningly cold schizoid numbness that feed the apparently mindless repetitiveness and self-destructiveness of human suffering. It is the inner world that does not even express itself in terms of clear-cut shame, guilt, and depression, but rather in terms of emptiness, chronic confusion and tiredness, exotic psychosomatic disorders, and inexplicable addiction to near-death (see Joseph 1982). This definition of suffering applies indigenously to those patients who spend their hours in treatment, as in their lives outside of treatment, repetitively rehashing a long list of grievances and a sense of unrequited entitlement, through which they safeguard a deep-seated narcissistic fragility and mask insatiable envies of the most primitive variety (Blechner 1987; Moses and Moses-Hrushovski 1990; Quinodoz 1993). It also refers to those patients whose therapies are most likely to end in negative therapeutic reaction. This level of pain, in its sheer obduracy and crippling effect on personality, easily challenges the potency, and perhaps even the legitimacy, of intellectual, rational, or otherwise palliative approaches to pain.

This level of suffering is the clinically relevant one. I must draw from the clinic, so to speak, because such work involves the best of all elements of listening: (a) it is empathic as opposed to sympathetic (the former lacks pity); (b) it involves a level of analysis that is experience-near but not merely participative; (c) it seeks the most basic, "deepest" source of pain and tends to look beyond superficial rationalizations of suffering; and (d) it seeks to organize and comprehend the patient's disparate ruminations, associations, and reminiscences in narrative terms but is not satisfied with a simple literary or aesthetic framework. I am unsure that we really succeed in extracting empathic reverberation from intellectual study of the texts of even the more painful episodes such as the "Ten Martyrs" or the tragic descriptions in *Midrash Lamentations Rabbah.* But we fail similarly when we lose distance and become over-involved in the other's experience of suffering—as many tend to do with the still raw accounts and memories of the Holocaust—and when we defensively put aside "analysis" in favor of granting undue privilege to the uniqueness of first-person reportage (Spero 1992b). To put this one last way, I wish to say something of relevance to those individuals least likely to derive any lasting emotional solace or tranquility from philosophical contemplation (even *deep* contemplation) of the "sayings of our fathers" or from mere intellectual acknowledgment (which such persons are often terribly proficient at doing) of the inherent truth of such values.

Finding the right balance between empathic listening, analysis, and interpretation, on the one hand, and sympathetic sharing and supportive presence, on the other hand, is *difficult* to do. And yet this is exactly why many types of vital questions and important formulations regarding suffering never get expressed, and why many facile responses and intellectually correct but emotionally wrong "helping ideologies" are grabbed up so readily by the needy. Careful listening, and a willingness to expose oneself to the limits of emotional comprehensibility, is necessary to discriminate among qualities of suffering. Only such participant listening can tease apart those speech patterns and metaphor usages that convey an individual's authentic, coherent sense of the meaning of his or her suffering and those that indicate defensiveness, artificial pain, displaced objects of suffering, or even a complete lack of any sense of suffering's meaningfulness.

The crux of the matter resides in the degree to which an individual has been able to (a) install the system known as secondary repression (upon which all symbolic language must be based), (b) representationalize pain, (c) convert global pain into discrete signal affects, and (d) symbolize the memory networks linked to specific kinds of pain, leading to the establishment of higher-order systems of meaning. From a religious point of view, the man-God dimension somehow ought to be related to and reflected in factors such as these. Here we need a bridge concept.

II: ISSUES PERTAINING TO A HALAKHIC METAPSYCHOLOGY

The bridge concept I have in mind is what I have termed the "halakhic metapsychology" (1992a). Some background issues will help introduce the value of this concept.

The first issue has to do with the *nature of the relationship* between psychological and Judaic, or halakhic, language and terminology. It arises in conjunction with the reasonable enough assumption that we are looking for "common ground" between Judaism and psychology. The search for common ground would seem to presuppose that we were dealing with two independent language systems,

thought to be unrelated pending the discovery of the al-
leged common ground. And when successful, the discovery of common ground makes all sorts of cross-fertilization
between the systems feasible. Assuming one were successful in finding common ground between Judaism and psychology on a given topic—say, between the various stages
of Job's descent into and ascent from anguish and suffering that the biblical narrative describes, on the one hand,
and Kübler-Ross's (1969) and Pollock's (1961) well-known
stages of adaptation to grief and death, on the other
hand—what would that signify?

Well, if we take up the parenthetical illustration of Job
and Kübler-Ross and Pollock, one might conclude as follows:

(a) Kübler-Ross's/Pollock's stages add *totally* new infor-
    mation to our understanding of the biblical text,
    imported from psychological language—a kind of in-
    formation that hitherto was simply not present in
    human imagination or the biblical text until that ser-
    endipitous moment when Kübler-Ross/Pollock pro-
    pounded their psychological discoveries.

This first paradigm is clear-cut but philosophically problematic. It states unambiguously that there is Torah and there
is psychology, each operating along independent lines and
becoming known or available to the human mind at different rates. According to this paradigm, the newfangled
psychological concept Kübler-Ross developed in 1969 might
have nothing to do with Torah or, in fact, might add new
depth to the Torah (i.e., Moshe Rabbenu would have to
raise his eyebrows in surprise and say, "Hmmm! Kübler-Ross
has a *ḥiddush* there!").

The problem with this paradigm, which many religious
individuals implicitly accept, is that it proposes a body of

knowledge—such as Kübler-Ross's or Pollock's theories of the stages of loss and mourning—that is somehow unknown or extraneous to the halakhic universe until such time as it is wedded to it. However, from the halakhic point of view, is it in fact legitimate to postulate phenomena that are in principle extraneous to Halakha? Do the truths of theology, anthropology, or psychology exist outside of Halakha (Shapiro 1967, 107)? Or are these disciplines mere handmaidens that are useful for isolating certain aspects of Halakha *post hoc* but have no particular legitimacy in their own right (the approach of those who forever are seeking an indigenous "Torah psychology" or "Torah medicine")?

Without going into the details of this debate here (see Lamm 1990; Spero 1986, ch. 1; Steinberg 1992), such a view leads to hopeless circularity. If one supposes that there is, in fact, only one language system—Halakha—and that all other putative language systems simply have been identified mistakenly as distinct disciplines, then the discovery of common ground is an illusion and the efforts invested in seeking common ground would be pointless.

We get further by considering an alternate paradigm:

(b) Kübler-Ross's/Pollock's stages add new information to our previous understanding of the biblical text that, though totally new to the average mind, can be considered *latent* in the biblical text (in some infratextual manner, known only to Moshe[2] and unreached or even unreachable by conventional methods of rabbinic exegesis until this day), waiting to be comprehended as only Kübler-Ross and Pollock were able.

---

[2]Or Adam (see Talmud, *Sanhedrin* 38b, *Avodah Zarah* 5a; cf. *Ede'yut* 2:9; and Num. *Rabba* 23:4).

This paradigm suggests that there are multiple layers of latent or dormant truths, necessarily "Torah" or halakhic *in their essential* a priori *form*, awaiting discovery. Some of these truths will be activated directly through conventional hermeneutical methodologies; others will be realized through "less conventional" paths of discovery (science, intuition, art) that might *seem* to have nothing whatsoever to do with Torah. Among these paths would be the methods of contemporary scientific psychology/psychotherapy.

To my mind, only this point of view justifies the search for common ground between the conventional and nonconventional means of discovering Torah truths. Without this approach, one is really at a loss to explain what one would be adding by stating, for example, that we *now* appreciate what Job went through personally, or intrapsychically, when we re-examine the texts in light of Kübler-Ross's five stages of grief. In another example, we have the sense of a new dimension when we advance the idea that Jacob's inconsolability over the loss of Joseph conforms to the contemporary definition of "complicated bereavement": a guilt-ridden inability to surrender the loved object.[3] The second paradigm hypothesizes that our psycho-

---

[3]This is an example worth elaborating upon. The relevant text is Gen. 37:35, "... *vä-ye'mä'en le-hit'näḥem*." The term "*vä-ye'mä'en*" means "refused" but also bears the sense of inhibition. Rashi *ad loc* cites the talmudic explanation (*Sofrim* 21 and cf. Gen. *Rabbah* 84). "*Ein mekäbbelēm tän'ḥumin äl hä-ḥäï*": consolation is ineffective in the case of an object who in fact is alive. Because the destiny of the dead is that is to be forgotten, the Talmud (citing Ps. 31:14). Jacob comprehended that Joseph was still alive. This is an extremely important interpretation, pregnant with psychologically useful insight, though to some degree it renders the situation a wholly intellectual affair. Strangely enough, that is how some Torah/science exponents would like to see things: Jacob as halakhocrat, absolute master of his feelings, *reasoning* his way out of tragedy, *inferring* his son's existence from halakhic machinations, and

not absorbing consolation simply because consolation was essentially irrelevant (cf. the Vilna Gaon's reading of the text in *Sofrim* 21: ". . . velō he'e'mēn lä'hen kól ēkär; mē'nä'in? . . .")!

Unfortunately, some critics (Meier 1988, 31) have misinterpreted my halakhic metapsychology as postulating the same kind of Halakhaover-mind approach. Actually, I am interested in the link between the halakhic model and the psychological model—and in the way *both* as models or representations necessarily abstract the real and structuralize it—but not in the elimination of the one via the other. Thus, I think it correct and valuable to be invited by Halakha as well as by contemporary scientific expectations to state that Jacob's internal representational processes included structural accommodations and adjustments between the psychic principles of mourning, object relations, and other psychodynamic factors (e.g., wish-fulfillment, guilt, separation anxiety). Piaget and Freud say more about these processes than any known Halakha, but without some halakhic paradigm—such as this biblical text as interpreted by the Talmud, he would have no warrant to merely assume that Jacob's pain could be analyzed according to contemporary psychological principles. At the same time, any given halakhicmetapsychological paradigm is but a schematic; it does not rule out the coexistence of other emotional properties, feeling states, or fantasies that (a) the text did not choose to reveal (oftentimes, the Midrash supplies just such missing information or clues), (b) our current conceptions have not enabled us to perceive yet, and (c) play a temporary and possibly unnoticed role during the course of a larger interval whose discrete *beginning* and *end* points Halakha has highlighted, taking no particular stand on the quality of the middle phase.

In Jacob's case, then, a more accurate assessment would be that, though *initially* he mourned his son deeply and in a complex, tormented way (Gen. 37:34), he eventually became inconsolable, either because (a) he began to doubt the fact of Joseph's death but could not reconcile emotionally with Joseph's actual absence and uncertain status (*pace* Rashi); (b) he no longer wished to express his feelings openly but, in fact, continued to mourn his loss in secret (*contra* Rashi; cf. Torah Temimah, *ad loc*); or, combining Halakha and psychology, (c) he had certain intuitions or complex wishes—resulting in a fantasy that Joseph was "among the living"—that were in conflict with certain other intuitions or complex wishes—resulting in a fantasy that Joseph was "among the dead." The coexistence of these fantasies caused the emotional suffering delineated across the two texts (37:34 and 35) and also might have motivated Jacob's desire to reinvestigate the veracity of Judah's story.

logical studies simply do not tack on a foreign or redundant body of knowledge to a static halakhic text or concept whose meaning can be understood unilaterally and exhaustively in "indigenous" terms. Rather, the dynamic of the halakhic text or concept has numerous tributaries of potential meaning that can be brought forward by terms *primed with their own inherently halakhic affinities* can bring forward. These terms simultaneously enrich our understanding of the text or concept and further elaborate the halakhic or Torah dimensions of the so-called nonconventional pathway of knowledge (e.g., clinical research) or the bit of knowledge (e.g., Kübler-Ross's stage theory) in question.[4]

Thus, when considering *psychological* interpretations or explanations of Halakha, I do not assume that such an interpretation is necessarily "secondary" or "inferior" to the halakhic phenomenon in question. As a religious Jew, I do presume that at the ultimate level the smallest unit of analysis must be halakhic; but at the same time that unit of analy-

---

Another midrash also acknowledges that normal suffering and bereavement should yield to the processes of internalization and contraction of time *unless* some other pathognomonic factor mitigates against this. See Esther *Rabba* 8:3 to Esther 4:3, "*Evel gădŏl*": "[Does the term] 'great' mourning [imply that this is to be distinguished from some hypothetical] 'small' mourning? [for in the case of Jacob the text found it sufficient to state "*evel* kăved"?!] In fact, ordinarily, the mourner's bereavement diminishes incrementally [*mitmă'et ve-hŏlekh*] in the course of 12 months. But this *evel* [caused by] Haman intensified with each day [that passed until the appointed doomsday], [for they would say] 'one more day has been taken from us.'"

[4]Elsewhere (1992b) I have anticipated objections to my hypothesis that might be raised in light of Rabbi Soloveitchik's analysis of the difference between Maimonides' and Naḥmanides' approaches to the rationale for the commandments.

sis can be mathematical, biological, or psychological. In taking this point of view, I am attempting to avoid the Scylla of unqualified panhalakhism, which elasticizes Halakha to such a degree that valuable phenomenological subidentities (the "bands") are eliminated, and the Charybdis of bifurcation, which creates an artificial distinction between Halakha proper and coexistent nonhalakhic entities. Thus, I have adopted the view that psychology and Halakha share a complementary relationship (expanding upon Shubert Spero's [1983, 167–97] analysis of the relation between morality and Halakha). To the degree that psychology occupies its own independent band within God's universe—"independent" in the sense that a chair is not a horse, a human is not an angel, and *din* is not *raham'im*—it can serve as an operating principle within Halakha that helps resolve certain areas of tension, conflict, or apparent incompleteness that pertain to Halakha's psychological dimensions and psychology's halakhic dimensions.

The first meta-issue, then, postulates that, in addition to being a system of practice, Halakha is also a symbolic framework. At every stage, Halakha lends representation to certain dimensions of psychological processes, needs, wishes, desires, and functions; these qualities are implicit in the created universe and could not be perceived at their fullest without Halakha's perspective. For example, while a scientist accurately might comprehend a significant number of the dimensions of the psychological pathways of emotional change (i.e., psychotherapy), only the complementary halakhic model for those same dimensions (i.e., *teshuva*) would bring into focus the additional elements particular to the relationship between man and God along the specific pathways under study (Spero 1977, 1980b, 1980c, and 1986). Insofar as psychotherapy can be modeled halakhically upon *teshuva*—or to the extent that our psychological conceptions of suffering can be modeled upon certain operating principles of the laws of *äveilut,* as we shall see—the religious or deocentric elements can be brought readily into focus *without distorting the necessarily* psychological *identity of the mechanics of psychotherapy* qua *psychotherapy.*[5]

The second meta-issue, then, is the careful identification of discrete models within Halakha that successfully represent psychological processes. As in previous research (Spero 1980b, 1986, and 1992a), we are interested primarily in models that incorporate halakhic structures bearing the closest possible affinity to their mooted counterpart in the domain of scientific psychology. In the present case, I have identified a cluster of halakhic principles that apply directly to the quality and dynamics of suffering encountered in the clinical setting. These halakhic metapsychological models shed light on the practical problem of how mindless, inchoate agony might be transformed into the kind of mature suffering that carries symbolic, existential, and religious significance.

---

[5]According to my viewpoint, this could be stated per formula: under certain circumstances dictated by the appropriate halakhic model, religious observance will be psychotherapeutic (e.g., giving vent to a deep psychological equivalent of *psychotherapy per se,* because psychotherapy is an *independent* moral obligation whose operational uniquenesses are upheld by their own independent halakhic structure. Under other circumstances dictated by the appropriate halakhic model, psychotherapy will run collaterally with religious observance (e.g., a prayerful or supplicative moment during a therapeutic hour, psychological suffering during prayer) *without necessarily being the equivalent of the specific religious observance per se,* for prayer is an *independent* moral obligation whose operational uniquenesses are upheld by their own independent halakhic structure. For examples, see my text (1986).

III: HALAKHIC METAPSYCHOLOGICAL MODELS
PERTAINING TO SUFFERING

I now will outline briefly some halakhic analogues that correspond to the fundamental psychological elements or processes that distinguish between pathological and mature suffering. I will illustrate them with the cases presented in section IV and further amplify them in section V.

The first psychologically relevant halakhic analogue is the concept of *äveilutye'shänäh*, or "old" mourning (Talmud, *Yebamot* 43b, Tos., s.v. "*shänē*;" see Resp. *Igerot Moshe: Y. D.* vol. 1, no. 224). Strictly speaking, it is identified with the historical status of the ninth day of the Hebrew month of *Av* (and also the seventeenth day of *Tammuz* [Talmud, *Ta'anit* 26a]), which has been associated with misfortune and calamity throughout Jewish history ("*yōm mukhän le-fur'änē 'ut*" [*Mishnah Berurah, O.H.,* 549:(2) and 551:17(95)]). In fact, this concept is expressed in two distinct ways:

> "And on the day when I visit (*päk'di* ["punish"]), I will visit their sin upon them" (Exod. 32:34). It was taught in the name of Rabbi Yose: it is a time (*et*) propitious for calamity (Talmud, *Sanhedrin* 102a).

and

> Said Rabbi Yizhak: There is no calamity that comes to the world that does not contain one-twenty fourth measure [of the sin of] the Calf (Talmud, *Sanhedrin* 102a). . . . Said Rabbi Yuden in the name of Rabbi Yosa: There is no generation that does not contain an ounce of the sin of the Calf (Talmud Jer., *Ta'anit* 4:5; also Exod. *Rabba* 43:4, Eccles. *Rabba* 9:11; Lam. *Rabba* 1:28; see Rashi to Num. 19:22).

Aside from the literal intent, the *mechanism* alluded to here is significant, for it expresses the idea that psychologi-

cal pain and related structures of meaning tend to be strati-
fied and nested within different but parallel levels of
memory and representation, connecting at several nodal
points. Freud referred to this as "multiple series" and "multiple determination" (1900, 307; see Laplanche and Pontalis
1973, 292; Waelder 1936), concepts that have retained vigorous support from the clinical literature and empirical
research on memory (see Schore 1994). This stratification
may run *within* events (the need for oral nurturance, the
libidinal aspects of anal secrecy, or phallic-oedipal implications   of   gender   identity: all   are   present
simultaneously within a given behavioral cluster or unconscious theme), or *across* time (e.g., the different levels of
meaning that a particular image, person, day, or memory
has acquired over time).

The stratification concept is especially valuable because
it provides the common denominators for the analysis of
multiple meaning (such as in dream symbols) and the
hierarchiazation of language, the power and influence of
transference, as well as the formation of psychopathology.
When the principle of multiple determination becomes ad-
versely linked with a sadomasochistic compulsion to repeat,
one usually witnesses the development of a "fate neurosis"
through which an individual or nation chronically and
blindly (i.e., unconsciously) repeats the same self-destructive
motive or complex in a multitude of different patterns.

In many ways, this is exactly what the Talmud has described. From the psychohistorical perspective, something
that is deeply problematic within the Jewish personality or
national mind and that has failed to be addressed during
hundreds of centuries of attempted betterment, ideological
revolution, and programs of *teshuva*, continuously fulminates
and possibly, by some unconscious design, calibrates its boil-
ing point to the "nodal moment" of *Tish'äh be-Av.* This is
the unresolved *äveilut ye'shänäh*'s negative impact.

On the healthy side, the same principles underwrite the capacity to invest new meaning in earlier, conservative patterns, though this will require the reactivation of dormant layers of meaning and affect in addition to mere revision. The pain of trauma can be construed existentially only when it is able to be signified, as we shall discuss further below, and when it is viewed in the context of historically meaningful cycles and in this manner is taken out of the frenzied tarantella of compulsive or obsessive repetition. "*Nah 'pe 'säh deräkhen 'u ve-näh 'kō rä ve-nä 'shuväh*" (Lam. 3:10; see Talmud, *Berakhot* 5a): The tendency to repeat, after all, is coevally a *restitutive* tendency of refinding (*hi'ppus*), researching (*hä'kiräh*), working through, and then re-establishing, via interpretation, the context of traumatic memories in relation to lost or damaged object representations (Freud 1914).

The possibility of re-entering and awakening the world of unchanged memories brings us to the second halakhic analogue; the principle of catalyzation, or "*hō zer ve-nē 'ór.*" This interactional or synergistic principle states that, under certain circumstances, a given substance can be modified when a second substance, introduced to the first at a subsequent point in time, catalyzes or "awakens" its otherwise dormant or previously nullified qualities. This principle is basic to numerous areas of Jewish law having to do with the intermingling of elements and is expressed best by Rashi's own definition: "[the new element] *wakes up* and augments, as in the sense of 'like one who is awakened [*yē 'ōr*] from his sleep' [Zech. 4:1] (s.v. "*mäz̧ ä min et min 'ō,*" Talmud, *Avodah Zarah* 73a; also *Zevahim* 31a). Importantly, the principle applies to the intermixing of intentions as well as physical substances (see Mishnah Torah: *Hil. Pesul'ei ha-Mukdashim* 16:4). I believe it very nicely establishes the grounding for psychological principles such as the "return of the repressed" and the mechanism by which inhibition and incitation of memory can occur proactively and retroactively. With every modification induced in the patient's feeling state within the consulting room, memories, object relational patterns, and other repressed material that corresponds to the new emotional state are stimulated. The newly stimulated memory material, in turn, instigates new expectations and possibilities in the patient-analyst relationship. Through this process, the *transference* mechanism during psychoanalytic psychotherapy catalyzes latent thoughts and feeling states, attaching them to the person of the analyst, through whom the patient can experience and rework them.

Yet no memory can be recalled or evoked if it has not been "registered" in a mind already predicated upon a working conscious and unconscious. In many senses, the mind (as opposed to the brain) cannot be said even to exist until the "system repression" has been installed (somewhat like a computer program's dependency upon the prior booting-up of the computer with DOS). Thus, experience and related memories—if we even may term them as such—from the earliest stages of life, cannot exert any truly mental influence because they have not been linked to some system of coding and signification. Without a stable system of signification, the entire mental apparatus will not develop properly.

Two halakhic principles anticipate these notions. The first concerns the law of the forgotten sheaf ("*shik'ḥah*"):

> "When you reap your harvest in your field and you forgot a sheaf in the field, you shall not turn back (*lō tāshuv*) to take it" (Deut. 24:19). This teaches: a sheaf left behind constitutes *shik'ḥāh* [and belongs to the poor]; a sheaf in front of him does not constitute *shik'ḥāh* [and does not belong to the poor]. The principle is: all to which "do not turn back" applies constitutes *shik'ḥāh*, and all to which "do not turn back"

does not apply does not constitute *shik'ḥäh* (Talmud, *Baba Meẓ'iah* 11a).

Restating this quite simply, that which has not been registered within a signification system based upon fundamental and immovable dichotomies or contrasts (yes/no, one/two, can/cannot, front/back) cannot be "turned back to," cannot be retrieved. The conversion of the thing-like qualities of real-world elements into abstractions or symbols demands the ability to *abandon*, negativize, or deconstruct the concept; to refuse to "turn back" literally to recollect or replace things, to let "thingness" fall instead, and to refind via symbol (see Spero, 1996). The law of *shik'ḥäh* indicates that Halakha is not valorizing mere absentmindedness or "forgetting" *per se*, but rather is elevating one's inattention or nonaction to a symbolic equivalent within the context of the *täshuv/lō täshuv* dichotomy. Only that which has been affirmed perceptually and then nullified via a system-like repression can be forgotten and refound meaningfully.

The third halakhic analogue derives from certain explicit biblical injunctions having to do with remembering, or *zekhiräh* (Exod. 20:9; Deut. 9:7, 24:9, and 25:17–19). In each of the cases of interest, there is a command to remember, followed by an adjuvant command either "to preserve" or "not to forget." In the case of Israel's archenemy Amalek, the biblical text states, "Remember," and then adds, "Erase the name of Amalek; do not forget." We shall return to this triple injunction in a moment. The *Torat Kohanim* (*Beḥukot'ai* 26:3) refers to each of these in a series of separate but essentially identical exegeses (I have combined them into a single teaching and emended the text for ease of reading):

> [Had the text written only the word] *zäkhōr*, I would understand [this as a reference to remembering in one's] heart. Yet the text also states [in the case of Shabbos] *shämōr* ["pre-

serve"], [and in the case of the story of Miriam] *hē'shā'mer*
["keep"], [and in the case of the calf] *äl tishkäḥ* ["do not
forget"], [and in the case of Amalek] *lō tishkah*—all of these
terms indicate not forgetting in one's heart—so what am I to
fulfill [additionally] with *zäkhōr?* [*Zäkhōr* teaches] to remember it orally [*bä-peh*].

The Talmud (*Megillah* 18a) actually only records the exegesis for the case of Amalek, probably because the apparently paradoxical instruction "Erase the name of Amalek;
do not forget" brings the desired point home more forcefully. The fundamental teaching here is that one must establish some permanent mental representation with the assistance of mnemonic devices and also remember orally by
reading at least once a year the relevant passages pertaining to the Amalek episode.

The operation of a deeper and far more complex psychological mechanism is hinted at here. The text could be
seen as setting the terms for the creation of what Täkhä
(1984) calls a "remembrance formation," the mental index-
ing of a given memory as-of-the-past and as not-having-a-
future. Without relinquishing a lost object or feeling state
to such a formation, mourning and mature suffering are
impossible (see also Volkan 1981 and 1993). For a remembrance formation to be created, however, the mind must
be able to accommodate the contradictory demands of at
least two prototypical meta-dimensions of memory upon
which all historical knowledge of trauma is based: *a necessary memory that forbids forgetting* and *a forbidden
memory that necessitates forgetting* (Enriquez 1990, 108).
In her exposition on memory, Enriquez further differentiates between two additional *kinds* of memory. The first are
primary or "prehistoric" memories that can *neither be
remembered nor forgotten* and that serve as the basic
inscriptive bedrock of the unconscious. The memories of

this class are not the "past" proper but merely *belong* to the past and are themselves always unknowable (and are not aimed for in treatment). But if they are unknowable, what function do they serve? In response, their value might be said to inhere in what Enriquez terms "figurative potential"—i.e., in the capacity they potentiate for the figurability of events or sensations that would otherwise defy absolute knowledge and certainty (one might think here of so-called procedural memories, which govern the way thinking takes place and cannot be remembered). This is the primary memory—or Ur-memory, so to speak—that enables the mind to contain the unknowable at least figuratively, approximately or coenesthetically.

The second kind of memory is *forgettable and memorable*. This is the level of memory that can be organized, stored, repressed, and evoked and that in general submits to dynamic processing. With this second type, it is possible to speak of absence and "memory holes" *as metaphors*, as references to the existence of organized subclusters of the overall organization of memory (or, of forgetfulness), but only so long as the linguistic laws governing the symbolic processes have been internalized within the unconscious. Without the symbolization and the conventions of signification, memory holes are just that.

The idea of these two levels of memory helps explain how the process of *forgetting* is transmitted transgenerationally. Whereas the first generation represses historical memories of suffering, the second generation represses its parents' suspicious silence and its own need to ask, while the third generation might repress even the will to remember, the basic connection to memory. Worse than repression, the third generation might foreclose on the psychic concept of a cultural past altogether.

In this light, reconsider the biblical passages regarding the immortalization of Amalek. There are two key loci that serve as the basis for the command to "remember and not forget" God's battle with Amalek. In Exod. 17:14–16, Moses is instructed to create a written record of Amalek's defeat and is promised that God surely will eradicate Amalek's memory through a battle eternal "from generation to generation" ("*mē 'dōr dōr*"). In Deut. 25:17–19, the specific instruction is to remember Amalek's ambush, to erase his name, and not to forget it ("*timḥeh et zēkher Ämälek mē 'täḥät hä 'shämäyim, lō tishkäh*"). In the first reference the emphasis is on the transgenerational link ("*mē 'dōr dōr*"); in the second reference to the twin modes of remembering and not forgetting, run parallel to Enriquez's concept of the dual, contradictory yet complementary components of the original traumatic memory: a necessary memory that forbids forgetting ("*lō tishkäh*") and a forbidden memory that necessitates forgetting ("*timḥeh et zēkher*"). It is thus that the complex, two-tiered *zäkhōr* imperative allows establishment of the "remembrance formation," making it possible to transform compulsive retraumatizing into a more symbolic *äveilut ye 'shänäh*.

I now will summarize this section. Individually and as a unit, the preceding halakhic analogues support the conclusion that memories that have been brutely excluded from the mental apparatus as a whole (foreclosure) cannot be retrieved and, properly speaking, cannot be remembered or known. In halakhic terms, that to which "*lō täshuv*" cannot apply will not be easily available to restorative operations such as *teshuva* or psychotherapy. If such "memories" or "objects" are painful, their impact cannot be mourned; if idealized as "all good," they sponsor manic emotional episodes and tend not to be internalized (Mitscherlich and Mitscherlich 1975). Substitute entities, including ersatz feeling states, might be dragooned into masking the void but cannot eliminate it, so the sufferer is in constant dread of collapse.

Both trauma and history, of course, are linked to time, but in an inverse manner: trauma limits history and historical understanding (Caruth 1991). Psychoanalysis teaches, however, that there are modes of history—notably, the one the patient creates during the course of the analytic encounter—in which trauma, compulsive repetition, and stalemated suffering can be given new contexts, worked through, and eventually made symbolic. This kind of remembering does not require total abandonment of the idiosyncratic, the subjective, the "mythic memories" (Friedlander 1992) or even the legitimate wish not to know. Rather, it blends these elements into a symbolic network that the patient's experience of the known/unknown and transference's real/illusory dimensions have created. And in the realm of religious experience, such a mode of history is implicit in the dual tracks of *zäkhōr/lō tishkäḥ.*

IV: CLINICAL ILLUSTRATIONS OF THE IMPACT OF SUFFERING ON RELIGIOUS BELIEF

I now will flesh out the preceding discussion with the aid of four clinical vignettes. The constraints that the task at hand imposes preclude our delving into intricate psychodynamic formulations and each treatment's numerous technical complexities. I will bring out only the characteristics of pathological suffering that indicate the absence or inadequate functioning of the halakhic metapsychological elements outlined above.

Vignette 1:

Leah, a religious young woman in her twenties, immediately strikes one as a charming, eminently eligible single, good at her chosen profession, with a caring, considerate, and intelligent personality. However, from the perspective of the couch, this charm is a mask—and a fragile one at that—that covers almost unceasing inner torment regarding her self-worth, her capacity to please, her inability to form lasting relationships, her basic disdain for piety, her various dependencies, her tantrums and hysterical reactions to minor changes, and her deep-seated confusion about her own sexual proclivities.

During eight years of psychoanalysis, Leah outlined a childhood of constant dislocation, loyalty conflicts, inadequate and overstimulated parenting, and, most important, ample evidence (in dreams, drawings, writings, slips of the tongue) of some traumatic sexual abuse at an early age. In the language of psychoanalysis, there was an obviously compensatory phallic quality to her tomboyish pursuits and mannerisms, yet even as this character style protected her against some levels of hurt, it simultaneously tortured her with a variety of unconscious significances that always threatened to surface. When this latter threat would reach threshold, which during the early years of treatment happened more than occasionally, she would resort to different forms of acting out and self-punishing behavior (teasing liaisons with married men), over which she then would excoriate herself further. Yet while these topics often occupied our work, a prevailing theme was her general moodiness, her tendency to whine and wimper about all manner of everyday upsets, and her talent for artificially generating a mawkishly pathetic atmosphere about herself and her life. She constantly attempted to assist herself by reading a welter of self-help books and attending all of the "learn to be good to yourself" seminars, during which times she stingingly would lambast the inadequacy of psychoanalysis compared with these alternative methods, only to experience repeatedly the nugatory value of these methods and revert to the abject hopelessness of her circumstances.

On the day-to-day level of our work, she almost never began a session from where the previous one ended. She would become hysterical when her own derivative associations and material were reflected back to her or would feign a particularly maddening "la-di-da" attitude about the most significant topics. If there was anything consistent about her sessions, as she herself often caviled, it was her annoying tendency to *repeat* a litany of woes and discontents each time, to claim she knew that these were just surface problems, and then to torture herself mentally over her pitiful inability to change anything. She was full of hate—generally speaking of this hate as if it were a physical substance—but could not, for a long time, direct it toward any of her personal objects. Later, when she was more able to release the full, psychologically relevant level of her rage, she directed it first at me—a period that lasted about one and a half years—and then gradually connected this level of real suffering to its historically "correct" metaphors (urinary incontinence and constipation, clamping down on thoughts and ideas as if these were dangerous objects or, alternately, special, private, cherished things that never could be shared with anyone) related to *specific* traumatic, identity-suffocating parental identifications, phases of her childhood.

Her attitude toward helpfulness, kindness, and the palliative ideologies of Judaism or common sense always has been remarkable. On one hand, as indicated, Leah was a great aficionado of these beliefs and ideologies, constantly comparing my strict Freudian approach with the more "humane" and "sympathetic" writings of Alice Miller, Miriam Adahan, and Heinz Kohut. She also took

copious notes at all manner of classes on Jewish philosophy. *But she was not much consoled by this material,*
viewing herself as too pathetic and disgusting to be
worth any kindness and as beyond the reach of God's
salvation. In these reactionary phases, she would lam-
poon with withering cynicism and spite all the "pious"
housewives and do-gooders of the world. Following angry outbursts against me—which occasionally included
turning over chairs, breaking plant vases, and, rarely,
approaching me menacingly and attempting to hit me—
she strove to express regrets but could not maintain
these "good" feelings for long.

At bottom, the true shame that Leah felt regarding
certain hidden secrets remained unconscious, so there
was not much value in seeking or receiving forgiveness
for ulterior acts or sentiments. Ironically—and significantly for the treatment—I *was* able to discern a mod-
est, hopeful, truly warm side in many adjacent aspects
of her personality and habits (the detection of which,
obviously, only Leah herself unconsciously could have
granted me). But for a long time her more authentic
side could not be cross-referenced with the shameless
and arrogant attacks she needed to launch due to a
sense of frustrated entitlement and psychosexual inferi-
ority. Thus, to Leah's great consternation, her apologies
were empty and destined to be repeated ritualistically
until the deeper subjective sense of wrongdoing could
be brought to consciousness. When we finally were able
to interpret this, it turned out that the aggress-forgive-
hope-disappoint-aggress cycle in the transference repeated the central feature of her parents' relationship
to her.

Among the crucial elements that have enabled the
analysis to progress—in addition to insight-conveying interpretations—has been my understanding that Leah

uses the consulting room as a kind of toilet-sanctuary
where she can dare to cry pitifully, be frightened, act
antagonistically, and be vile and disgusting *without being punished.* Her strong transference neurosis does
not always allow her to experience herself as not being
punished ("You stopped the session when I was in the
middle of a thought! You hate me, don't you! After eight
years I still do these *stupid* things! My case is hopeless!
Why don't you throw me out already?!). As we slowly
reconstructed the "original events" around which her
pathetic personality took form, Leah steadily has become
able to feed more useful data into her sessions, to
acknowledge consciously the significance of the story
she is developing, and to experience solace. Her
monologue's "mindless" repetition and apparent aimless-
ness (= the urinary leakage) of her monologue has become more clearly directional, with fresh revelations (including dreams) in each session. *Her suffering makes
sense because it has been realigned with certain representational data that she now can recollect vividly.* She
no longer wallows in patheticness because she has come
closer to the awareness of how these overvalent, affective states screened a deep-seated sexual conflict—including a fantasied image of herself as an incompetent hole
out of which all good and valuable mental contents (including the palliatives of faith) simply dripped in em-
barrassing puddles. She is substantially less dependent
upon intellectualized pursuit of religious catechisms or
ideological allegiances to comfort her soul, though she
remains religiously devout. Indeed, she now *feels* religiously devout for the first time because she meets God
as a whole person, without splitting off her hostilities
and idealized expectations, which permits her to feel
that a divine response might be directed at all of her

rather than partialized away from her undernourished, unclean, undeserving side.

Vignette 2

Tikvah is a religious divorcée in her forties, a single parent who, through four years of daily, intensive psychoanalysis, courageously has managed to rehabilitate a mentality that in many ways could be considered the epitome of consciously experienced suffering. Beginning in early childhood and continuing to adolescence, Tikvah was sexually abused, a situation augmented by incestuous sexual relations. Her history included rape, an abusive marriage, manipulative and disappointing religious leaders, substance abuse, failed therapies, bizarre sexual liaisons, and a long list of other kinds of victimization. (As is often the case, these were sometimes the product of a combination of external impositions and complex, unconsciously communicated forms of invitation and compliance.) Her mother provided her with little of the love a child needs in order to flower, though obviously sufficient care (including much guilt-ridden maternal overcompensation) was available to prevent complete psychological decompensation.

Like most of the patients in my care, Tikvah is a bundle of contradictory forces and needs: she was a caring woman much sought after for her organizational and counseling skills, yet she unconsciously lent herself to being overused, abused, and exhausted by those who needed her. She was a veritable battery of intellectual advice, spiritual guidance, culinary wizardry, and practical remedies for others, yet few could discern that these very wondrous qualities were a fragile bastion against her private inner world of helplessness, phobias, hypersensitivities, and bouts of panic and listlessness. Despite the lengthy array of sexual abuse and other traumas noted above, Tikvah managed to educate herself and become an excellent teacher, raise several children with special needs, and successfully resettle her family in Israel. Under the surface, however, lurked themes of death, confusion, interminable tiredness, suicide, falling helplessly into black holes, and drowning in contaminating, oily fluids. She loathed the pain, but she also resented the "good" for its disappointing inability to withstand contamination by the "bad." Ironically but predictably—and much more apparent once her analysis with me got under way—many of her devices or "crutches" for survival, which on the surface were intended to secure "good" feelings and comfortableness, had built-in destructive catches. However, whereas in the past these inevitable collapses spelled random havoc and severe regression, the vital therapeutic framework Tikvah and I managed to design—she often informing me via projective identification exactly how we needed to do this!—enabled us to bring these paradoxical tendencies and "impossible" situations into the consulting room, tolerate them together, and gradually incorporate them into structures of lasting meaning.

As regards Tikvah's capacity to bear suffering, I would like to say that, despite every protestation of hopelessness, she possessed some deep source of indomitable faith that in every instance enabled her somehow to peer through the gloom. Tikvah certainly *knew* and *understood* the gamut of halakhic and midrashic aphorisms and approaches to suffering and affliction—and, for many obvious reasons, maintained a not small library of material on the laws and mores of *ona'at de'varim*. Her dilemma, however, was not in the realm of *gewusstes* but rather *gedachtes*; the dimension of Jewish ideology was oftentimes psychically unreal and unthinkable to her, its concepts unmalleable, coldly removed from her personal vulnerability and need. If Tikvah was able to maintain an image of a "good" God, it was largely because she dared not yet direct toward him the incessant, heart-rending, and violent anger that she was learning to direct toward me.

Yet if Tikvah felt that human hypocrisy and, to some extent, divine indifference were etched into the warp and woof of her mind, from where did she derive her faith and her elementary capacity to forgive? How has she been able to retain her commitment to the analysis? I do not yet have the complete answer. Part of it is certainly our mutual and well-deserved love and respect (even though I am a rank Freudian!). Another part is interpretation. And yet another part is probably due to intense transference "loans" from deeply sequestered "good" childhood memories of healing and relief from suffering (though these, too, are many-sided). For example, Tikvah had managed to amalgamate those few "good" objects (a kindly grandfather, a supportive brother, a revered rosh yeshiva) she had encountered in her life and built a core around which her divided self could find refuge. *She protected this core vigorously, and it was in this light that I often needed to interpret some of her apparently indifferent, aggressive, or destructive movements.* Over the years, in fact, we created a safe baseline for work—conforming in many ways to the fantasy and function of a benevolent, maternal breast—modeled quite a bit upon this inner core's deep structure and conditions.

Gradually, the "good" experiences in the psychoanalysis itself were represented as symbols sufficiently strong to survive the next deeper level of regression. In this manner, the level of suffering Tikvah was to experience later as we gently began to remove some of the artificial scaffolding that had been improvised around the therapy was a more mature suffering, more akin to true existential despair, born of a depressive rather than a totally schizoid or apathetic level of object relationships. This suffering, which involved no small amount of transference-based disappointment, resembled weaning more than it did the earlier deathly mental collapse. Most important, I experienced her suffering as an emotion two humans could share, as opposed to a moribund one-dimensional, undigestable psychosomatic state of unsignifiable proportion. Finally, as we analyzed the unconscious ways in which her mind always had known from the outset of treatment that painful crises were inevitable—as part of the necessary processes of reworking trauma and evacuating congealed toxic feelings and destructive identifications—we discovered her secret, unconscious reservoir for hope, faith, and trust.

Vignette 3:

Jacob is a young man who has abandoned the external evidence of Orthodox Jewishness following years of lonely, silent withdrawal into a world of depersonalization and autistic-like fantasizing. He is a highly intelligent, handsome individual who walks about giving off an air, alternately, of being privately enraptured with "otherworldliness" or of pathologically contemplating some hostile act in the immediate future. When he began treatment with me, he just had aborted a suicide attempt (which Jacob attributed to divine intervention) after having reached the end of his efforts to secure a stable course of education or employment. He was despondent, taciturn, without plans. When he was not outright hostile or busy aggravating me, he would sit through hours of sessions in stoney silence.

Jacob's family is religious; his parents are highly educated, community-minded persons who became religious around the time of their marriage. Jacob always portrayed his mother's relationship with him in the worst light: a story of chronic, obsessive hounding for him to perform religiously and an equally rigid mandate regarding all forms of normal childhood spontaneity and pleasure. Jacob portrayed his father in a more favorable light: often violent with him as a child and overly caught up in his new religious enthusiasms, but also somehow making available to his son his deep appreciation for aesthetics, historical process, and fantasy. Jacob got lost somewhere in the throes of his parents' juggling of their own identities and personal loyalties, as well as in tumultuous adjustments to the rapid arrival of numerous sibling competitors. His memories of paternal beating (redeemed by his awareness of his father's anguished conflict) and maternal despotism (damned by his awareness of her indifference and murderous wishes) were etched profoundly. These he also wrapped up in an apparently true (or "screen") memory of some kind of homosexual abuse in a summer camp belonging to the Hasidic group that his family was affiliated with at the time and that Jacob henceforth associated with all that is evil in religion.

On a deeper level, however, Jacob's inherent nature evoked his parents' own repressed traumas; this, in turn, initiated the well-known kind of unconscious projection of these selfsame conflicts onto the child. As a result, Jacob carries within him "dead" or unreachable madness that in truth belongs to his parents. Worse, he always must mask that madness—wear it as if it were his own— lest he experience a renewed, mindbending parental counterattack against his psyche in order to prevent the pain from resurfacing in their own minds (Winnicott, 1969).

For our purposes here, the uniqueness of Jacob's case is that for many years, and during the first few years of analysis, he expressed no pain and did not suffer visibly. When he began acting out as a youngster, he displayed only arrogant denial and manic pleasure in defeating others. During the period when he still studied at the yeshiva, his intellectual achievements were nearly prodigious. Generally, there was always a fair enough degree of functionality. In fact, Jacob was only clinging to a rapidly deteriorating veneer, using whatever frameworks he could tolerate to maintain his sanity. Below the surface, his hate for and paranoid fear of religious feeling were terribly intense, and even this hatred covered the more fundamental and stifled rage against his parents.

Jacob devoted months of the treatment sessions to lambasting religious belief; excoriating the foibles and vacuousness of so many religious bromides regarding pain, suffering, and pleasure; and attacking with painful cynicism the entire hermeneutical basis of Jewish law. In addition, he routinely mocked my own religiosity and strove diligently—and, to some necessary degree, I think, successfully—to unmoor my own presumptions about religious belief and my own suppositions of safety nurtured in me since my own earliest childhood. I believe that this kind of occurrence in psychotherapy is essential with patients such as Jacob so that they can develop a sense that they are communicating with a truly open mind. This requires much more than the well-known analytic neutrality or reserve recommended since Freud, and much more than the therapist's simply not directly imposing his or her personal beliefs upon the patient.

The schizoid or borderline psyche (at least during critical phases of treatment) can work only with another
mind that has been relatively cleared of all the facile
hopes and even mature abstractions that might obstruct
the patient's ability to secure adequate representational
space for exploring old experiences and creating new
objects. On the one hand, this state is artificial; after all,
the analyst by no means has decided consciously to de-
nounce his faith or his personal loved objects, nor does
the patient consciously wish to have an impact upon another individual in this way. On the other hand, this
state parallels the patient's inner world, and this fragile
world can be accessed and repopulated only by allowing it to take expression by borrowing from the
therapist's own psychic functioning and available representational space.[6]

However, it is important to note that Jacob did man-
age to sequester certain "good" religious feelings, though
in nontraditional form. These he hid in a bizarre fascination with the world of science fiction, its heroes and
fantastic exploits, secret codes and nonhuman languages,
microrealities and temporal translocations, and quasi-
philosophical ideologies. It was crucial to Jacob's treatment that I comprehend this and play with him, so to
speak, in this periphery zone, for all that was potentially
healthy and remedial in his personality was hidden here.
Only in this world, and our dialogue through it, was
Jacob able to begin to express suffering, endow a men-

---

[6]Although this treatment approach contains some of my own contributions, it is based on techniques basic to contemporary psychoanalytic treatment (e.g., Grinberg 1962 and Ogden 1989 and 1994). For a
fuller review of this approach, broader literature, and additional details of Jacob's case, see Spero (1994 and 1995).

tor with the capacity to be respected by him (I was Mr. Spok; he, Captain Kirk), and turn manic, robot-like functioning into a *desire* to live and feel. As this work continues, Jacob now has begun to dare to lower the iron mask, re-experience the suffering he hid away as a child, and bring forward in metaphoric fashion and in an interpersonal setting the despair and hardship he for so long had "suffered" alone.

Vignette 4:

Endora was an extremely intuitive, narcissistic female patient who was especially challenging not only by virtue of the dominance of certain parallels to aspects of my own personality, but also by being knowledgeable herself about the fields of mental health and education. Her parents survived the Holocaust and resettled in Israel with a largely nonreligious lifestyle except for a few emotionally charged cultural links to Jewish values. These few links, however, were the secret base of some very significant "good" object representations, remaining dormant for many years until they later helped motivate Endora's interest in a superficially conventional religious way of life.

From the outset, Endora provided few specific details about her life and tended to cling to repetitious generalities and tragical, evaluative monologues. She geared most of her investigative skills toward my personality rather than her own (she never adopted my efforts to explore this reversed, paranoid, projective mechanism, though I think she comprehended my interpretations). About all I could glean from the data she offered were images of a failed yet deeply idealized paternal figure; a hateful, wicked, magically powerful maternal figure whom Endora nevertheless perceived as deeply dependent upon and jealous of her practically from birth; a "council" of aunts who cared for Endora during her infancy and early childhood; the possibility that her mother was raped by Nazis; and the apparent fact that her father had another daughter living somewhere else.

From sundry details that I managed to collect from her discourse and from the snippets of imagery in her dreams, I surmised that during Endora's early infancy her mother had at least one severe psychiatric breakdown or illness of some other kind that required a relatively long hospitalization and separation from her child. Endora portrayed her childhood with a broad sweep of chronic emotional privation and tended to diminish the significance of any specific traumatic event or memory. Most of her achievements, aspirations, and interpersonal relations were enwrapped in shifting, mysterious winds of metaphoric allusion; I often had the impression that a swirling vapor was all that remained of a once emotionally real sense of history. She lived within a myth of tragic fatedness. She exuded a weird adeptness at "perceiving" when evil things were about to happen and always was foretelling some doom. Whenever a difficulty arose in her life or in the treatment, Endora would smile in an otherwordly, omniscient manner and state that she had had a "sense" that this or that was going to happen. While not as prophetically gifted as Endora, I certainly could see the heavy shadow of a patient's intense need to create a failed analysis in conformity with a deeply pathological sadomasochistic wish-fantasy. And, of course, she knew the treatment *was* doomed, as I would be able only to take her near the gates of suffering and then abandon her there. These baleful prophecies, she added, accorded with what kabbalists call the "cup of the slingshot" (*kaf ha-kela*) in which our souls had been ensconced fatefully since time immemorial.

Endora's air of mystery and despair was essentially a semivalid (if one-sided) "representation" of her home atmosphere; the unsymbolized absences within that home rendered it in her mind a null space that no home that no human being could have come from or conceivably could return to. I gained the impression that innuendo and partial images from the post-war years in Europe circulated freely within her home; stories told in half-ridicule of her father's long faded sexuality created fantasies that consumed the objective fidelity of her own sense of interpersonal and intrapsychic perception. Not much of her early childhood lent itself to re-representation, including that may never have achieved representation, masked by a young child's highly sensitive but nontensile protective layer of superior intelligence, verbal skills, intuitive warning barriers, and powerful projective mechanisms. In the main, I believed that Endora had manufactured her own version of a childhood from a few personal myths (she often stated baldly that she had *had* no childhood) and that what I did *not* know of her seemed far more important to her than what I did know. The dynamic pull of precocious oedipal strivings and the sadomasochistic hunger for regressive fulfillment of earlier psychosexual desires soon lent themselves to this defensive structure. Endora perpetuated these quasi-representational states through the select, mostly morbid religious metaphors and activities she preferred. She thus was swathed effectively and continuously in mysterious and deathly affective states: a woman locked into eternal mourning for losses she barely could conceptualize.

It was relatively easy to be aware of the effect of Endora's destructive, Medea-like "*shwartzearbeitung*," as her mother had defined it long ago, on my mind, and I could perceive some of the partial objects that these forces fluidly represented. But it was a far greater challenge for me safely to sequester for her—which I believe she was asking me to do via projective identification—the more vulnerable, capable, optimistic, and joyful childhood images I occasionally could discern. This secret program of Endora's testified to her efforts during infancy to hide (in schizoid fashion) the "good" parts of the self from destructive adults. At the same time, she seemed intent upon destroying the analytic relationship precisely because it held forth the potential for discovering her own repressed, normal sexuality and her capacity for goodness. The danger would be, as I imagined it, that immediately upon discovering such hidden goodness, destructive inner objects (her parents) would swoop down and steal them from her, leaving her with absolutely nothing. The religious metaphors she used and the melancholy Hasidic tales or music she enjoyed further expressed this dilemma.

In Endora's everyday life and interactions, these same qualities supported and hid in her various pseudoexistential, philosophical preoccupations and her thirst for the mixed sexual metaphors of Jewish kabbala, the vagaries of popular versions of rabbinic hermeneutical style, and the pseudoscience of astrology. Repeated efforts to explore this situation led to the conclusion that the impasse was the result of—and in a sense *represented*—her deep dread of actually ever achieving dimensionality and identity. Preserving the impasse confirmed Endora's inner conviction that experiencing any kind of lasting joy—indeed, being *known*—inherently *limited* her preferred conscious sense of mysterious plenipotentiality.

As we saw in the first vignette with Leah, Endora often would seek my forgiveness after her angry outbursts, citing chapter and verse, yet there seemed to be little emotional backing behind these solicitations. To forgive an object requires letting go of it to some degree, as well as the ability to relegate one's dialogue with it to abstract dimensions of memory, where healing takes place. Endora truly could not risk such transformations because to her they implied *depletion* or lack of control over the object. Indeed, her suffering was a massive, intractable "object" in its own right; reparation would have required a willingness to explore and heal deep splits within her personality, which she was not prepared to do yet, and an ability to surrender her mask of mystery. Thus, Endora could find relief in the bleak, tragic, repetitive, cyclical qualities of Jewish ideology and practice to the degree that these elements enabled her to maintain her state of perpetual mourning and to suspend her "dead" objects within the miasmic webbing of incompletely represented inner secrecy.

Further exploration seems impossible for her at this time, due in part to the great deal of secondary gain she draws from her current lifestyle. What she has glimpsed dimly through the successful moments of the analysis frightens her. Her treatment has come to a halt, and thus she has not been able to free herself of the myth that the discovery of true subjectivity, while painful, does not have to be catastrophic. I believe the knowledge that she has abandoned—at least for the time being—the possibility of creating actual representational space that might absorb some of the shapeless mysteriousness genuinely saddens her. On the other hand, precisely through ending treatment at this point, she has been able to experiment with mourning for an object (the therapist) that was objectively "good" enough to let her be "bad."

V: CLINICAL DISCUSSION

The common denominator among the four cases presented is an inability to suffer productively: Leah cannot connect her overvalent weepiness and pitiful state with specific memories; Tikvah cannot escape her sense of falling into suffering and of being trapped within an overabundance of memory; Jacob refuses to feel, as if he therefore will be immune to suffering; and Endora has transformed suffering into an amorphous, all-encompassing pseudoideology that relegates mourning to the status of a way of life. In each of these cases, we witness suffering without mourning and the transformation of the suffering state itself (or the state of nonsuffering, in Jacob's case) into the subjective object. Because of the constant and heavy cloaking of their deeper, more authentic states of pain, and their dependency upon projective identification as the vehicle for communication, it was terribly difficult to offer these patients what they desired most: the sense of *sympathetic*, uninduced suffering or *Mitleid* within the therapist (see Freud 1942).

In each instance, there is some kind of paralysis of psychic functioning—living as if a character in a story or through a one-way glass—and the maintenance of a conservative state of frozen relationship with internal objects that cannot be bypassed, replenished, internalized, or mourned (see Bollas 1987, 110–111, and Volkan 1981). Masochism and repetitively-compulsive suffering are basically last-ditch efforts to maintain the self against intense, unrepresented, and otherwise uncontrollable pain that threatens to annihilate it (Joseph, 1981 and 1982). But such mechanisms do not enable truly *meaningful* or coherent suffering.

The British psychoanalyst Wilfred R. Bion expressed the dilemma of these patients very well (1970, 9):

> People exist who are so intolerant of pain or frustration (or in whom pain and frustration is so intolerable) that they feel

pain but will not suffer it and so cannot be said to discover it. . . . the patient who will not suffer pain fails to "suffer" pleasure and this denies the patient the encouragement he might otherwise receive from accidental or intrinsic relief.

Bion essentially is reformulating the famous rabbinic dictum "The reward is proportionate to the suffering" (Talmud, *Avot* 5:22). That is, emotional relief is only possible in a mind that can conceptualize suffering in the first place and fit it into a single, subjective framework that subsumes the terms of suffering in the same chain of metaphoric signifiers of meaning that subsume the concept of relief.[7]

---

[7]The topic of suicide comes to mind *a propos* this dictum, and it is a perennially problematic one. A key issue always has been whether suicide, as the ultimate brute expression of human suffering, is a *symbolic* act? A discussion of this topic would require another paper, but the following idea is pertinent. I believe that suicide always marks that moment when the individual no longer can represent his or her suffering in a symbolic manner, the nadir of the capacity to communicate metaphoric meaning, and the collapse of conceptualization. Technically speaking, if the individual somehow could have expressed his meanings in symbols or metaphors at that particular moment, he would not have needed to annihilate his mind. As Winnicott taught (1963), individuals who are forever preoccupied with an inevitable, anticipated breakdown or with the "need" to commit suicide (and, to some extent, the somaticisers) in fact are expressing a radical effort to translate into some kind of terminology a breakdown, psychic catastrophe, or mental death *that actually transpired a long time ago but that never had achieved representation.* The individual "remembers" this event or state only dimly, yet its significance is usually central to his core of being and persists until lent adequate expression. I also believe that in such cases, the individual's wish is not to die (despite every fervent insistence of the contrary), but to experience something death-like (or black-like, quiet-like, enveloping-like, passive-like—whatever the case might be) that he cannot conceptualize in any other manner and to experience (and eventually internalize) the loving reactions of the healthy other, with whom this inchoate memory or state is represented successfully.

Fantasies and ideologies might cover temporarily the mental space where interpersonally relevant suffering needs to be experienced; thus, such persons often seem quite able to intellectualize or even *believe* relatively deeply in all sorts of nurturant and supportive notions. But these new beliefs do not appear to be translatable into the capacity to *live* one's suffering in a way that is morally or aesthetically meaningful.

Rabbi Soloveitchik expressed what we might view as the moral side of Bion's aforementioned thought (1978, 65):

> Judaism held that the individual who displays indifference to pain and suffering, who meekly reconciles himself to the ugly, disproportionate, and unjust in life, is not capable of appreciating beauty and goodness. . . . A human morality based on love and friendship, or sharing in the travail of others, cannot be practiced if the person's own need-awareness is dull, and he does not know what suffering is.

Only then, as Rabbi Soloveitchik continues, can "need-awareness turn into passional experience, into a suffering awareness" (67). A psyche that is simply incapable of mature suffering, that has inured itself to the perception of

---

I think that this approach also explains those incidents related in the Talmud where certain individuals precipitously took their lives as a result of very sudden and strong religious motivation (e.g., Yakum Ish Ẓerorot [Gen. *Rabbah* Rabbi Hannaniah ben Tradyon's executioner [Talmud, *Avodah Zarah* 18a]). Upon reflection, the primary impulse in these cases seems to have been the sudden awakening of the desire to approach some hitherto under- or nonrepresented dormant "religious" object that, under the heady sway of each case's specific conditions, prompted the individual to move toward concrete reunion as opposed to a metaphoric relationship. It is probably for this reason that these individuals were granted an immediate but nevertheless token "share" in the World to Come, inasmuch as their actual deaths cannot be viewed as the preferred level of representation for their acute religious stirrings.

pain via neurotic, schizoid, or psychotic self-enclosure, cannot realize whole domains of Halakha, such as prayer, charitableness, and compassionate regard for the widow and the orphan. If the intimate balance between self-regard and empathy, which presupposes affective responsiveness, were wholly irrelevant to halakhic life, then the clause "for you know the soul of the sojourner" (Exod. 22:20 and 23:9)[8] would be pointless indeed. Rabbi Soloveitchik thus has underscored a moral imperative: namely, that the responsible Jewish individual must be aware of his own needs, which include his pain's dimensions and interpretations, to be able to relate fully to himself and to others. Obviously, if the capacity for such awareness is not possible without psychotherapeutic assistance, then psychotherapy becomes a moral imperative as well.

What else is needed, then, for suffering to be rendered meaningful?

First, painful memories cannot be assimilated and mourned unless they can be experienced as memories in time and subsequently experienced as memories that no longer have an actual future. This would contrast to a "conservative object" (Bollas 1987) locked in a permanently un-

---

[8]Cf. Lev. 1:4, "*ve-nērẓäh lŏ le-khäper ä'läv*" ("... and it shall be accepted for him ...") (also Lev. 26:41 and 43). Zvi Hirsch Meklenberg (*ha-Ke'tav ve'ha-Kabbalah*, ad loc) argues that *ve-nērẓäh* does not refer to mechanical propritiation of God, but means the sinner's (the patient's) internal remorse and reconciliation that must precede atonement (cf. 1 Sam. 29:4). Once again, a psychological-psychotherapeutic endeavor, and neither belief nor hope alone, is required for any significant transformation in personality to take place. This explains the link the rabbis generally forged between suffering (*yissurin*), internal investigation and analysis (*le-fäsh'fesh* [see Talmud, *Berakhot* 5a to Lam. 3:40]), and acceptance or working-through (*ve-nērẓäh*) (see Torah *Sheleimah* to Lev. 1:4, no 111).

reachable or "dead" psychic nonspace. By nesting memory within true temporal dimensionality—by granting memory its subjective historicity—the representation of a lost or painfully inadequate object can be transformed into a "remembrance formation" (Täkhä 1984). This cannot be done as long as the pain is too great, the pain has not been brought forward yet in its full dimensions, the individual's need to mourn conflicts with a stronger cultural or family message that forbids mourning, or the individual continues to cling to the object in one form or another. Suffering's historicity is additionally important because it permits the transformation of painful affect, which is a pseudo-object in its own right (as we saw in the clinical illustrations), frozen in time, into a "signal affect," which is of moderate proportion and abstract significance and combats the compulsion to repeat trauma ahistorically. Signal affects also help the individual change the fundamental sense of incapacitating, overwhelming, or castrating "dread" into mature, uplifting, and inspiring "awe" (without losing the deeper, enriching maternal or paternal symbolic content that underwrites these special feeling states [see Greenacre 1956; Harrison 1975]).

The element of time brings to our attention the crucial significance of the concept of transference. Aside from its well-known overall role in psychoanalytic psychotherapy, I only would reiterate here its contribution to framing the individual's suffering within a context that is simultaneously of the past and of the present. Although hundreds of authors have elucidated this point, I will refer to James Strachey's singular phrasing (1934) because it utilizes so many of the terms mentioned in the present analysis:

> Instead of having to deal as best as we may with conflicts of the remote past, which are concerned with dead circumstances and mummified personalities, and whose outcome is already determined, we find ourselves involved in an actual

and immediate situation, in which we and the patient are the principal characters and the development of which is to some extent at least under our control.

Because halakhic analogues for transference have been worked out elsewhere (Spero 1992), it is legitimate from the Judaic point of view to anticipate coincidence of transference and transcendence on both the deocentric and the anthropocentric levels (cf. Jones 1991).

Second, as Masud R. Khan (1979, 210) eloquently has put it:

> Over the past two centuries and more, with the increasing disappearance of God as the witnessing *other* from man's privacy with himself, the experience of psychic pain has changed from tolerated and accepted suffering to its pathological substitute: masochistic states.

Masud Khan is indicating that the suffering person needs help to develop a sense that a helpful other unobtrusively is witnessing his pain. Ultimately, this all-seeing other is God. The pathological sufferer generally has little or no internal representation of a helpful, responsive other with whom to combat or to dilute pain's prepotent inner images and voices, or has only the sense of "dead," insensitive, poisonous, or impotent internal objects (Green 1983 and Vergote 1978, 62). Hence the chronic sense of helplessness, *tedium vitae*, aloneness, the reality-defying conviction of fatefulness and unceasing badness, and the inability to utilize help and succor effectively when they are offered. Developmentally speaking, an internal "good" presence generally refers to the internal sense of benevolent mothering—or the image of the breast and its "good" functioning—that eventually serves as the basis for the development of transitional objects and the entire intermediary or transitional space (Winnicott 1953 and 1959, 58). This transitional area is the realm of illusion, play, art, and religious feeling, yet it, too, must include the capacity for destruction, reparation, and restoration, for these alone kindle the level of symbolization requisite for mature suffering.[9] Indeed, this intermediary dimension succeeds "in proportion" to its ability to permit and contain such creative destructivity.

Thus, alongside the broken images and affective states of pain and loss, mature suffering will reveal equally potent images or representations of healing, helpfulness, and solace that partake of the transitional sphere's salutary functions. These might take the form of imaginary companions (Stern 1985, 111–122 and 193–195). Yet to bear the brunt of everyday loss, strife, and pain, these early forms of transitionally need to mature into solacing *concepts* (such as the idea of the relationship between God and Knesset Yisrae͏̈l and the mutuality of their returning [Malakhi 3:7] or the concept of "*Emó Änō͏khē bez̜äräh!*").[10] These ulti-

---

[9]I hope to expand upon the psychological dimensions of *teshuva* in my forthcoming book *Repetition, Repentance, and Return: A Psychoanalytic Inquiry into the Refinding of the Religious Object* (University of Chicago Press). The central theme here will focus on the capacity to represent the lost object and to "refind" it, as Freud so fundamentally understood (1905, 222), as the groundwork for the process of *teshuva*, both in its healthy and pathological variants.

[10]The actual text is "*Emó änókhē be-z̜ärä*" ("I am with him [Israel] in the affliction") (Ps. 91:15). The image of the divinity bound, or as sharing in Israel's afflictions, is found in many sources. See Isa. 43:14 and 43:9 (and *Pesikta Rabba* 31), Ezek. 36:20, and especially *Introduction* to Lamentations *Rabba* (24) to Lam. 1:2, citing Isa. 22:12 and Jer. 13:17. At the same time, as I have emphasized in the text, it is not likely that an individual who has no representational space for such images can maintain this kind of imagery; nor can it be adopted productively by an individual whose resident internal objects bar access to solacing imagery or split these into concrete introjections that then need to be projected onto idealized objects in the outside world (our contemporary "gods"). While the unconscious fantasy might be that such idealization

mately broaden even further to incorporate the individual's actual representations of his or her own experiential relationship with God (see Benson 1980; Sugarman and Jaffe 1989). The capacity for healthy solitude, so vital for what I have been calling mature suffering, presupposes the internalized representation of this sense of presence and relatedness (see Modell 1993, 120–123, and Winnicott 1958).

A third factor of growth—in the movement away from wallowing in agony and toward mature suffering—is the capacity to surrender the need to *possess* or *keep* the loved object (or to hold on morbidly to the pathological conservative, "dead" object) and instead to *return* and *restore* it, to *know* it. Central to the religious concept of *teshuva*—as well as to the work of art or the psychotherapeutic odyssey—is the ability to interweave "good" and "bad" harmoniously, as opposed to preserving a dichotomy and to acknowledge a destroyed or incomplete reality's dimensions and to revive it (Segal 1952). Psychologically speaking, the perception of beauty is impossible without the ability to comprehend ugliness unanxiously. Similarly, many of the patients illustrated above could achieve no lasting sense of inner sanity or cleanness until they gave full expression to their own sense of inner insanity and contamination (without projecting these impressions onto anything else or

---

of "helpful" objects—such as "special" friends or psychotherapists—renders the comforting object ready-to-hand, the maneuver must, in fact, backfire. It generally results in (a) the subjective sense of emptying what little good there is within oneself, (b) an aggravating sense of dependency upon the idealized object, and (c) the ever-present anticipation of failure and rejection by that object (as such patients are skilled at evoking through the intense pressures of their unmonitored projective identification). With these complications in mind—and the Midrash aside—might such factors possibly appear *vis-à-vis* God Himself as a result of the extended attritions of Exile and the protracted period of *hastarat panim*?

masking them behind rationalistic ideology). This brings to
mind our earlier comments regarding the ability to create
a "remembrance formation" around lost or imperfect objects
to facilitate mourning—to which I now have added the need
to do so in a manner aesthetically pleasing to the spirit.[11]

VI: DISCUSSION

We have examined some of the differences between pathological and mature suffering and have looked at the
halakhic analogues that lend representation to the relevant
psychological processes involved in the two kinds of suffering. The purpose of viewing the well-known psychological
mechanisms in halakhic terms, as section III clarified, is
that concepts such as *ävēilut ye'shänäh shik'ḥäh, ḥozer
ve-nē'ōr* and *zäkhōr* are linked explicitly with the man-God
dimension and bring into sharper focus the ways in which
our complementary psychological mechanisms and operations interface with this unique dimension. Whereas some
religious psychotherapists have struggled to find the appropriate place in their work for what they saw as the discon-
tinuous elements of agape, caritas, and eros (Guntrip 1956;
cf. McDargh 1993; Oden 1967; and Zilboorg 1962, 75)—
God having to enter the consulting room, as it were, *after*
the requisite therapeutic processes are instated—the
halakhic metapsychology outlined here obviates this dilemma. From its standpoint, psychotherapeutic activity is a
religious endeavor not only when it deals directly with
manifestly religious issues, but also by virtue of its basic

---

[11]In the same vien, as I have stated here and elsewhere (1992a),
teshuva or repentance, which is itself a form of sacrifice, is impossible
without an inner representation of destruction, reparation, restoration,
and symbolization.

framework and receptivity to the man-God dimensions inherent in transference, reworking, regression, repetition-compulsion, remembrance formation, and so on.

Our approach enables us to respond to yet another issue. Religious individuals aspire to the ability to sacrifice the way our forefathers did, to bear painful tests of faith, and, if demanded, to surrender their lives to sanctify the holy name. Would the afflictions of persons such as Leah, Tikvah, Jacob, and Endora—prior to treatment—have qualified for these purposes?

Aside from what already has been said, I only would add at this point that mature suffering and sacrifice are essentially impossible when an individual has an impaired capacity to relinquish his objects and experiences great difficulty allowing for those psychological processes that result in internalization and abstraction.[12] As Jacques Lacan understood (1960, 308),[13] even the forefathers and all subsequent martyrs only sacrificed after they already had accepted, at least on some basic level, the symbolic framework of God's word or convenant. Psychotherapeutic experience as well teaches that, in the case of pathological or complicated suffering, sacrifice actually has been *desymbolized*. This occurs because the substitute or "sacrificial" acts of masochism and the resistances of manic optimism are intended to *penetrate* one's inner objects or their substitutes (includ-

---

[12]Because the present audience might not be familiar with Lacan's work, I will cite the pertinent comment in the text referred to: "In other words, the pact is everywhere anterior to the violence before perpetuating it, and what I call the Symbolic dominates the Imaginary" (cf. Vergote 1975). That is, the *brit* has been secured before the forefathers are asked to offer their children upon the altar.

[13]On the topic of the stranger, see Fromm's brilliant essay "The Way: Halakhah" (1966, pp. 143–45).

ing the therapist) and *expropriate* them. This is the opposite of relinquishment. Suffering as true sacrifice (that is, suffering that can be offered as a sacrifice) must be a free, historical, symbolic act, a personal expression that is part of an intersubjectively mutual give and take.

It is obvious from my viewpoint that I am skeptical about the effectiveness or relevance of various psychotheologies, logotherapy, and related levels of psychological counseling and support that claim to heal the individual through directly investing his perspectives with meaning. It is true, as Freud himself pointed out (1915), that philosophical inquiry and psychological awareness were born from the conflict of feelings surrounding death and transience. Yet there are many steps between the infantile wail of bewilderment and palliative fantasies and illusions, on the one hand, and the mature, philosophical query and evolution of an *Anschauung* toward suffering, on the other hand. Such progress presupposes the development of what contemporary psychoanalysis calls representational space and the capacity for symbolization, which in turn support the instantiation of drive-delay mechanisms, secondary-process thinking, and signal affects. Without these frameworks, philosophical inquiry, psychological reflectivity, and meaning are all impossible.

This notion of intellectual or purely philosophical conquest of psychological suffering brings to mind a personal anecdote that might be instructive.

Several years ago I wrote a review essay (1977) regarding the halakhot of *tumäh* (ritual uncleanliness) and mourning in which I found the opportunity to cite a datum quoted by Rabbi Joseph Soloveitchik quoted (1944, 66) in his father's name. Rabbi Soloveitchik related that Reb Ḥayyim of Brisk occupied himself with the intricate laws of *tumät hä-met* (the laws of ritual impurity imposed by contact with a corpse); to quell his fear of death, Reb Ḥayyim incorporated this event into a halakhic framework. In the text itself, Rabbi Soloveitchik concluded (67):

> When the Man of Halakhah fears death, the single weapon for dealing with this awesome fear is the eternal Law of Halakhah. The act of [halakhic] objectification conquers the subjective anxiety of death.

In a footnote (n. 86), citing Zweig, Rabbi Soloveitchik compares Reb Ḥayyim's behavior with Tolstoi's artistic undertakings (the reference must be to *The Death of Ivan Ilych*), which represented a literary genius's endeavor to transform death into terms essential to his world view.

At some point, I sent a copy of this little review essay to my rosh yeshiva, Rabbi Mordekhai Gifter, may he live and be well. Some time went by, and he eventually invited me to come and discuss the topic. After first dismissing what he termed Rabbi Soloveitchik's "mathematical" approach to halakha, he brought up the Reb Ḥayyim Brisker/Tolstoi analogy and exclaimed, "The entire approach leaves me cold! Reb Ḥayyim didn't have any 'fear of death' to *conquer!*" But is this probable? Do not myriad biblical and talmudic sources, as well as practical halakhot, teach us that humankind inevitably fears death but also has the capacity, under nonpathological circumstances, to transform this fear into mature anxiety over its existential predicament? Indeed, if I may state what I believe is almost explicit in Rabbi Soloveitchik's view (as well as in the psychoanalytic framework outlined here): the man who has no fear of death simply cannot appreciate the laws of *tumāt met* and even might be at risk of miscarrying them in some way!

There is still the matter of under what circumstances halakhic objectification can conquer "the subjective anxiety of death." Obviously *not* when the "subjective anxiety" is essentially pathological and the suffering does not permit the mind to focus upon any symbolic framework, no matter how apparently "objective." I do not wish here to take up the large debate between contemporary psychoanalysis and the existential schools of psychiatry and psychotherapy. I do, however, think it important to say a few words about a similar trend in the writings of some Judaically oriented psychotherapists.

David Fox, who seems cognizant of intrapsychic conflict's role in the sufferer's life, nevertheless adopts the terms of Meier's "psychohalakhah" (1987 and 1988) and argues (1987, 93):

> To relegate the subjective response [of the suffering patients] to a psychodynamic level is to reduce the patient's experience to an intrapsychic entity. In essence, this may aid in the patients' grasp of their role in the phenomenon of suffering while denying and obviating the *objective reality* of their situation.

Aren't "intrapsychic entities" a fundamental component of an individual's "objective reality"? And isn't "objective reality" a part-illusion largely influenced by intrapsychic determinants? Even if we wish to speak of God and His role in our lives, if He has consented to being perceived intrapsychically—which means not only Freud's "intrapsyche" but also the intrapsyche as predicated upon unconscious halakhic structures of the kind described herein—then perhaps He willingly has consigned a certain degree of reality to subjectivity and illusion. In the end, we are judged by how well we consciously brought halakhic objectivity to bear upon these other characteristics of the mind, but it is expected that this cannot take place where the irrational has become strong and pathology deeply entrenched. Causality and purpose cannot be differentiated as easily and artificially, I think, as Fox and Meier sup-pose—and certainly not in the case of the disturbed mind. It might be that Fox and Meier have overlooked the fact that "self," "structure," and "subjectivity" evolve simultaneously (Moran 1993). It is true that suffering is a subjective experience, but it does not follow immediately that the pathologically suffering individual easily will learn that "subjective awareness of suffering is a facilitative feature of self-analysis and penance" (Fox 1987, 98). For suffering to be comprehended even as a "subjective experience" requires in the cases of many individuals an entire reworking of their basic, internal, representational makeup. As I have attempted to show, the necessary representational "material" is comprised of structures whose identity is halakhic as well as psychological, guiding the individual toward the development of a sense of subjectivity in the context of a relationship with God as well as his fellow man.

REFERENCES

Bakan, D. (1968). *Disease, Pain, and Sacrifice.* Chicago: University of Chicago Press.

Grolnick, S., Barkin, L., and Muensterberger, W., eds. (1978). *Between Reality and Fantasy.* New York: Jason Aronson.

Becker, E. (1973). *The Denial of Death.* New York: Free Press.
——— (1975). *Escape from Evil.* New York: Free Press.

Benson, R. M. (1980). Narcissistic guardians: Developmental aspects of transitional phenomena, imaginary companions, and career futures. *Adolescent Psychiatry* 8:250–264.

Bion, W. R. (1970). *Attention and Interpretation.* London: Maresfield.

Blechner, M. J. (1987). Entitlement and narcissism. *Contemporary Psychoanalysis*, 23:244–254.

Brayer, M. B. (1982). The psychology of the Halakhah of bereavement. In *A Psychology-Judaism Reader*, ed. R. P. Bulka and M. H. Spero, pp. 183–211. Springfield, Ill.: Charles C. Thomas.

Bulka, R. (1977). Logotherapy and the Talmud on suffering: Clinical and meta-clinical issues. *Journal of Psychology and Judaism* 2:31–44.

——— (1982). Rabbinic attitudes towards suicide. In *A Psychology-Judaism Reader*, ed. R. P. Bulka and M. H. Spero, pp. 211–225. Springfield, Ill.: Charles C. Thomas.

——— (1987). Guilt from, guilt towards. In *Guilt, Suffering, and Death: The Impact and Challenge*, ed. L. Meier. Special issue of *Journal of Psychology and Judaism* 11:72–90.

Breuer, J., and Freud, S. (1893–1895). *Studies on Hysteria*. In J. Strachey, ed. and trans. (1953). *The Standard Edition of the Complete Psychological Works of Sigmund Freud, Vol. II*. London: Hogarth.

Caruth, C. (1991). Unclaimed experience: Trauma and the possibility of history. *Yale French Studies* 79:26–43.

Enriquez, M. (1990). The memory envelope and its holes. In *Psychic Envelopes*, ed. D. Anzieu, pp. 95–120. London: Karnac.

Finn, M., and Gartner, J. (1992). *Object Relations Theory and Religion*. New York: Praeger.

Fox, D. (1987). Suffering and atonement as a psycho-Judaic construct. In *Guilt, Suffering, and Death: The Impact and Challenge*, ed. L. Meier. Special issue of *Journal of Psychology and Judaism* 11:91–102.

Freud, S. (1905). Three essays on sexuality. In J. Strachey, ed. and trans. (1953). *The Standard Edition of the Complete Psychological Works of Sigmund Freud, Vol. VII*, pp. 123–243. London: Hogarth.

——— (1915). Thoughts for the times on war and death. In J. Strachey, ed. and trans. (1953). *The Standard Edition of the Complete Psychological Works of Sigmund Freud, Vol. XIV*, pp. 275–300. London: Hogarth.

——— (1900). *The Interpretation of Dreams, Part I*. In J. Strachey, ed. and trans. (1953). *The Standard Edition of the Complete Psychological Works of Sigmund Freud, Vol. IV*. London: Hogarth.

——— (1914). Remembering, repeating, and working through. In J. Strachey, ed. and trans. (1953). *The Standard Edition* of the Complete Psychological Works of Sigmund Freud, Vol. XII, pp. 145–156. London: Hogarth.

———— (1916). Some character-types met with in psycho-analytic work. In J. Strachey, ed. and trans. (1953). *The Standard Edition of the Complete Psychological Works of Sigmund Freud, Vol. XIV*, pp. 311–333. London: Hogarth.

———— (1916–1917). Introductory Lectures and Psycho-Analysis, Part III. In J. Strachey, ed. and trans. (1953). *The Standard Edition of the Complete Psychological Works of Sigmund Freud, Vol. XVI*. London: Hogarth.

———— (1920). *Beyond the Pleasure Principle*. In J. Strachey, ed. and trans. (1953). *The Standard Edition of the Complete Psychological Works of Sigmund Freud, Vol. XVIII*, pp. 7–64. London: Hogarth.

———— (1927). *The Future of an Illusion*. In J. Strachey, ed. and trans. (1953). *The Standard Edition of the Complete Psychological Works of Sigmund Freud, Vol. XXI*, pp. 3–56. London: Hogarth.

———— (1942). Psychopathic characters on the stage. In J. Strachey, ed. and trans. (1953). *The Standard Edition of the Complete Psychological Works of Sigmund Freud, Vol. VII*, pp. 303–310. London: Hogarth.

Friedlander, S. (1992). Trauma, transference, and "working through." *History and Memory* 4:39–55.

Fromm, E. (1966). *You Shall Be as Gods: A Radical Interpretation of the Old Testament and its Tradition*. New York: Holt, Rinehart and Winston.

Glatt, M. J. (1979). "God the mourner—Israel's companion in tragedy." *Judaism* 28:72–79.

Green, A. (1983). The dead mother. In *On Private Madness* (1986), pp. 142–173. Madison, Conn.: International University Press.

Greenacre, P. (1956). Experiences of awe in childhood. *Psychoanalytic Study of the Child* 11:9–30.

Grinberg, L. (1962). On a specific aspect of countertransference due to the patient's projective identification. *International Journal of Psycho-Analysis* 43:436–440.

Guntrip, H. (1956). *Psychotherapy and Religion.* New York: Harper.

Harrison, I. B. (1975). On the maternal origins of awe. *Psychoanalytic Study of the Child* 30:181–195.

Jones, J. W. (1991). *Contemporary Psychoanalysis and Religion: Transference and Transcendence.* New Haven: Yale University Press.

Joseph, B. (1982). Addiction to near-death. *International Journal of Psycho-analysis* 63:449–56.

——— (1981). Toward the experience of psychic pain. In *Do I Dare Disturb the Universe? A Memorial to Wilfred R. Bion,* ed. J. S. Grotstein, pp. 92–102. Beverly Hills, Calif.: Caesura Press.

Khan, M. M. R. (1979). *Alienation in Perversions.* London: Karnac.

Kübler-Ross, E. (1969). *On Death and Dying.* New York: Macmillan.

Lacan, J. (1960). The subversion of the subject and the dialectic of desire in the Freudian unconscious. In *Ecrits: A Selection* (1977), trans. A. Sheridan and ed. J.-A. Miller, pp. 292–325. London: Routledge.

Lamm, N. (1990). *Torah u-Mada.* Northvale, N.J.: Jason Aronson.

Laplanche, J., and Pontalis, J.-B. (1973). *The Language of Psycho-Analysis.* New York: Norton.

McDargh, J. (1984). *Psychoanalytic Object Relations Theory and the Study of Religion.* Lanhan, Md.: University Press of America.

——— (1993). On Developing a psychotheological perspective. In *Exploring Religious Landscapes: Religious and Spiritual Experiences in Psychotherapy,* ed. M. L. Randour, pp. 172–193. New York: Columbia University Press.

Meier, L. (1987). Does death confer meaning on life? A psycho-biblical approach. In *Guilt, Suffering, and Death: The Impact and Challenge,* ed. L. Meier. Special issue of *Journal of Psychology and Judaism* 11:103–120.

——— (1988). *Jewish Values in Psychotherapy.* Washington, D. C.: University Press of America.

Meissner, W. W. (1984). *Psychoanalysis and Religious Experience*. New Haven: Yale University Press.

Meltzer, D. and Williams, M. H. (1988). *The Apprehension of Beauty: The Role of Aesthetic Conflict in Development, Violence, and Art*. Perthshire: Clunie Press.

Mitscherlich, A., and Mitscherlich, M. (1975). *The Inability to Mourn*. Trans. B. R. Placzek. New York: Grove Press.

Modell, A. H. (1990). *Other Times, Other Realities*. Cambridge, Mass.: Harvard University Press.

———— (1993). *The Private Self*. Cambridge, Mass.: Harvard University Press.

Moran, F. M. (1993). *Subject and Agency in Psychoanalysis*. New York: New York University Press.

Moses, R., and Moses-Hrushovski, R. (1990). Reflections on the sense of entitlement. *Psychoanalytic Study of the Child* 45:61–78.

Oden, T. (1967). *Contemporary Theology and Psychotherapy*. Philadelphia: Westminster Press.

Ogden, T. (1989). *The Primitive Edge of Experience*. Northvale, N.J.: Jason Aronson.

———— (1994). *Subjects of Analysis*. London: Kranac.

Pollock, G. H. (1961). Mourning and adaptation. *International Journal of Psycho-Analysis* 42:341–361.

Pruyser, P. (1983). *The Play of the Imagination: Toward a Psychoanalysis of Culture*. New York: International University Press.

Quinodoz, J.-M. (1991). *The Taming of Solitude: Separation Anxiety in Psychoanalysis*. London: Routledge.

Randour, M. L. ed. (1993). *Exploring Religious Landscapes: Religious and Spiritual Experiences in Psychotherapy*. New York: Columbia University Press.

Rizzuto, A.-M. (1979). *The Birth of the Living God*. Chicago: University of Chicago Press.

Rubenstein, R. L. (1967). *The Religious Imagination*. New York: Bobbs-Merrill.

Schafer, R. (1970). The psychoanalytic vision of reality. *International Journal of Psycho-Analysis*. 51:279–97.

Schimmel, S. (1987). Job and the psychology of suffering and doubt. *Journal of Psychology and Judaism* 11:239–249.

Schore, A. (1994). *Affect Regulation and the Origin of the Self.* New Jersey: Lawrence Erlbaum.

Segal, H. (1952). A psychoanalytic approach to aesthetics. In *The Work of Hanna Segal: Delusion, Artistic Creativity, and Other Psycho-Analytic Essays* (1986), pp. 185–205. London: Free Associations Press.

Shapiro, D. S. (1967). The ideological foundations of Halakhah. *Tradition* 9:100–122.

Soloveitchik, J. D. (1944). *Ish ha-Halakhah.* In *Ish ha-Halakhah— Galu'ive-Nistar* (1979), pp. 10–113. Jerusalem: World Zionist Organization.

———— (1978a). Redemption, prayer, and Talmud Torah. *Tradition* 17:55–72.

———— (1978b). Majesty and humility. *Tradition* 17:25–37.

Spero, M. H. (1977). Halakhah as psychology: Explicating the laws of mourning. *Tradition* 16:172–184.

———— (1980a). Sin as neurosis—neurosis as sin: Further implications of the halakhic metapsychology. In *Judaism and Psychology: Halakhic Perspectives*, pp. 49–63.

———— (1980b). *Judaism and Psychology: Halakhic Perspectives.* New York: Yeshiva University Press/Ktav.

———— (1980c). Psychology as Halakhah: Toward a halakhic metapsychology. In *Judaism and Psychology: Halakhic Perspectives* (1980), pp. 11–30. New York: Yeshiva University Press/Ktav.

———— (1986). *Handbook of Psychotherapy and Jewish Ethics.* New York/Jerusalem: Feldheim.

———— (1992a). *Religious Objects as Psychological Structures.* Chicago: University of Chicago Press.

———— (1992b). Can psychoanalytic insights reveal the knowability and the aesthetics of the Holocaust? *Journal of Social Work and Policy in Israel* 6–5:123–170.

———— (1994). Religious patients' metaphors in the light of transference and countertransference considerations. *Israel Journal of Psychiatry* 31:145–161.

———— (1995). Countertransference-derived elaboration of religious conflicts and representational states. *American Journal of Psychotherapy* 49:68–94.

———— (1996). Original sin, the symbolization of desire, and the development of mind: A psychoanalytic gloss on the Garden of Eden. *Psychoanalysis and Contemporary Thought,* 19:499–562.

Spero, S. (1983). *Morality, Halakhah, and the Jewish Tradition.* New York: Yeshiva University Press/Ktav.

Steinberg, A. (1922). Religion and science—Appendix. *Encyclopedia of Jewish Medical Ethics,* vol. III, pp. 399–467. Jerusalem: Falk Schlesinger Institute of Medical Ethics/Shaarei Tzedek Hospital.

Stern, D. N. (1985). *The Interpersonal World of the Infant: A View from Psychoanalysis and Developmental Psychology.* New York: Basic Books.

Strachey, J. (1934). The nature of the therapeutic action in psychoanalysis. *International Journal of Psycho-Analysis* 15:117–126.

Sugarman, A., and Jaffe, L. S. (1989). A developmental line of transitional phenomena. In *The Facilitating Environment: Clinical Applications of Winnicott's Theory,* ed. M. G. Fromm and B. L. Smith, pp. 88–129. Madison, Conn.: International University Press.

Tähkä, V. (1984). Dealing with object loss. *Scandinavian Psychoanalytic Review* 7:13–33.

Vergote, A. (1978). *Guilt and Desire: Religious Attitudes and their Psychological Dimensions* (1988). Trans. M. H. Wood. New Haven: Yale University Press.

Volkan, V. (1981). *Linking Objects and Linking Phenomena.* New York: International University Press.

———— (1993). What the Holocaust means to a non-Jewish psychoanalyst. In *Persistent Shadows of the Holocaust: The Meaning to Those Not Directly Affected,* ed. R. Moses, pp. 81–105. Madison, Conn.: International University Press.

Waelder, R. (1936). The principle of multiple function. *Psychoanalytic Quarterly* 5:45–61.

Winnicott, D. W. (1953). Transitional objects and transitional phenomena. In *Playing and Reality* (1971), pp. 1–25. London: Tavistock.

——— (1958). The capacity to be alone. In *The Maturational Processes and the Facilitating Environment* (1965), pp. 29–36. Madison, Conn.: International University Press.

——— (1959). The fate of the transitional object. In *Psycho-Analytic Explorations* (1989), eds. C. Winnicott, R. Shepherd, and M. Davis, pp. 53–58. Cambridge, Mass.: Harvard University Press.

——— (1963). Fear of breakdown. In *Psycho-Analytic Explorations* (1989), eds. C. Winnicott, R. Shepherd, and M. Davis, pp. 87–95. Cambridge, Mass.: Harvard University Press.

——— (1969). Mother's madness appearing in the clinical material as an ego-alien factor. In *Psycho-Analytic Explorations* (1989), eds. C. Winnicott, R. Shepherd, and M. Davis, pp. 375–382. Cambridge, Mass.: Harvard University Press.

Wohlgelernter, D. K. (1981). Death wish in the Bible. *Tradition* 19:131–140.

Zilboorg, G. (1967). A psychiatric consideration of the ascetic ideal. *Psychoanalysis and Religion*, pp. 63–79. London: George Allan and Unwin.

7

Theological Responses to the Hurban from within the Hurban

Nehemia Polen

INTRODUCTION

It is a striking fact that in the staggeringly vast sweep of the Holocaust, thus far only two extended documents of Orthodox Jewish theological reflection have come to the attention of the scholarly community. The specification of the set we have in mind—which will be the focus of this essay—requires some clarification. Its defining characteristics include the following:

(1) The document must be essentially theological in its orientation. This is meant to exclude, for example, halakhic responsa, but it includes *derashot* and other theological/philosophical reflections grounded in rab-

binic literature broadly defined: *aggadah* and Midrash especially, as well as medieval Jewish philosophy, biblical exegesis, kabbala, Hasidism, *mussar*, and related bodies of literature.

(2) The document must have been written during the Holocaust. This stipulation is not without ambiguity. Did the Holocaust begin in January 1942 with the Wansee Conference, in the summer of 1941 with the German invasion of the Soviet Union and the Einsatzgruppen mass killings, or perhaps with the German invasion of Poland and the start of the war in September 1939? In any event, for the purposes of this paper, documents written before September 1939 will not be included in our analysis. We will consider the date for the end of the Holocaust to be May 1945, with Germany's unconditional surrender and the end of the war in Europe.

This specification excludes many significant documents from the purview of the present paper: documents from before the war that might be seen to have prophetically foreseen the catastrophe (such as certain writings of Rabbi Meir Simcha of Dvinsk, among others), as well as responses to the rise of Nazism in Germany that were written before the war (such as essays of Rabbi Elhonon Wasserman, among others).[1]

Also excluded are postwar theological responses to the Holocaust by those who were threatened by the Nazi onslaught but who managed to escape, such as

---

[1] See the material cited in Gershon Greenberg, "Myth and Catastrophe in Simha Elberg's Religious Thought," *Tradition* 26:1 (1991), 60, n. 2; cf. also Hillel Goldberg, "Holocaust Theology: The Survivors' Statement," *Tradition* 20:4 (1982), 341–357.

the writings of the Satmar Rebbe, among many others.

This provision also excludes postwar testimonies and reminiscences, which, however valuable and significant, cannot be considered contemporaneous documents.

(3) We also exclude documents written during the Holocaust but outside the European theater, and thus outside the perimeter of oppression and degradation and the immediate threat of the Nazi extermination machine. This excludes wartime writings from *Eretz Israel* and America, for example. We include, however, writings from Hungary: while the German occupation came only in March 1944 and the existence of a wartime regime allied with the Nazis actually shielded the Jewish population (temporarily) from the systematic workings of the Final Solution, yet Nazi-style juridical exclusion, degradation, dehumanization, expulsion, and massacres were already endemic throughout most of the war period.

With our universe of analysis thus delineated with a reasonable degree of specificity and precision, we return to the claim in this essay's opening statement: thus far, only two documents of Orthodox theological reflection from the Holocaust have come to the attention of the scholarly community. These two are Rabbi Kalonymus Shapira's *Esh Kodesh* and Rabbi Yissachar Shlomo Teichthal's *Em ha-Banim Semehah*. In a moment we shall discuss these documents and append one more item to this very short list, but first let us examine the significance of our specification set.

While the paucity of exemplars within our set is indeed striking, it is hardly incomprehensible. For those who were directly caught in its net, the period of the Holocaust was hardly a time for creative religious thought. While many diaries, chronicles, poems, and other works of historical and literary interest have survived, the time was clearly not conducive to sustained theological reflection. This only increases the significance of those very few documents that did survive.

By focusing our analysis on documents written during the Holocaust, we do not in any way intend to diminish the value of works written before or after the war; to this date, a comprehensive treatment of all such documents has not been attempted and is a desideratum. Our intention, rather, is to restrict the domain of analysis to a field appropriate to one paper. In addition, we are suggesting that documents written during the Holocaust indeed have a special value, as they are direct responses to the unparalleled catastrophe, unmediated and unrefined by the opportunity for reflection that distance (either geographical or chronological) affords.

It cannot be overlooked that in all likelihood other such documents were written but did not survive. It is said, for example, that during the war Rabbi Menahem Zemba of Warsaw wrote on the laws and theology of mourning. But this work, if it did exist, and no doubt others like it, is lost to history, and we cannot analyze what we do not have. This again only serves to underscore the preciousness of those few works that we have in our possession. It is to them that we now turn.

I. *SIFTEI SHLOMO*

Before we discuss the two works mentioned above that already have received scholarly attention, we shall introduce one that comes within the domain of the above specifications but that, so far as I can tell, until now has escaped notice in the scholarly literature on the Holocaust. I am referring to Rabbi Shlomo Zalman Unsdorfer's collection of *derashot, Siftei Shlomo.*[2] Rabbi Shlomo Zalman Unsdorfer (1887–1944) was a *maggid* in Pressburg (Bratislava), in Slovakia. In his youth he was a student of Rabbi Yosef Zvi Dushinsky and Rabbi Akiva Sofer. During the war he remained at his post in Pressburg, giving support and encouragement to the beleaguered community, until he was taken to Auschwitz in the fall of 1944. *Siftei Shlomo* was published in 1972 by the author's son, Rabbi Shmuel Alexander Unsdorfer, who had been sent by his father to yeshiva in England in 1939, before the war's onset. According to the publisher's account in the introduction, the author originally wrote the *derashot* in Yiddish and the younger Unsdorfer translated them into Hebrew. The book contains an approbation by the rabbi of Pressburg, Akiva Sofer, dated September 25, 1947. Published privately and evidently never reprinted, the work appears to have had a very small circulation.

Rabbi Unsdorfer's homiletic approach is rooted in Nahmanides' typological approach to Scripture.[3] His ability to find parallels to the contemporary situation in biblical passages provided his flock with a measure of consolation and hope. An example is the *derashah* for *Parashat Lekh-Lekha,* 5702 (November 11, 1941); a short explana-

---

[2]Edited and published by Shmuel Alexander Unsdorfer (Montreal, 1972). My thanks to Rabbi Avi Weinstein, who introduced me to this work and graciously shared his insights with me. Rabbi Weinstein plans to publish extended selections from *Siftei Shlomo* in translation. [It just has come to my attention (8 Menahem-Av, 5756) that *Siftei Shlomo* is cited in Abraham Fuchs, *The Holocaust in Rabbinic Sources (Responsa and Sermons)*, Jerusalem 1995 (Hebrew).]

[3]See Amos Funkenstein, "Medieval Exegesis and Historical Consciousness," in idem, *Perceptions of Jewish History* (Berkeley: University of California Press, 1993), 88–130.

tory remark prefaces the *derashah,* noting that it was delivered "at a time of great trouble, may God spare us, when they decreed and began to expel Jews from our city." Rabbi Unsdorfer writes that during normal times, his community would read the words of *Lekh-Lekha* enjoining Abraham to leave his homeland as historical recounting, but this year the words were aimed directly at his community, an accurate description of its own tragic circumstance. The rabbi counsels his flock to be strong in faith, to accept everything in love, sure in the knowledge that it was all for the good, now or "for the coming generations":

> ... We who believe in God are compared to the stars: it is precisely in the night's deepest darkness that the stars shine most brightly. So it is with us in times of trouble. God spare us: at that time our trust in God shines, and the great power of Israel's sanctity is revealed in their faith and righteousness. (30–32)

Later in the same year, on December 21, 1941, shortly after the outbreak of war between America and Japan (to which he refers directly), he wrote the following for *Parashat Vayeshev:*

> This Torah section, from start to finish, is all about dreams. When a person lives in peace and tranquillity he has no need for dreams. Who wants to interrupt a quiet, contented life with dreams? Who loves dreams? Who needs dreams? Someone who is suffering, God spare us, someone who is persecuted, just as Joseph was persecuted by his brothers, just as the royal cupbearer in prison. So it is with us today: we are as in a dream, because we are saturated in suffering. They have forbidden us to speak, no one dares utter a sound out of fear of the enemy. But they could not prohibit us from dreaming, and with our dreams we see the future: our sheaf has risen and stands firm. This is our consolation: just like the dreams of Joseph, they will certainly come to pass. (64–66)

Until the very end, Rabbi Unsdorfer preached his message of hope, consolation, and the sacredness of Israel. His *derashot*, so far as I can see, display no change over time, whether in terms of homiletic style or theological posture. Their creativity lies in their ability to marshal biblical and rabbinic sources as parallels adumbrating the troubles of his day. *Siftei Shlomo* demonstrates that even during the Holocaust, preachers could maintain the traditional approach to suffering, applying ancient sacred texts to a radically new situation while vigorously affirming the standard theodicy.

Rabbi Unsdorfer was taken to Auschwitz and killed on October 18, 1944.

II. *EM HA-BANIM SEMEHAH*

The second work that satisfies our criteria is Rabbi Yissachar Shlomo Teichthal's *Em ha-Banim Semehah*. As noted above, this work has received the attention of Holocaust writers, in particular Pesach Schindler.[4] Originally published in Budapest in 1943, it was republished in Israel in 1983, in an expanded edition that included footnotes, indices, and other explanatory material.[5] Like many of his rabbinic colleagues, Rabbi Teichthal, a follower of the Munkaczer Rebbe, originally was unsympathetic to the Zionist movement. But the rise of Nazism and the persecution of his people caused him to change his mind. *Em ha-Banim Semehah* is a monograph that draws upon a wide range of

---

[4]See especially "*Tikkun* as Response to Tragedy: *Em Habanim Smeha* of R. Yissakhar Shlomo Taykhtahl—Budapest, 1943," *Holocaust and Genocide Studies* 4:4 (1989), 413–433. Cf. also idem, *Hasidic Responses to the Holocaust in the Light of Hasidic Thought* (Hoboken: Ktav, 1990), 7–8, passim; idem, "Rabbi Issachar Teichthal on Hurban and Redemption," *Tradition* 21 (1984), 63–79.

[5]Jerusalem: Pri Ha-Aretz, 1983.

traditional sources to make a single point: that Jews must work actively to redeem the Land of Israel and restore it to Jewish sovereignty and that the persecutions of his day were a consequence of having rejected earlier opportunities for emigration to the Holy Land. While not a tract of political Zionism, it is broadly sympathetic to the Zionist movement's aims and sees a messianic dimension in rebuilding of the Land. Rabbi Teichthal sharply criticizes the rabbinic leadership that opposed earlier opportunities for aliyah:

> Had the rebuilding of the Land proceeded earlier with the consent and the participation of all of Israel, the Land would have been ready to receive a large portion of diaspora Jewry. A significant portion of our recently murdered Jewish brethren would have been spared by virtue of their being in the Land of Israel. But now, who takes responsibility for all the innocent blood which has been shed in our time? It appears to me that those leaders who prevented Jews from going and joining the builders, will not be able to wipe the blood-guilt from their hands. (18)

Aside from the author's acknowledgment that he originally was dismissive of the movement to build Israel (21) and that only exile from his home provoked him to re-examine the question anew, the reader does not discern any movement or undercurrent of complexity within the text, which is all of one piece. Like Rabbi Unsdorfer, he cites Nahmanides' Torah commentary, but rather than simply drawing parallels between the biblical narratives and the sufferings of his day, he writes that "[Nahmanides] teaches us that we can detect from the nature of the suffering that Heaven is pointing out the desired path: to make Aliyah to the Holy Land." (147) The meaning of the catastrophic destruction and suffering is stated simply: it is all a divine sign prodding the Jewish people to return to its motherland.

In his introduction, Rabbi Teichthal informs us that the writing of *Em ha-Banim Semehah* was the fulfillment of a vow taken in a time of distress, with the hope that the merit of the Land of Israel would protect him from mishap (25–27 and 33). This might explain in part the single-minded concentration and passionate intensity with which he gathers sources and texts to make his argument for aliyah and building Israel.

III. *ESH KODESH*

The third and final exemplar is Rabbi Kalonymus Shapira's *Esh Kodesh,* written in Occupied Warsaw and the Warsaw Ghetto, 1939–1942, and published in Israel in 1960. I have written about *Esh Kodesh* elsewhere[6] and will summarize and extend my findings here as they relate to the theme of suffering.

Rabbi Shapira's responses to suffering can be grouped in two major categories. The first is a set of psycho-spiritual responses, heuristic strategies for facing and overcoming suffering. The second is a more purely theocentric response. We shall examine each type individually.

Strategies for Transformation of Suffering

In the pages of *Esh Kodesh,* we find a variety of strategies for confronting suffering and persecution. Near the beginning of the work, Rabbi Shapira draws upon the ancient tradition that martyrs do not feel the pain of their martyrdom. He casts this tradition in a characteristically hasidic

---

[6]See Nehemia Polen, *The Holy Fire: The Teachings of Rabbi Kalonymus Kalman Shapira, the Rebbe of the Warsaw Ghetto* (Northvale, NJ: Jason Aronson, 1994).

framework: martyrs elevate their senses to the metaphysical World of Thought, thereby stripping themselves of corporeality and pain.[7]

Other strategies involve transforming raw fear into sacred
awe;[8] emphasizing Israel's greatness;[9] and noting that even
in conditions of acute suffering, mutuality of caring and
human relationship are always achievable.[10] We call these
psycho-spiritual strategies because, while they are anchored
completely in the rabbinic-kabbalistic-Hasidic worldview,
their focus is on the individual's suffering and how to transcend it.

One particularly significant motif in this category is that
of suffering as sacrificial offering; the individual is urged to
envision his losses as being placed upon the altar as a sacrifice lovingly offered to God. The precedent for this is a
famous talmudic passage in which the loss of fat and blood
that a Jew suffers on a fast day is to be considered a sacrificial offering.[11] A related motif is Rabbi Shapira's statement
that those who have been killed because they are Jews are
to be considered "God's servants"—saintly martyrs—even
though they did not freely choose their deaths.[12] This is an
early version of what would become a standard motif of
post-Holocaust theology: that all of the six million, whatever
religious convictions they had in life and whatever the precise circumstances of their deaths, are to be considered
kedoshim (holy martyrs).

---

[7]*Esh Kodesh*, 8–9; *Holy Fire* [=HF], 67–68.
[8]*HF*, 37–38.
[9]*HF*, 44–49.
[10]*HF*, 49–53.
[11]*Cf. Berakhot* 17a; *HF*, 62–63.
[12]*HF*, 63.

Divine Weeping

The second major approach to suffering in *Esh Kodesh* is more purely theocentric. In it, the emphasis is not so much on how to grapple with the suffering, but with the question of its origin and meaning. Here we find a dramatic shift over the course of the three years during which *Esh Kodesh* was written. At first Rabbi Shapira tends to the traditional theological motif of the divine Father reprimanding his son for his waywardness.[13] This theme eventually is overshadowed by an acknowledgment that there are sufferings that might be incomprehensible and counterproductive, incapable of assimilation into any framework of human benefit or understanding—like the commandments known as *hukkim*, which have no rational explanation and which indeed might be designed to challenge our concept of rationality itself.[14]

The *hukkah* is an expression of God's will, which might be both incomprehensible and paradoxical. If there are *hukkim*-type commandments, there are also *hukkah*-type sufferings. Responding to such sufferings requires a total surrender of the critical cognitive faculties, a complete submersion in the purifying waters of faith.

Rather than attempting a theodicy for this category of suffering—which he came to see as the appropriate one for what was besetting the Jews in the Warsaw Ghetto—Rabbi Shapira shifts the emphasis from human suffering to divine suffering.

Drawing heavily upon passages in rabbinic literature that speak of God's suffering,[15] Rabbi Shapira turns the idea of

---

[13]*HF*, 106–110.

[14]*EK*, 84–85; *HF*, 70–94.

[15]A summary of this theme can be found in Jacob J. Petuchowski, *Theology and Poetry: Studies in the Medieval Piyyut* (London, 1978),

divine transcendence on its head. Precisely because God is infinite, his suffering is infinite and beyond human conception. It is the infinite magnitude of Divine suffering that paradoxically explains the absence of a visible Divine response to Israel's catastrophe. God has not abandoned his people. Quite the contrary: God's distress is so great that He is forced to escape to the innermost domain of Heaven, to weep in secret. If one tear from the flow of divine weeping were to enter the world, the world would explode. So God must hide the awesome secret of His weeping and suffering; this is what we perceive as *hester panim*.[16]

One should not confuse Rabbi Shapira's writing on divine suffering and hiddenness, on the one hand, and modern ideas of process theology, on the other. In certain versions of this theology, one reads of a finite divinity who has relinquished omnipotence completely and unconditionally in order to grant radical freedom to his creation.[17] It is important to recall that Rabbi Shapira's concept of divine pain and hiddenness is generated by emphasizing God's infini-

---

ch. 8: "The Suffering God." See also Henry Slonimsky, *Essays* (Cincinnati, 1978), 41–48; also Michael Fishbane, "The Holy One Sits and Roars," *Journal of Jewish Thought and Philosophy* 1 (1991), 1–21.

[16]This is based on a reading of *Hagiga* 5b. See *HF*, ch. 6 and 8.

[17]See, for example, Hans Jonas, "The Concept of God after Auschwitz," in A. Rosenberg and G. E. Myers, eds., *Echoes from the Holocaust: Philosophical Reflections on a Dark Time* (Philadelphia: Temple, 1988), 292–305. (This is the most recent version of an essay that has appeared elsewhere in several different forms; see ibid., 292, for full publication history.)

It is interesting that Jon Levenson takes pains to forestall and disentangle a similar misunderstanding in his *Creation and the Persistence of Evil: The Jewish Drama of Divine Omnipotence* (Princeton: Princeton University Press, 1994). See especially the new preface to the 1994 edition, xv–xxviii.

tude, not finitude. In line with kabbalistic thought, Rabbi Shapira understands that the eruption of God into the physical realm in no way limits or affects His infinitude; rather, it is the capstone of unlimited divine power to be able to enter the finite realm as well. In a famous formulation of Rabbi Azriel of Gerona, "If one were to assume that His power reigns in the unbounded but does not extend to the domain of the bounded, one would thereby diminish His perfection."[18] The multitiered interleavings and recursive self-mirrorings of the sefirotic system allow for the appearance of the upper levels within the lower, the infinite within the finite. For this reason, Rabbi Shapira never entirely gives up hope in divine salvation in a historical sense; he continues to hope and pray for deliverance until the very end.[19]

In the later pages of *Esh Kodesh,* Rabbi Shapira does not offer a theodicy; in fact, there are passages where he refutes its possibility of theodicy, denying the enterprise any legitimacy.[20] Instead of attempting to justify God, he assumes the posture of total submission, of absolute surrender, of complete immersion in the waters of the divine will. At the same time, he does not shrink from calling God to task, imploring Him in the name of His suffering people

---

[18]*Perush Eser Sefirot* (cited in Rabbi Meir ibn Gabbai, *Avodat ha-Kodesh* 1:8). Cf. J. Dan and R. C. Kiener, *The Early Kabbalah* (New York, 1986), 90.

[19]In *Esh Kodesh,* 161–163, Rabbi Shapira explains that God is linked to the realm of the finite through the Torah, which is at once the will of the infinite God and the template of creation for the bounded world of space and time. As God's revelation, the Torah is thus the vehicle for the penetration or eruption of the infinite into the finite. The hope for salvation lies precisely in communion with God by means of the Torah.

[20]For details, see *HF*, 70–94.

to bring deliverance. At one point he even suggests that God perform the mitzvah of *teshuva* (repentance.)[21]

He also freely admits where he has been wrong. Perhaps the most powerful instance is a passage written in late 1942, revising an earlier passage from the winter of 1941. In the earlier passage, Rabbi Shapira had argued that, for all the sufferings of the contemporary period, nothing in them overshadowed what Jews had endured in earlier periods of catastrophe, such as the time of the Temple's destruction. The marginal note from late 1942 (after the great deportation of the summer of 1942, when most Jews were sent to their deaths in Treblinka) acknowledges that the most recent events were indeed different, surpassing in horrific cruelty anything previously recorded in Jewish history.[22]

Toward the end of *Esh Kodesh*, there is also a heightened emphasis on human initiative, what the kabbalists call *itaruta de-le-tata* (arousal from below). At a time when there appeared to be only silence from Heaven, Rabbi Shapira works to break through that silence by means of a self-generated call to spirit. Because *itaruta de-le-eila* (the gift of grace from above) seemed to be temporarily unavailable, the Hasid, through his own initiative and labor, would have to wrest the spirit of song from the abyss itself. At a time when the enemy was doing all he could to push God out of the world, Rabbi Shapira knew that it was the Hasid's task to awaken the numinous in one's soul, inviting the indwelling of the Holy Spirit to recover Her place in the world.

This posture places the emphasis on human initiative, human creativity, and divine anchoring in the human (Jewish) condition. Man's suffering is transcended by a shift of focus to the suffering of God, and God's suffering provokes

---

[21] *HF*, 94–105.
[22] *EK*, 139; *HF*, 84.

a move to new birth, to new creation, to the eruption of new initiatives out of the abyss.

Esh Kodesh provides us with a typology of suffering. The relevance of the traditional approach continues to be affirmed: there is indeed suffering that is divine chastisement and for which the appropriate response is *teshuva*. This kind of suffering might act as a prod, a sign, a reminder, a tocsin. Just as times of prosperity are particularly conducive for serving God with enthusiasm and joy, times of suffering are opportunities to serve Him with a broken heart and the outpouring of the soul.

Furthermore, much suffering can be attenuated, softened, meliorated by cognitive reframing. A path to achieving dignity in suffering is consciously accepting the suffering as sacrifice and decisively offering it up to God on the altar of one's soul. Even when the suffering is caused by a human enemy's hatred and persecution, one never must forget the dignity of Israel, the fact that each Jew is a prince and a child of the Master of the Universe. The evil that the enemy embodies will be transformed one day. Because the Hasid recalls the Baal Shem Tov's essential teaching that the bad is the throne for the good, that evil is only provisional and phenomenal, that in the end Satan will be transformed into a sacred angel whose name encodes the divine, the Hasid is secure in the inner knowledge that Israel will triumph over her persecutors.[23]

All this having been said, there was still a deep mystery in the unparalleled cruelty the Jews were experiencing as Rabbi Shapira taught and wrote. As he acknowledged, there are some sufferings that completely resist interpretation and that are incomprehensible. Here the only answer is surrender, as well as communion with other human beings in

---

[23]*HF,* 122–135.

suffering and with the divine holy One whose suffering is infinite and infinitely hidden.

We might summarize Rabbi Shapira's views on suffering in the following manner: In contrition and surrender, man fully accepts the reality of his personal suffering and participates by compassion in the suffering of others. But with the eyes of faith, he sees through the evil that is the proximate cause of the suffering and believes that the vector of evil one day will be transformed and transmuted into a powerful vector of good. In faith, man engages in self-examination and self-improvement. He prays for deliverance. Equally in faith, he protests, imploring God to desist, to turn back, to relent.

But what if deliverance in the hoped-for, concrete sense refuses to come?

In the end, what remains is a relationship. A relationship with the other, compassion for the other, suffering with the other, is itself a kind of redemption. For what is redemption if not the finding of our most fully human self in the act of *imitatio dei*? It is not just that God suffers with us, for us, because we suffer, but that God is most God when He suffers; He comes most into Himself when He identifies with Israel, with her humanity, her vulnerability, her personal and collective destiny. Similarly, we become most like God when we transcend our own suffering and participate in that of others and of God. Because God is God, He suffers most intensely and infinitely; His suffering must remain hidden. But because God remains God, He remains the hope for redemption in a concrete sense. Because man is man, he does not decide when or how to end his suffering and he does not claim to know its meaning. But because man is man, he can rouse himself, take hold of inner, hidden, mysterious resources—in other words, grasp his faith—and thereby hope to rouse God to manifest, physical redemption.

Rabbi Shapira observes that in Jewish history, it is often precisely during periods of suffering and persecution that the most profound and powerful sacred texts have emerged.[24] Furthermore, Rabbi Shapira introduces the notion of suffering itself as a kind of sacred text.[25] Like all texts, suffering captures and conveys the soul of its author; it demands interpretation, which resides as much with the reader as with the writer. Like all communication, it may be ignored or dismissed. But to interpret is to wrest meaning from the abyss.

Rabbi Shapira made his own suffering into Torah, a communion-text that bares his soul, yielding a triadic fusion of student, text, and divine author. All who study it make contact with the soul of the human author, with their own soul, and with the soul of the One who, in unfathomable ways, teaches Torah to His people of Israel.

IV. COMPARISON OF THE THREE DOCUMENTS

As noted in the introduction to this essay, it is indeed striking how minuscule is the pool of documents that fit our criteria for analysis. Each of the three works we have examined displays a different mode of response to the suffering of the Holocaust. *Siftei Shlomo* demonstrates that a preacher could and did respond with courage, compassion, and creativity and still remain entirely within the traditional worldview of his youth, with theology and theodicy apparently unaffected. The homilies of *Siftei Shlomo* are effective as *derashot* but are utterly conventional theologically. This is precisely the tale they tell: that one can go through

---

[24]*EK*, 178; cf. 75–76; 127–130.
[25]*EK*, 100.

the unprecedented, the unparalleled, the overwhelmingly
incomprehensible, and still be unshaken in one's pure faith
and commitment.

Rabbi Teichthal's *Em ha-Banim Semehah* is different: he
grapples with the events of his day and is transformed by
them. They provoke him into reading the traditional
sources in ways he had not perceived before, and they
awaken him to the spiritual beauty in the lives of individuals whose paths and accomplishments he previously had
dismissed. But for Rabbi Teichthal, the transformation pertains to one matter: the enterprise of rebuilding the Land
of Israel.

In Rabbi Shapira's *Esh Kodesh*, however, the shift is
more fundamental, touching upon the deepest layers of
faith: a faith beyond reason, beyond the mind's grasp, beyond despair. Faith that God would intervene to save the
Jews was transformed into faith in God despite the evidence
that He had *not* intervened to save the Jews. The image of
God as the righteous judge of Israel's actions receded; the
mythic and participatory consciousness of divine weeping
replaced the rational accounting of reward and chastisement.
Esh Kodesh reminds us, as Rabbi Jonathan Sacks has
pointed out, that not all theology of suffering is theodicy,[26]
that there are faith-filled responses that seek not to justify
God, but to surrender the self as a sacred offering, to protest, to rouse the divine realm to responsive action, to commune in weeping—to do all of these things serially or even
simultaneously, but withal to maintain and even deepen
one's relationship with the Holy One of Israel, the One who
is beyond all conception.

---

[26]Jonathan Sacks, *Crisis and Covenant: Jewish Thought after the
Holocaust* (Manchester and New York: Manchester University Press,
1993), 40.

Each of the three documents that has survived, then, must speak for, stand for, be emblematic of others that might have been written, or that we wished had been written. The response of a powerful conventionalism that eloquently transcends its conventionalism; the response of renewed commitment to ingathering the Diaspora, redeeming Israel, and uniting her children in unconditional love; and the response of human spiritual initiative that penetrates the deepest mystery of divine suffering in partnership with Israel: the elements of this triad of responses complement and frame each other, by comparison and by contrast giving honor and tribute to the awesome power and courage of their authors, and to the suffering and eternal people which gave birth to them.

8

Popular Jewish Religious Responses during the Holocaust and Its Aftermath*

Yaffa Eliach

Every day, every child, after studying the daily lessons prescribed by our sages, should learn about the Holocaust, for it says in our holy Torah: "Then it shall come to pass, when many evils and troubles are come upon them, that this song shall testify before them as a witness." (Deut. 31:21) The

---

*This paper is based on my original research and writing about Jewish tradition during the Holocaust era, as well as my detailed, systematic study of the shtetl of Eishyshok and its vicinity during a 900-year period. It draws on the documentation for the *Tower of Life*, my exhibit at the United States Holocaust Memorial Museum, and on my book on *There Once Was a World: A Nine-Hundred-Year Chronicle of the Shtetl of Eishyshok*, Little, Brown, 1998.

*suffering and the testimonies when told by Holocaust sur-
vivors are a song, a hymn of praise, a testimony to the eter-
nity of the Jewish people and the greatness of their spirit.*
—Rabbi Israel Spira, the rabbi of Bluzhov
(Yaffa Eliach, *Hasidic Tales of the Holocaust*, New York:
Oxford University Press, 1982)

During the Holocaust and its aftermath, the executioner,
the bystander, and the ultimate victim in each acted and
reacted within the framework of their particular tradition
and culture.

The Holocaust is the first major catastrophe to take place
in secular times; the Bogdan Chmielnitski massacres were
the last major Jewish calamity to take place during a religious age. During the massacres of 1648–9, the entire Jewish world was governed by Jewish law, tradition, community
responsibility, and the concept that "all Israel are sureties
one for another." [1]

The Jewish chronicles of the time mention 100,000
people killed and 300 communities destroyed. The Tartars
took many Jews captive and sold them into slavery on the
markets in Turkey. Some managed to escape. But a large
segment of them were redeemed by Jews in various locations.
The Lithuanian Council passed a resolution with regards to
the refugees sold into slavery and imposed tariffs and taxes
on the communities for the redemption of the captives
(*pidyon shvuyim*). "Many souls of Israel which were taken
into captivity assimilated among [the nations] and were
almost lost among them. . . . we have written an authoriza-
tion to all communities and to every place where there is a
minyan (quorum) of Jews . . . to redeem every soul." [2]

The refugee problem was another dimension of the

---

[1] *Shavuot* 39a.
[2] *Pinkas Medinat Lita* (1649), 452.

Bogdan Chmielnitski massacres that the Lithuanian Council attempted to solve.[3] Many Jewish communities and individuals throughout the Diaspora—especially those of Turkey, Italy, Amsterdam, and Hamburg—offered food, clothing, money, and shelter.

Gluckel of Hameln (1646–1724), a contemporary, describes how her family opened its doors and hearts to the refugees:

> About this time, the Vilna Jews were forced to leave Poland. Many of them, stricken with contagious diseases, found their way to Hamburg. Having as yet neither hospital nor other accommodations, we needs must bring the sick among them into our homes. At least ten of them, whom my father took under his charge, lay in the upper floor of our house. Some recovered; others died. And my sister Ilkele and I both took sick as well.
>
> My beloved grandmother tended our sick and saw that they lacked for nothing. Though my father and mother disapproved, nothing could stop her from climbing to the garret three or four times a day, in order to nurse them. At length she too fell ill. After ten days in bed she died, at a beautiful old age, and left behind her a good name. For all her seventy-four years she was still as brisk and fresh as a woman of forty.[4]

The massacres had a devastating impact on the family unit. The Lithuanian Council took up the issue of surviving children too young to remember their families and their identity.[5] Children born to mothers who were raped by Chmielnitski's soldiers and the Tartars were yet another

---

[3]*Pinkas Medinat Lita* (1650), 460.

[4]*The Memoirs of Gluckel of Hameln* (New York: Schocken Books, 1977), 19–22.

[5]*Pinkas Medinat Lita* (1650), 461.

problem the communities had to come to terms with, both socially and halakhically.

In 1650 the Lithuanian Council decreed three years of consecutive mourning. It prohibited the wearing of elaborate clothes and ornaments[6] and decided that "no musical instruments be heard in the House of Israel, not even the musical entertainment at weddings for one full year."[7] It also established the twentieth day of the month of Sivan (May–June) as the official day to commemorate the Chmielnitski massacre. In many communities this day was observed until the Holocaust.

The Bogdan Chmielnitski massacres is the last major paradigm for how the Jewish religious community and the Diaspora coped with a major catastrophe in pre-modern times, for how eyewitness chroniclers documented it and pre-secular society memorialized it. Unlike during the 1648–9 massacres and other calamities, during the Holocaust, the ultimate victims were given no options for survival, such as conversion, expulsion, or slavery. Hence the Holocaust's uniqueness. German law legally placed the Jews in German-occupied countries, outside the family of mankind. And it was a time and a place when and where the Jewish community in the free world did not respond in an organized fashion to the needs of the ultimate victims and survivors.

It was a time and a place in which lawyers were dedicated to robbing people of their lives, liberty, and property, not protecting them. It was a time and a place when the Auschwitz doctors, men and women who took the Hippocratic oath to save human lives, dedicated themselves instead to taking them; they transformed themselves from healers to killers. The *Yishuv* in *Eretz* Israel and the Jews

---

[6]*Pinkas Medinat Lita* (1650), 463–468.
[7]*Pinkas Medinat Lita* (1650), 469.

in the free world were involved in rescue attempts along modern, secular, ideological, and political lines. But they failed to create a super, all-inclusive rescue organization that followed historical models based on the ancient dictum "all Israel are sureties one for another." Nor were there any organized preparations, in anticipation of liberation, to help survivors, document the Holocaust within a Jewish context, or memorialize the victims.

The lonely Holocaust victims had to create options in a world with no options. At a time when human beings were stripped naked of everything, even their names, the only resource remaining to them was their inner spiritual strength. In the struggle to survive, this strength became the very essence of their existence. Their beliefs and their traditions became religious Jews' weapons for spiritual resistance in a debased society. But the idea of documenting, commemorating, and memorializing this struggle has yet to find its proper place within the observant Jewish community. This is in contrast to the experience of the secular Jews, for whom the process of documenting and commemorating those aspects of the Holocaust that they find relevant and interesting—the physical resistance and courage, the various political parties and ideologies—has become a veritable religion unto itself. To understand the religious popular response, we must examine major Jewish traditions that governed Jewish life and community as well as traits of the individual survivor, such as familial position, age, gender, whereabouts during the Holocaust, and the duration of the tormented life under Nazi occupation. Was there a difference, for example, between the experience of the Polish Jews west of the Bug River, who came under Nazi occupation in September 1939, and that of the Hungarian Jews, who came under the regime four and a half years later in March 1944.

Paul Tillich has written that "Judaism is more related to time and history than to space and nature." And, indeed, by its very nature Jewish tradition is time-oriented. Time is divided into two major units: sacred and profane, *Kodesh ve-Hol.* These fundamental dimensions dominate Jewish Halakha and life. Its most simplistic manifestation is the Jewish Lunar-Solar calendar, the division of the year into sacred and secular days, holidays, and normal days. However, on both the sacred and secular days, most of the rituals must be performed at prescribed times and are not left to the individual observant Jew's discretion.

This special bond between Judaism and time, which governs every aspect of life, and the Jewish tradition's ability to impose its concept of time wherever Jews lived, was the very essence of Jewish survival during long years of exile from the homeland. During the Holocaust, too, this bond between time and the Jew was crucial in the struggle for survival. The German system placed the ultimate victims outside the sphere of normal time and place. It robbed them of all shreds of individuality—clothes, hair, names, family—and reduced them to faceless, nameless slaves before reducing them to ashes. The victims' ability to superimpose their own time-consciousness on the Nazi system helped them retain their humanity and sanity and possibly cling to life itself. Rabbi Joseph B. Soloveitchik states:

> The basic criterion which distinguishes free man from slave is the kind of relationship each has with time and its experience. Freedom is identical with a rich, colorful, creative time-consciousness. Bondage is identical with passive intuition and reception of an empty, formal time-stream.[8]

----

[8]Joseph B. Soloveitchik, "Kodesh and Chol," *Gesher* 3, no. 1 (June 1966): 16.

In the vast slave kingdom of hundreds of ghettos, concentration camps, death camps, and labor camps, one day was indistinguishable from another: long days from dawn to darkness, with the same endless roll call, the same meager food, the same long marches to and from work, the same deadly blows. It was a place where time was measured heartbeat by heartbeat, where the only variant was the hour of one's death. Yet under the threat of death, a significant number of Jews clung to their tradition and did not succumb to the monotonous camp cadence that spelled total dehumanization. They imposed their concept of time and their traditions on this debased world.

In Radun, the shtetl of the Hafetz Hayyim, Hoshana Rabba was celebrated in the house of Rogowski (where Rabbi Gorelick "ate days" when he was a student at the Radun Yeshiva) after the September 1941 massacre in next-door Eishyshok, just as it had been celebrated for hundreds of years before. Moshe Sonenson, who has just escaped the massacre and was astonished to discover Jewish time flowing uninterruptedly, picked up one of the beaten willow branches and said, "This is how we look bare, beaten and broken." Mr. Rogowski assured him, "Here it will not happen. The grave of the sainted Hafetz Hayyim will protect us. Besides, we are in Byelorussia, where the Jews will be much safer than in Lithuania."[9]

Until the *shehita* in Radun on May 10, 1942, there was a daily, clandestine minyan in private homes. On the eve of Hanukkah in 1942, in a freezing attic facing the gallows and the Hafetz Hayyim's home and yeshiva building, the ghetto's small children were taught about the Festival of

---

[9]Moshe Sonenson, 29 June 1977.

Lights. At Passover, matzot were baked; flour was smuggled in from the mill outside the ghetto.[10]

In the Radun Ghetto, hunger amplified the suffering that shootings, hangings, beatings, cold, and sickness already caused. Trying to feed one's family was a never-ending task and worrying about it was a ceaseless preoccupation, awake or asleep. Observing dietary laws in the ghetto became increasingly difficult. Rabbi Hillel Ginzberg, a member of the Hafetz Hayyim's family and the ghetto's spiritual leader, gave permission to the young and the sick to eat nonkosher meat (though they were prohibited from sucking on the bones so that they would not enjoy it too much).[11]

Young Rabbi Kalman Farber from Olkenik was in the Vilna Ghetto, where he worked as a blacksmith. One day the German officer who supervised the Jewish workers gave him a sandwich with nonkosher meat. Kalman declined the offer. The officer was surprised: "In time of war aren't you supposed to give up your rituals? Is the Jewish religion different from other religions?" Kalman explained that Judaism indeed has special provisions for critical times when one's life is in danger but at the moment he felt that he was not yet at the life-threatening starvation level. His response touched a human chord in the German officer's heart. He was impressed when he heard that the blacksmith was a graduate of a rabbinical seminary. His attitude toward Kalman changed. Never again did he offer him nonkosher meat."[12]

Even in the darkness of underground pits and caves, time was sanctified. On the farm of Korkuc, between Radun

---

[10]Yaffa Eliach, *There Once* Was a World (New York: Little, Brown, 1998), p. 600.

[11]Miriam Shulman Kabacznik, 24 May 1987.

[12]Kalman Farber, "Yoman Vilna," in *Olkeniki in Flames* (1962), 165.

and Eishyshok, there were several of these hiding places; The Kabacznik family hid in a pit under the stable. At their request and for a handsome fee paid in dollars, a Christian maid smuggled a small *sefer Torah* and a siddur out of the Radun Ghetto. On the same farm, in a cave under a pigsty, Moshe Sonenson and his family hid. He had a small Jewish calendar. Between the two spaces, Jewish holidays were observed whenever possible. Even traditional "food" was "served" at such "celebrations." Imagination and memory transformed the rotten potato peels into freshly baked hallah, gefilte fish, and other favorite Shabbos and holiday dishes.

Many of the Jews who found refuge in the forest—in the partisan family camps and other kinds of groups—also observed tradition.

From mid-1942 until liberation, groups of friends and relatives as well as occasional, isolated individuals constantly roamed the forests of Nacha, Rudnicki, and Mieszczanca, which were the large, dense *puszcza* (forests) in the vicinity of Eishyshok and Radun, as well as smaller, wooded areas nearby. Some of the groups consisted of just three or four people, who preferred the smaller size because they felt the risk of detection by hostile farmers and shepherds was less. But others wanted more of a sense of community, a feeling that they "lived among Jews," and they opted for life in larger groups.

The Blacharowicz women from Eishyshok, Fruml and her daughters Szeina and Gutka, lived in one of these extended communities, along with a number of other Eishyshkians and people from nearby shtetlach. They included Liba Shlosberg and her aging parents, Shmaye-Mendl and Freidl, and the Davidowicz family, Moshe the Lubaver and Dvora, with their three surviving daughters, all of them adults. (The fourth had been killed when they escaped ghetto Radun.)

By the summer of 1942, their group numbered about forty people, who moved from one temporary shelter to another in the Nacha and Mieszczanca forests.

Despite the difficult conditions, the Davidowicz family and Liba (as well as her parents until their deaths) observed not just the Jewish holidays, but also many of the traditions and dietary laws for the entire twenty-six months they spent in the forest. Somehow they even managed to bake matzot for Passover. Avraham Lipkunsky, a former yeshiva student who was with the partisans at that time, used to come to them to "warm" himself with a bit of Jewish tradition, sometimes making his own contribution to the holiday observance, as when he brought white chickens for *kapparot*, the eve of Yom Kippur ceremony. Years later he remembered the theological reservations he had as he took part in the group's prayer that Yom Kippur. "We are guilty," he recited, while thinking to himself that the prayer should read, "*They* are guilty."[13]

Out of the group of forty, only eight survived. Shmaye-Mendl froze to death. Liba gave her father a proper Jewish burial: she made a wooden coffin and recited the kaddish over his fresh grave.[14] None of the other victims, all murdered by the "White Poles," members of the *Armia Krajowa* (AK), had this privilege.

To impose one's sanctified concept of time on the profane landscape of death in the vast network of concentration camps was an even more heroic task than to do so in ghettos or in hiding. Yet even above Auschwitz there was a full moon hanging over the crematorium chimneys on the fifteenth day of the Jewish month, that being for many the

---

[13]Avraham Aviel Lipkunsky, 7 August 1980 Yad Vashem 03/508, 97–108; Liba Ahuva Shlosberg, *Mi-Labat Esh* (Jerusalem, 1988), 58–59.

[14]Ahuva Shlosberg, *Mi-Labat Esh*, 65–69.

only calendar. In the last months of typhus-ridden Bergen-Belsen, an inmate made a calendar by tying a knot on her dress for each passing day. On the seventh (Saturday night) she said the only prayer she knew, "God of Abraham." Bertha Saltz was on her way to the electrified fences to end her wretched existence when she suddenly heard the woman reciting "God of Abraham." She marveled that she knew it was Saturday night. Instead of touching the electrified fence, Bertha followed the faint sound of prayer. She was so overcome by the woman's ability to impose her own time on this profane place that she, too, made her dress into a calendar. Bertha's mentor perished, but she survived. The many fragments of calendars that survived the camps are a testimony to their importance. The struggle of men and women to observe time-related mitzvoth in the face of death is overwhelming.

An incident that occurred in the Janowski camp in Lwow shows the struggle to preserve Jewish tradition in its extreme. During a children's *Aktion*, a mother struggled with an SS officer for his pocketknife. After obtaining the knife, she circumcised her eight-day-old son. Then she looked up to the heavens and said: "God of the universe, you have given me a healthy child. I am returning to you a wholesome, kosher Jew." She walked over to the SS officer, gave him back his blood-stained knife, and handed him her baby.[15]

The day in the concentration camp began at dawn with a roll call. Some observant Jews began their day earlier with morning prayers, despite the penalty of death. Under the striped uniform and cap, they maintained souls in search of meaning.

---

[15]Yaffa Eliach, *Hasidic Tales of the Holocaust* (New York: Oxford University Press, 1982), 151–153 (hereafter, *Hasidic Tales*).

Gad Goldman recalls that someone in his barrack in Auschwitz "organized" a pair of *tefillin*. At four o'clock in the morning, people would line up to put them on.[16] Herman Weiss was in Buna (Auschwitz II) from May 1944 until January 18, 1945. During this nine-month period, he was able to put on the *tefillin* once. The *tefillin* belonged to a Jew in Block No. 60. They probably were smuggled into camp via a British POW for a very high price."[17]

There was also a pair of *tefillin* in the forced-labor camp of Bunzlau and in Mielec (part of the Gross-Rosen network of camps), Martin Grossman recalls.[18] David Laufer testified that in Plaszow, near Cracow, they had only one set of *tefillin*. People would get up at three o'clock in the morning to put them on so that they would be ready for the four o'clock roll call.[19]

Sinai Adler, in a memoir written immediately after the liberation, recalls that after arriving in Birkenau (Auschwitz II) from Theresienstadt, all his belongings were confiscated, including his *tefillin*. On the following day, in the garbage, he found the *tefillin* for the head. He was satisfied that he could observe the precept at least partially.[20] In Birkenau, in the bunk with Sinai Adler, were many young men from Central Europe and Greece. The observant ones would

---

[16]The following are a few excerpts of material that was published previously. Yaffa Eliach, "Jewish Tradition in the Life of the Concentration Camp Inmate" in *The Nazi Concentration Camps* (Jerusalem: Yad Vashem, 1984), 195–206. Testimony of Gad Goldman in the Oral History Project, The Center for Holocaust Studies, New York OH 78-10 SuC, RG 439. All testimonies used in this paper are part of this project.

[17]Testimony of Herman Weiss, OH 75–26 SuC, RG 151.

[18]Testimony of Martin Grossman, OH 78–129 SuC, RG 502.

[19]Testimony of David Laufer, OH 78–45 SuC, RG 401.

[20]Sinai Adler, *Be-Gei Zalmavet–Shenat Hayim shel Na'ar be-Mahanot Rikkuz* (Jerusalem: 1979), 13 and 17.

gather in a corner, pray, and put on *tefillin*. As a result, an especially close bond formed among these lads from distant lands.

In the camps, the Sabbath was a regular forced-labor day. The observant Jew, however, even while slaving like everybody else, managed at times to sanctify a few of the day's moments by reciting the kiddush over two slices of stale bread that he had managed to save. Not only did that act sustain him during the rest of the week, but planning and "organizing" for it gave him the triumphant sense that he could outmaneuver the Nazi system—if only by reciting a single blessing over two pieces of bread.

Gad Goldman says that "of the holidays, we kept an account in our heads—an exact account—we kept track day after day. We knew every date precisely; we were sitting and thinking and figuring out." Another inmate reflects: "The moon also helped. It was sometimes our final authority, especially on the fifteenth."[21]

On Rosh Hashana of 5704 (1943) in Bergen-Belsen, a shofar was smuggled from one sector to another in the morning coffee cauldron. Hayyim Borak, a Dutch Jew with Argentinian papers, obtained it for a Polish Hasidic Jew.[22]

Miriam Leser, a privileged inmate with Palestinian papers interned in Bergen-Belsen, recalls, "When we blew the shofar the other Jewish inmates without privileged status heard the voice of the shofar. They stopped for a moment from their labor, listened to the shofar. The German guard discovered and immediately gave them a terrible beating. Others still continued to listen."[23] In Buna, food and tobacco collected from inmates were used to purchase a sho-

---

[21]Testimony of Goldman, op. cit.

[22]*Hasidic Tales*, 42–43.

[23]Testimony of Miriam Leser, OH 75–22 SuC, RG 298.

far from a Cracow Jew, according to the testimony of Naftali Landau. In the forced-labor camp Skarzysko Kamienna, in the Radom district, the Grand Rabbi of Radoszyce asked one of his Hasidim, Moshe Winterer (ben Dov), to make a shofar for him. Under threat of the death penalty, Moshe made a shofar in the camp workshop with a Polish supervisor's help. The mitzvah of blowing shofar was observed in Block No. 14 at Skarzysko Kamienna.[24]

Helaine Nadler recalls that in her Auschwitz barrack on Rosh Hashana of 5705 (1944), one woman lit candles: "She stood in the middle of the barrack with all the women around her sobbing. The woman recited prayers. She made them up as she went along. I do not recall the words, but the impact was fantastic." When the guard in charge of the barrack (*stubhova*) walked in, the candles were extinguished.[25] In Christianstadt (part of the Gross-Rosen network of camps), Sary Joszef's group was luckier. An older woman from Warsaw, a cantor's wife, knew the Rosh Hashana prayers by heart. At night, after a long day's work, she prayed. "We repeated word for word, praying and hoping that the Ribbono shel Olam [Master of the Universe] will give us help and freedom."[26]

Martin Grossman recalls that in Bunzlau on Rosh Hashana, he conducted services. As a former yeshiva student, he knew the prayers by heart. During late-night services, the block elder, also a Jew, walked in. The inmates explained that it was the Jewish New Year and they were

---

[24]I am grateful to Vladka Meed for telling me about the event and to Ilana Guri at Yad Vashem for locating the shofar and the accompanying testimony by Moshe ben Dov (Winterer), Yad Vashem Museum, 1530.

[25]Testimony of Helaine Nadler, OH 78–5 SuH, RG 364.

[26]Testimony of Sary Joszef, OH 78–5 SuH, RG 358.

praying for the Third Reich's welfare. The block elder was very moved. The following day he brought them three pieces of bread. "It was some holiday!" Martin concludes.

Fanny Berger was a prisoner in Hanover (part of the Neuengamme network of camps), one of thousands of girls living in tents, starved and emaciated. One day, she relates, "someone said it is Yom Kippur today. It is hard to explain what happened to me that moment, it was as if a ghost went through me. Suddenly everybody knew it was Yom Kippur. We fasted the entire day. They made better food, but nobody ate."[27] At the Janowski camp, after the midnight shift returned from work in the town, beaten-up Jews with freshly inflicted, open wounds gathered in Block No. 12 and listened to the rabbi of Blazowa (Bluzhov), Israel Spira, recite *Kol Nidre*. The following morning, one of the camp elders, Schneeweiss, a nonobservant and anti-religious Jew, assigned work to the rabbi and a few of his Hasidim. He sent them to a secluded building so that they could pray and gave them jobs that could be performed without transgressing any of the thirty-nine main categories of forbidden work. At noon the SS guards entered the building with trays of food, the likes of which had not been seen throughout the war, and ordered the inmates to eat. Schneeweiss, composed, his head held high, objected: "We Jews obey the law of our tradition. Today is Yom Kippur, a day of fasting." He was shot on the spot.[28] "On that Yom Kippur in Janowski, I understood the statement of the Talmud: 'Even the transgressors in Israel are as full of good deeds, as a pomegranate is filled with seeds,' "[29] Rabbi Spira said.

---

[27]Testimony of Fanny Berger, OH 79–16 SuC, RG 438.

[28]Yaffa Eliach, "Yom Kippur ba-Mahane," *Hadoar*, no. 39 (September 13, 1978): 691–692.

[29]Eruvin, 19a.

Yitzhak Mann recalls that when his labor battalion reached Bornemissza near the border of Carpatho-Russia, it was Yom Kippur of 5705 (1944). The prisoners were uprooting telephone and telegraph poles and destroying all lines of communication as the German army retreated on the eastern front. It was raining heavily. His father, Kalman, prayed, and those around him repeated the prayer as they worked. They were joined by a detachment of Jewish converts to Christianity, who also fasted and spilled their coffee into the streaming gullies. At night they were punished; they were forced to climb the muddy slopes of Mt. Bornemisza and slide down on their stomachs—ten times! Late at night the rains stopped. Around campfires, the prisoners dried their clothes and broke their fast. A young German officer came over to Yitzhak Mann's group and said: "I don't know who will win this war, but a people with your determination will never give up, never."[30]

Rabbi Jacob Jungreis, a passenger in the Kasztner train, recalls that the rabbi of Szatmar and some of his Hasidim in Bergen-Belsen made a sukkah out of a two-tiered bed in order to teach the children in the group. Straw from the mattress served as a *sekhakh* (a roof), but the wind and rain blew it away. Martin Grossman relates that there was a sukkah in Buna. It lasted two days, until the Germans discovered and destroyed it.

In Bergen-Belsen, Hanukkah also was observed.[31] A wooden clog served as a menorah, a thread from a concentration-camp jacket as a candle, and black shoe polish as the oil. Hundreds of Jews assembled to see Rabbi Israel Spira kindle the Hanukkah lights in the darkness of Bergen-

---

[30]*Hasidic Tales*, 101–105.
[31]*Hasidic Tales*, 13–15.

Belsen. Among the many present was the Bund leader Zishe Zamieczkowski, who recalled years later that the Hanukkah lights at Bergen-Belsen were a constant source of strength and inspiration.[32]

Hanukkah observance was not unique to Bergen-Belsen's sector for foreign nationals. In Janowski, Birkenau, and many camps, men and women managed to kindle Hanukkah lights.[33]

Passover was one of the most significant holidays for the concentration-camp inmates. Its message of freedom, hope, and deliverance from bondage held a most timely promise. Indeed, the number of testimonies of Passover observance in the concentration camps is overwhelming. The fact that numerous camps indeed were liberated around Passover 1945 adds to this unique dimension.

In Bergen-Belsen in 1944, privileged inmates, holders of South American passports, were given permission to bake matzot. Something that resembled a seder was arranged, especially for the children in the privileged sector of Polish Jews. That night the Haggadah, recited from memory, took on a new meaning:

> Why is this night different from all other nights? Why is this night of the Holocaust different from all the other previous suffering of the Jewish people? For on all other nights we eat either bread or *matzah*, but tonight only *matzah*. Bread is leavened; it has height. *Matzah* is unleavened and is totally flat. During our previous suffering, during all our previous nights in exile, we Jews had bread and *matzah*. We had moments of bread, of creativity, and light, and moments of *matzah*, of

---

[32]Ibid., 243.

[33]On the kindling of Hanukkah lights in Janowski, see Kahana, op. cit., 119–120. On the kindling of Hanukkah lights in Birkenau, see Adler, op. cit., 33–34.

suffering and despair. But tonight, the night of the Holocaust, we have reached our greatest suffering. We have reached the depth of the abyss, the nadir of humiliation. Tonight we have only *matzah*; we have no moments of relief, not a moment of respite for our humiliated spirits. . . . But don't despair, my young friends, for it is also the beginning of our redemption. We are slaves who are serving a Pharaoh. Slaves in Hebrew are *Avadim*. The letters of the word *Avadim* form the acronym of the Hebrew phrase: David the son of Jesse, your servant, your Messiah.

This was the message of the rabbi of Blazowa, Israel Spira, to his young listeners on that dark seder night in Bergen-Belsen.[34]

Livia Bitton-Jackson recalls that as a 14-year-old girl in Augsburg (Germany) labor camp, she had abstained from eating bread for eight days because, according to her calculations and her mother's, it was Passover. Only afterward did she learn that they had miscalculated and Passover had just begun. She therefore abstained from eating bread for another eight days, all the while slaving in a German factory.[35]

In March 1945, Adolf Hershkowitz was sick with typhus. Although he managed to bake some matzo as the Hungarian guards fled the Russians, it was not enough to last the entire holiday. Hiding in a leaky boat in the marshes with a friend, a Jewish doctor from Poland, he refused to eat bread. The doctor cut the bread into thin slices, like matzo, and convinced the sick Adolf that he must eat so that he would live to see the deliverance from the bondage of Nazi

---

[34]Yaffa Eliach, "Lel ha-Seder be-Bergen-Belsen," *Hadoar*, no. 22 (April 6, 1979): 353.

[35]Testimony of Livia Bitton, OH 79–45 SuC, RG 581. See also Livia E. Bitton-Jackson, *Elli* (New York: 1980), 162–164.

tyranny. The Russians liberated them on the last day of Pass-over.[36]

The concentration camp established on the ruins of the Warsaw Ghetto was part of the Majdanek network. The inmates' tasks were to clean up the rubble of the destroyed ghetto and ship all salvageable materials to Germany. On July 28, 1944, they were evacuated from the advancing lines of the eastern front and began their long death march along the banks of the River Vistula. July 30, 1944 was the fast of *Tish'a Be-Av* (the ninth of Av). Despite the severe heat, 4,000 Jews refused to obey orders and neither drank nor ate.[37]

In the vast network of camps, these Jews snatched moments away from oblique reality and sanctified them. These moments helped them cling to a pre-World War II reality and create a link with the future: the hope that even they, the modern slaves, would hear the Messiah's footsteps, the dream that one day the war would come to an end.

But World War II seemed to drag on endlessly. The condition of the victims deteriorated. The executioner perfected his methods, and the concentration-camp reality could have shamed Dante's Inferno and made Job's Satan look like a novice. Many inmates lost the last surviving members of their families, their last friends. Man descended deeper into the abyss, stripped of everything—family, friends, and even his flesh as disease and starvation ate away at it.

Hundreds of thousands of living human skeletons began death marches across the frozen face of Europe. Walking skeletons, ribcages suspended from bare bones, they continued to cling to life. The Nazis could snuff out their lives

---

[36]Testimony of Adolf Hershkowitz, OH 78–199 SuC, RG 527.
[37]Testimony of David Junger, OH 79–77 SuC, RG 624.

but not their spirits. They were oblivious to their physical existence, clinging only to their visions, their dreams. They functioned in limbo, more skeleton than flesh, more spirit than body, more dream than reality. Their consciousness of time changed reality; vision and dream took over. Even there, in this semiconscious, suspended existence, the holidays, family, and Jewish tradition remained of major significance.

For the prisoners, exhausted from the death marches and delirious with typhus, dreams and visions about holiday observances were common. A young lad named Ignaz in Mauthausen—starved, emaciated, and dying—dreamed of the third Sabbath meal at his grandfather's cozy home back in Dolha in Carpatho-Russia.[38]

In April 1945, in Bergen-Belsen, a girl delirious with typhus was convinced that she was back home on a Friday night, that her father is placing his warm, reassuring hands on her head and blessing her, as he did every Friday night. But this time his blessing was for life and freedom.[39]

There is an overwhelming number of examples of such experiences. It is difficult to suggest a precise percentage of Jewish inmates who managed to observe some aspects of the Jewish tradition while in the concentration and labor camps. But it is clear that they were a significant number and from many countries.

The type of camp in which an inmate was incarcerated was a dominant factor in the degree of observance. Conditions varied with the type of camp—death or concentration, labor, detention, transit or family—as well as with Hungarian forced-labor battalions and other administrative units. The camp's structure, its commander's character, its geo-

---

[38] *Hasidic Tales*, 172–176.
[39] Ibid., 177–178.

graphical location, and its guards' nationalities, in addition to the amount of time an inmate spent in the environment, are all variables to take into account when discussing observance in the camps.

A distinction as to the manner in which tradition was observed also seems to emerge between men and women. Men appeared more concerned with ritual (washing hands, *tefillin*, shofar, matzo, etc.), the precepts they had observed in the pre-Holocaust days. Woman appeared to relate more to the family "togetherness" of the holidays, sitting around the table on the Sabbath, the memory of the aroma of freshly baked hallah or cooked fish in the pre-Holocaust days. Their observance of tradition in the camps seems to have been more limited. Rather, it was more of a genuine attempt to endow the sacred days with some special meaning, some expression of Jewish identity and pride, some assertion of a sense of their humanity.

One might suggest that in the concentration-camp system, the majority of observant Jews were not as concerned with observing tradition only according to Halakha, which, naturally, was even less possible than in the ghetto. Their observance expressed their great wish and need to manifest their Jewishness and humanity in the face of Nazi bestiality. They were dedicated to a tradition diametrically opposed to Nazi ideology and its deadly manifestation in the concentration-camp network. Observing their Jewish tradition sanctified a few salvageable moments in the reality of the camps. Their relationship with their special Jewish "national" time was a link with the past and the future. It endowed them with historical consciousness and placed them in the continuum of Jewish history.

Within the concentration camps, the opportunities for making halakhically correct provisions for burying and mourning the dead were minimal. Dying as a Jew and being buried as a Jew were impossibilities.

Outside the camps, however—in ghettos, hiding places, and forests—it was possible, despite the many obstacles, to observe the customs related to death. There were remnants of traditional Jewish leadership, and some members of families were still together.

For example, when the people of Eishyshok were awaiting their deaths, their beloved rabbi was with them, wearing his silk top hat and black coat. Rabbi Razowski addressed his congregation for the last time. In a loud, clear voice, he said, "My dear Jews, we are lost and doomed!" The yeshiva students in the horse market then began to recite the *Shema Israel*, the Jewish proclamation of faith, the prayer that was forever on the lips of Jewish martyrs everywhere. All joined in the prayer, young and old alike, down to the littlest ones in their mothers' arms, and even the lunatics from Selo. The entire crowd's tearful voices issued from the depths of their hearts and souls: "Hear, O Israel, the Lord is our God, the Lord is One!"

At six o'clock the following morning, as people were in the midst of their morning prayers, the selection began. Healthy young men and community leaders were selected. Soldiers from the *Einsatzgruppen*, the Lithuanian *shaulisti*, and the police ordered them to line up five abreast and prepare to march. Rabbi Szymen Razowski, *Hazzan* Moshe Tobolski, and Rabbi Avraham Aaron Waldshan, the rabbi of Olkenik, were at the head of the procession. As they neared the old cemetery, they began to chant the *viddui*, the confession recited on the verge of death.

Zvi Michalowski, age 16, and his father, Maneh, were among those who marched to the old cemetery in a later group. Once they arrived at their destination, Zvi saw that the deep trenches that once served to keep cattle away from the sacred ground now served as a mass grave. The bodies of the men who had left earlier filled the trenches, now overflowing with a river of blood. Nearby was a huge pile of clothing. Now this group, too, was told to undress and add their own clothes to the pile. As Zvi undressed, he stood next to his rosh Yeshiva, Rabbi Zusha Lichtig, who was comforting his sons and reciting Psalms with them:

> I will say of the Lord, who is my
> refuge and my fortress,
> My God, in whom I trust,
> That He will deliver thee from the
> snare of the flower . . .[40]

Grabbing his father's hand as they neared the grave's edge, Zvi envied Zusha's sons for having a father who was such a pillar of strength even in the face of death.

Just before a volley of gunfire rang out, Zvi noticed a German soldier kneeling near the pile of clothing, a machine gun cradled in his lap. And at precisely that moment, Maneh pushed his son into the grave then fell on top of him, mortally wounded. Hours later, Zvi would emerge from the grave, his father's action having saved him. When he walked off into the night and went to various nearby homes for help, he was told everywhere, "Jew, go back to the grave where you belong." Finally he came to a farmhouse about three kilometers outside the shtetl. When the frightened woman who answered the door gave him the same response, he told her he was Jesus Christ come down from the cross on an earthly mission. The woman let Zvi into the house, gave him food and fresh clothing, and allowed him to clean up before he went back out into the darkness.[41]

In Radun, too, the Jews went to their deaths as holy martyrs observing their traditions. On May 10, 1942, the Jews were lined up, among them many Eishyshkians who had

---

[40]Ps. 91:2–3.
[41]Zvi Michalowski, 4 October 1992; *Hasidic Tales*, 53–55.

escaped the *shehita* in September 1941. Rabbi Hillel Ginzberg was at the head of the line, wearing his phylacteries, his white *kittel*, and his prayer shawl. They prayed in unison, "Shema Israel, Hear thee O Israel, the Lord our God, the Lord is One!" They marched toward the cemetery as shots fired all around them.[42]

But then the murderers called a momentary halt; the gravedigging was behind schedule because of the first group of gravediggers' uprising that morning. Everyone was told to kneel while *Burgenmeister* Kulikowski delivered an obligatory anti-Semitic speech over the loudspeaker, telling them that they were being punished for the killing of Jesus Christ. After a long stay on their knees, they were told to get up. The march proceeded to the cemetery.

It was a beautiful spring day. Sunlight glanced off the tin roof of the Hafetz Hayyim's mausoleum, and the trees were in bud. Near the mausoleum was a huge, freshly dug grave. During the killings, Avraham Lipkunsky, a yeshiva student, spotted his older brother Pinhas among the gravediggers. Because he was still dressed, he thought he might be able to join Pinhas without being noticed. His mother, unaware that her husband had escaped and lacking any hope for the future, told him to say the Shema and die like a Jew. But he let go of his mother's hand and left her and his younger brother Yekutiel behind. Gradually, furtively, he made his way to join his brother Pinchas in the group of permit-holders.[43]

Meanwhile, in a hiding place back in the ghetto, baby Shaul Sonenson slept peacefully in the attic hayloft where his family had taken shelter—until the sharp noise of a

---

[42]Moshe Sonenson 29 June 1977.

[43]Avraham Aviel Lipkunsky, 8 February 1987; Avraham Aviel Lipkunsky, *Dogalishok* (Israel: 1995), 98–102.

German motorcycle in the street below awoke him and he began to whimper. His mother, fearful that his cries would reveal their presence, attempted to nurse him, but he refused. Nor would he suck on the cloth in which she had wrapped the poppyseeds that were supposed to induce sleep. As he continued to whine, all but one of the sixteen adults hiding in the hayloft with his parents, Zipporah and Moshe, surrounded the mother and child. Shmaye-Mendl, an older man with a yellowish beard, father of Liba Shlosberg and one of the most highly respected men in Radun, stated their case: "He is just a baby. We are all adults. Because of him we are all going to be murdered."

Just then the doors below swung open. Through the cracks between the attic's wooden floor planks, two young Germans could be seen, machine guns on their shoulders and their motorcycles decorated with streamers, as though they were headed for a parade or a party. Shmaye-Mendl took off his coat and threw it over the baby, then put his hand on the coat and motioned for the others to do the same. They did, and the baby's older brother and sister, Yitzhak and Yaffa, watched in horror. Zipporah remained motionless, big tears frozen on her face, holding her dead son in her arms. From that moment on, Yaffa began to fear all adults.[44]

To give brutally murdered Jews a proper burial was a major concern in the ghettos, hiding places, and forests. Many people endangered their lives during such undertakings. The people most dedicated to this task were usually indi-

---

[44]Moshe Sonenson, 29 June 1977; Yaffa Bat Moshe Sonenson (age 10), "Be-Mahboim," in *Eishyshok Koroteah Ve-Hurbanah*, 68–69; Liba Ahuva Shlosberg, *Mi-Labat Esh*, 46, tells the story—which concerns her father, Shmaye Mendl—in a different version; Leon Kahn, *No Time to Mourn* (Vancouver: Laurelton Press, 1978), 65–66.

viduals with a yeshiva education who were members of the
Kehila. On June 16, 1943, the blockade of the Nacha Forest began, which resulted in one of the biggest massacres
of Jews hiding in the vicinity. The blockade lasted fifteen
days. Jewish partisans who had maintained a camp nearby
returned to the site of the murder. Among them were
young men from Eishyshok and Radun, including Avraham
Lipkunsky, Benyamin Frankl, Avraham Asner, and several
of the Paikowskis. The devastation they found there and
elsewhere in the area was beyond their worst imaginings.
What once had been human beings were now unrecogniz-
able as such. The bodies of yeshiva students whose heads
had been replete with Torah learning and of mothers whose
hearts had contained nothing but love and hope now were
filled to overflowing with masses of crawling worms. The
stench was unbearable.

Although the partisans prided themselves on their tough-
ness and thought they had seen everything in the way of
human suffering, the scene so overwhelmed them that only
four of them could bring themselves to bury the dead.
"Ezekiel's vision of the Dry Bones was nothing in comparison to what we saw . . ." Avraham Lipkunski later recalled.
They did what they could to identify the bodies, though the
partisans had only a few clues—a shoe, a hat, a scrap of
cloth—to help them with their grisly task. Then they recited
the kaddish and engraved the date—June 16, 1943—on a
tree trunk. Among the dead were many men, women, and
children who had managed to survive the *shehita* in both
Eishyshok and Radun.[45]

Years later, Avraham Aviel Lipkunsky would be a witness
at the Eichmann trial in Jerusalem. The questions directed

---

[45]Avraham Aviel Lipkunsky, *Dogalishok*, 200–211; Yaffa Eliach, *The
Shtetl.*

at him then dealt mainly with the uprising of the gravediggers (who included his father) during the Radun massacre on May 10, 1942, and his own heroic experiences as a young, teenage partisan. He was not asked about his attempts to observe Jewish tradition during the Holocaust— a central concern of his both in the ghetto and as a partisan—for that aspect of Jewish experience did not interest those conducting the trial.

On the other side of the coin, the painful death of baby Shaul Sonenson in the Radun attic is still discussed in yeshiva circles. The event has been embellished in retelling to suggest that a profound halakhic debate took place among Radun scholars prior to the baby's tragic death. The halakhic discussion seems to grow longer with each recounting of the incident. In reality, the death verdict was one brief sentence: "Because of him we are all going to be murdered."

In the post-Holocaust era, the handful of survivors from Eishyshok, Radun, and Olkenik settled in the Americas, Israel, and western Europe, with one Jew from Eishyshok remaining in Radun. They established new families and built new lives, often remaining in close contact with one another but cut off from any feelings of continuity with the past, particularly the religious, spiritual, and communal aspects of their previous lives. Fewer than a dozen people from all three shtetlach remained observant Jews.[46] Many of them felt lonely, misunderstood, and abandoned by the Jewish people and by God.

In contrast to their experience, the Hasidic survivors retrieved as much of their past as they could. They built new

---

[46]See Yaffa Eliach, "Survivors of a Single Shtetl Case Study: Eishyshok," in *She'erit Hapletha*, 1944-1948 (Jerusalem: Yad Vashem, 1990), 489–508.

Hasidic courts in the lands where they settled. The rebbe's court in the New World was their spiritual home and a continuation of their life in Europe. It created a community that resembled many aspects of their pre-war existence and was very familiar—same name, same language, same tradition. Their spiritual leaders, their towers of strength—men such as the rebbes of Satmar, Bobov, Klausenburg, Bluzhov, and so forth—were survivors just like them who understood their spiritual difficulties, their economic needs, and their painful Holocaust memories. The feeling that they have lost for all eternity that unique Jewish way of life that was destroyed along with their beloved shtetlach constantly torments Lithuanian and other non-Hasidic survivors who have been cut off totally from their pasts.

After the Holocaust, Yossef Kaplan, the sole survivor of a large family from Radun, settled in London. His aunt, who had left the shtetl long before the war, asked him: "Yossele, how do the Jews of London treat you?" He responded:

> Dear Auntie, they treat me like a bastard. How else can they treat me? Do they know the gentle, dear Jews who were my parents? Do they know my father? Do they know my mother's lofty origin? The war turned all of us survivors into bastards, for it destroyed our illustrious past. Do you know what Hitler has done to us? He turned us into broken vessels that can never be mended, never.[47]

Elka Jankelewicz, the daughter of the last gravedigger/undertaker from Eishyshok (Nahum *der Kvoresman*), voiced a similar complaint:

> I am not religious, I am not modest, but I am a Jewish daughter. After the war, Judaism is not Judaism, Torah is not Torah, Humanity is not Humanity. A curse was placed upon the

---

[47]Yossef Kaplan, 7 September 1981.

Jewish people. We are busy destroying one another. Hitler can indeed be proud of his achievements.[48]

Only two Eishyshkian couples survived the Holocaust. One of them was a man named Kaplan, who was a Cohen, and his wife, a divorcée. In pre-war Eishyshok, they had rented an apartment in a Christian's home, for no Jew would rent to them. Now the Cohen and the *grusha* (divorcée) had outlived all the other couples, except for Moshe and Zipporah Sonenson. But shortly after liberation Moshe discovered that his tragedies would not end with the Holocaust. On October 20, 1944, Polish partisans murdered his wife Zipporah and another baby son named Hayyim. The NKVD (KGB) arrested and exiled him to Siberia; he left behind two young children, Yitzhak and Yaffa. Moshe was a scion of one of Eishyshok's original Jewish families, which had been among the shtetl's founders in the eleventh century. He, like his family before him during their nearly 900 years in the shtetl, had been among the community's leaders. After returning from his long prison years in Siberia, he settled in Kadima, Israel. His assessment of the post-Holocaust Jewish community was a painful one:

After the tragedy, the world is upside down, a lawless place. The rich became poor, the nobodies who stood no chance back in the old home have prospered beyond their own wildest dreams. To the sweet sound of their cash registers, they roam the world, preferably with a blonde *shikse* at their side; occasionally, they open their purse, but never their heart. This, my child, is the new Jew that Hitler has fashioned into being.[49]

One of Moshe Sonenson's new friends in Kadima was another farmer, a religious Jew who once had been a

---

[48]Elka Jankelewicz née Szulkin, 23 June 1983.
[49]Moshe Sonenson, 19 August 1980.

hevruta (study partner) of young Samuel Belkin in the Radun Yeshiva. Moshe Sonenson commented about his new friend: "His understanding of Jews and God ends with his days in the Hafetz Hayyim's yeshiva. The Jews after the *hurban* are strangers to him, as is the God of the Cohen and the *grusha* (divorcée)."

Moshe's words, like those of the other survivors just quoted, describe a world that was shattered forever. There is a sense of irretrievable loss, of the spiritual impoverishment of survivors and nonsurvivors alike, of drastic changes in values and lifestyles, of being thrust into a new, unfriendly reality without any credentials—advantageous to some and painful to others.

More and more, the Holocaust became the dominant theme of his life, just as Zionism and the yearning for a homeland in Israel had been during the years before the war.

On a black marble tombstone in a small, serene Kadima cemetery, his children engraved his epitaph:

> Here is interred Moshe Eliyahu Sonenson,
> A Holocaust survivor.
> The commemoration of the Holocaust and the
> teaching of its lessons were the essence of his life.
> I will give in my House
> And within my walls a monument and a memorial.

We are currently in an age of museum-building, constructing new ones and rebuilding old ones, that some refer to as "Museumania."[50] Various groups have vested interests in the museums, each manifesting their particular moral, ethical, philosophical, and historical outlooks and political

---

[50]See Jonathan Webber, ed. *Jewish Identity in the New Europe* (Oxford: The Littman Library Of Jewish Civilization, 1994), 228–231; on the United States Holocaust Memorial Museum in Washington, D.C., see Edward T. Linenthal, *Preserving Memory* (New York: Viking, 1995).

convictions. The interests of Germans and the citizens of countries under Nazi occupation are different from those of the people who fought them and liberated the camps from them. So, too, are the needs of Jewish Holocaust survivors different from those of Jews spared the war's agonies.

For the Holocaust survivor, commemoration is an urgent matter, its meaning and purpose focused on bringing the dead an eternal, respectable rest. With each passing year, these survivors seem to me to become evermore myth-like in stature, tragic figures going about their everyday lives among normal human society while lovingly cradling their dead in their empty arms. As the years go by, the survivors grow older and their burden becomes heavier, but the dead in their arms remain forever young, forever unburied. They hear one cry from the scattered ashes, they see one message in the smoke evaporating from the camp chimneys, but they never feel they succeed in answering their loved ones' call for a proper burial, a perfect rest. And so the survivors call for help. But no one in the museums or the universities hears their cries. Their friends and colleagues are busy commemorating the Holocaust and its murdered martyrs in their own ways, looking to the victims for inspiration, for meaning—and also for research projects, for funding, for their own livelihoods.

Meanwhile, the survivor still hopes only to find the proper Jewish burial place and a *mazeva* (tombstone) for his dead.[51]

As yet, Holocaust survivors have not found the perfect resting place for their dead in the museums.

---

[51]See Yaffa Eliach, "Private and Public Commemoration of the Holocaust: In Search of 'The Perfect Rest' " in *What Have We Learned? Telling the Story, Teaching the Lessons of the Holocaust,* ed. Franklin H. Littel, Alan L. Berger, and Hubert G. Locke (United Kingdom: The Edwin Mellen Press, 1993), 392–402.

Holocaust survivors, religious and secular, prefer traditional Jewish commemoration and memorializing of their dead. They erect traditional tombstones in Jewish cemeteries to commemorate their destroyed communities. Such tombstones are found in many major cemeteries in the Americas and western Europe and also in the Holon cemetery near Tel Aviv, where there are more than 800 of them. It is in the Holon cemetery, rather than at Yad Vashem, where annual memorial services are held.

The museums are secular in nature, and many have become temples of inspiration for moral and ethical values and shrines to a Jewish identity, forced in common suffering. Even the March of the Living to Auschwitz has some of these overtones.

Unlike all the other major catastrophes, the Holocaust has taken place in a secular age. Its patterns of documentation, commemoration, and memorializing are, for the most part, secular in nature. They were established by secular individuals who basically followed European patterns: a combination of Christian traditions, Enlightenment models, and World War I commemoration practices honoring the fallen heroes on the European battlefields.

The Holocaust is one of the twentieth century's most powerful experiences. For many Jews, it has become a secular religion. It is the strongest and most common bond they have with Judaism, stronger than Sinai and Israel. To many, the shadows of Auschwitz are brighter than the lights of Jerusalem. Death and destruction are more inspiring to them than living, dynamic Judaism. More money is invested in Holocaust projects than in Jewish education. Many Jews are eager to contribute to Holocaust projects because the Holocaust offers a passport to Jewish identity without any demands and obligations. The Orthodox community must have a greater input in Holocaust museums and studies if it wishes to safeguard the Holocaust from becoming de-Judaized.

Holocaust museums and studies offer a major challenge to the Orthodox community and the religious scholar. It is the twelfth hour for Jewish individuals and institutions of higher learning to respond to the challenge: place the Holocaust within a Jewish context, and place Jewish scholarship within museums. Failing to do so will hasten the process of de-Judaizing the Holocaust even in the free world, where the door and the mind are still open to all.[52]

---

[52]Yaffa Eliach, "A Challenge to the Orthodox Community," *Jewish Action* (Fall 5754, 1993): 49 and 66–67; "Defining the Holocaust Prospectives of a Jewish Historian," in *Jews and Christians After the Holocaust*, ed. Abraham J. Peck (Philadelphia: Fortress Press, 1983), 11–23.

9

Annotated Bibliography to the Problem of Evil

Yitzchak Blau

This bibliography makes no attempt at comprehensiveness. It offers a guide to the most important sources on this subject's many facets.

Tanakh: Several prophetic authors (Jer. 12, *Tehillim* 37 and 73, *Kohelet* 4:1 and 9:2, *Havakuk* 1:2) raise the question of injustice. The suffering servant passage in Isa. 53 seems to mention vicarious atonement. All of Job is dedicated to theodicy. Shalom Carmy and David Shatz provide a philosophical evaluation of the biblical texts in "The Bible as a Source of Jewish Philosophical Reflection" in *The Routledge History of World Philosophy*, vol. 2, ed. D. Frank and O. Leaman. Yissacher Jacobson cites the major commentaries on these passages in his *Baayat haGemul baTanakh* (Tel Aviv 1989).

331

S. Driver and A. Neubauer collect medieval commentaries on Isa. 53 in *The Fifty Third Chapter of Isaiah According to the Jewish Sources* (Ktav 1969). Shalom Carmy places that chapter in the context of the other *eved* passages in Isaiah and resists the *eved*'s limitation to any one individual in "The Courage to Suffer: Isaiah 53 and its Context" *Gesher*, vol. 7, 1979.

A few commentaries on Job attempt to work out philosophic approaches in the *sefer*. See the commentaries in Rambam's *Moreh Nevukhim* (*Guide to the Perplexed* 3:22 and 23), Ralbag (found in most *Mikraot Gedolot*, trans. A. Lassen, New York, 1945), Ramban (*Kol Kitvei haRamban*, ed. C. Chavel, vol. 1), and Malbim. Rebbenu Bahye ben Asher (*Kad haKemah* s.v. *hashgaha*) follows Ramban's approach and adds a distinction between the themes of God's two speeches to Job. For some modern approaches, see N. Glatzer ed. *The Dimensions of Job* (Shocken 1969) and David Shapiro's *Studies in Jewish Thought*, ch. 7–11 (New York, 1975). Rabbi Moshe Eisemann's ArtScroll *Iyyov* primarily follows Ramban and Rashi; see also Carmy and Shatz listed above.

Commentators throughout Jewish history have tried to resolve the contradictory passages in *Tanakh* regarding individual or collective punishment. The Torah at times claims that man suffers only as a result of his own sin; on other occasions, he is punished for parental or communal transgressions. Meir Weiss addresses this problem in *MiBaa'yot Torat haGemul haMikrait, Tarbiz* 31/32 (1962/3).

Hazal: It would be nearly impossible to list all the primary sources in the Talmud and Midrash that deal with reward and punishment. A partial list appears in C. G. Montefiore and H. Loewe's *A Rabbinic Anthology,* ch. 8, 28, and 31 (Philadelphia, 1960). Ephraim Urbach also cites many of the sources in chapter 15 of *The Sages: Their*

Concepts and Beliefs trans. I. Abraham (Jerusalem, 1979). Urbach argues that rabbinic sources do not accept the notion of original sin, sees the loss of sacrifices following the *hurban* as pivotal in the need to view death as an atonement, and investigates the concepts of *middat hadin u-middat ha-rahamim.*

Robert Goldenberg deals with rabbinic explanations for the *hurban* in "Early Rabbinic Explanations for the Destruction of Jerusalem" *Journal of Jewish Studies* 33 (1980). He suggests that many rabbinic explanations should not be taken as exhaustive but rather as preaching devices.

Aharon Agus's *The Binding of Isaac and Messiah: Law, Martyrdom and Deliverance in Early Rabbinic Religiosity* (SUNY, 1988) locates two different viewpoints among Hazal regarding living with suffering and oppression. Some rabbis focus on adherence to the law and patiently wait for history to unfold. Others search for perfection in one dramatic action, such as martyrdom, or the immediate salvation of a miracle.

Yaakov Elman has investigated and isolated different views within the talmudic passages on suffering. He points to those that break the simple causal connection between sin and punishment. See "When Permission is Given: Aspects of Divine Providence" *Tradition* 24:4 (summer 1989), "The Suffering of the Righteous in Babylonian and Palestinian Sources" *Jewish Quarterly Review* 80 (1990), and "Righteousness as Its Own Reward: An Inquiry into the Theologies of the Stam" *PAAJR* 57 (1991).

Joel Wolowelsky uncovers talmudic uneasiness with applying the category of *yissurin shel ahava* in "A Talmudic Discussion on Yissurin shel ahava" *Judaism* Fall 1984. In *Studies in Aggadah, Targum and Jewish Liturgy in Memory of Joseph Heineman* ed. E. Fleisher and J. Petuchowski (Jerusalem 1981), Louis Jacobs analyzes the talmudic structure and literary devices in the *sugya* of *yissurin shel ahava.*

David Kraemer's *Responses to Suffering in Classical Rabbinic Literature* (Oxford 1995) represents another view from the perspective of modern academic Talmud scholarship.

Medieval Jewish Philosophy: Rav Saadia Gaon offers his approach to the problem in *Emunot ve-Deot,* pt. 9, ch. 2 and 3 (trans. S. Rosenblatt, 1948). He emphasizes the future reward that will compensate for the suffering. A listing of standard traditional explanations appears in Rabbi Bahya ibn Pekuda's *Hovot haLevavot shaar ha-bittahon* (trans. M. Hyamson, 1962).

In the *Moreh Nevukhim,* sec. 3, ch. 8–24 (trans. S. Pines), Rambam discusses the problem from a variety of angles. Chapters 8–12 deal with the causes of evil, including the nature of matter (*homer*) and human foolishness. Rambam alludes to Augustine's notion that all evil is a privation without positive existence. Rambam also argues that we will appreciate how the relative amount of good in the world outweighs the evil if we realize that man is not the center of the universe. Chapter 24 deals with the problem of *nissayon.*

In chapters 17–22, Rambam outlines different views of providence and identifies these views with opinions expressed in Job. Chapter 51, which states that the wise and pious are saved from all earthly evils, seems to contradict the more naturalistic theory offered in chapter 17. For resolutions to this conflict, see S. Diesendruk, "Samuel and Moses ibn Tibbon on Maimonides' Theory of Providence" *HUCA* 11 (1936) and Charles Raffel's doctoral dissertation *"Maimonides' Theory of Providence"* (Brandeis University, 1983). J. Dienstag compiled a bibliography of secondary literature on Rambam and providence in *Daat* 20 (1988).

Rabbi Levi ben Gershom and Rabbi Hasdai Crescas also discuss the problem of evil in the context of a broader discussion on the nature of providence. Ralbag's controversial view that God's providence reigns over general categories but not particulars appears in *Milhamot haShem* pt. 4 (trans. Seymour Feldman, JPS, 1987; see his commentary, 139–151). According to Ralbag, loss of concentration on God removes a person from individual protection and makes him subject to accidents. Robert Eisen provides an excellent analysis of this view, as well as those on inherited providence and providential suffering, in his *Gersonides on Providence, Covenant and the Chosen People* (SUNY, 1995). Rabbi Hasdai Crescas criticizes Ralbag's position in *Or haShem,* pt. 2, ch. 2.

Ramban deals with the problem of suffering in his *Shaar haGemul* (Chavel ed. *Kol Kitvei HaRamban* II), 264–311. He justifies the search for an answer as part of knowing God, argues that *nissayon* comes to develop the potential of the *menusseh* rather than to teach others (as Rambam stated), and raises transmigration of souls as a possible solution. Both Ramban and Rabbi Yosef Albo analyze the prophets who complain about unjust suffering. Rabbi Albo deals with this issue in *Sefer haIkkarim* (trans. Isaac Husik), pt. 4, ch. 7–15. He also differentiates between the problems of *tzaddik v'ra lo* (suffering righteous) and *rasha v'tov lo* (flourishing wicked).

The concept of *yissurin shel ahava* attracted a great deal of attention. Rambam (3:17) rejected the usual interpretation of this concept, Ramban (*Shaar haGemul,* p. 270) viewed it as punishment for involuntary transgressions, and Rav Nissim Gerondi's *Derashot haRan* ed. Aryeh Feldman, 174, and Maharal's *Netivot Olam Netiv haYissurim* see it as part of spiritual growth. The commentaries of Maharsha and Pnei Yehoshua on *Berakhot* 5a raise the possibility of vicarious atonement.

Biblical emphasis on material reward and punishment and the apparent lack of mention of the world to come troubled many medievalists. Almost all the classic Jewish philosophers dealt with this problem. Rabbi Yitzchak Abravanel surveys the literature at the beginning of his commentary to *Behukkotai* (p. 133–136 in the Jerusalem 1984 edition of *Sefer Vayikra*).

Different schools in medieval philosophy debated whether animals receive reward and punishment. Rabbi Saadia represented the affirmative view, while Rambam and others vigorously disagreed. For the medieval and talmudic sources relevant to this debate, see Viktor Aptowitzer's "The Rewarding and Punishing of Animals and Inanimate Objects" *HUCA* 3 (1926).

Three surveys of medieval theodicies approach the problem from different vantage points. Harry Blumberg's "Theories of Evil in Medieval Jewish Philosophy" *HUCA* 43 (1972) starts with the metaphysical question of whether we can view God as the cause of evil. Hayyim Kreisel's "The Suffering Righteous in Medieval Jewish Philosophy" *Daat* 19 (1987) traces different theodicies back to varying perspectives on God. One begins with the biblical personal God or the Aristotelean removed God and proceeds accordingly. Oliver Leaman's *Evil and Suffering* (Cambridge, 1995) analyzes the approaches of Rabbi Saadia, Rambam, and Ralbag in the context of their commentaries on Job.

The Spanish expulsion triggered a variety of theological approaches as to the purpose of *galut*. Shalom Rosenberg examines these approaches in "Exile and Redemption in Jewish Thought in the Sixteenth Century" in Bernard Cooperman ed. *Jewish Thought in the Sixteenth Century*. For a perspective that incorporates moderns such as Rav Hirsch and deals with our place in the Diaspora when a Jewish homeland exists, see Shalom Carmy, "A View From the Fleshpots: Exploratory Remarks on a Gilded Galut Existence" *Tradition* 26:4 Summer 1992 (reprinted in C.

Waxman, *Israel as a Religious Reality* [Jason Aronson, 1994]).

Modern Jewish Philosophy: Rabbi Moshe Hayyim Luzzato address the problem of evil in both *Derekh Hashem* (trans Aryeh Kaplan; Feldhiem, 1977) and *Daat Tevunot* (trans Shraga Silverstein; Feldheim, 1982). Ramhal emphasizes the need for God to withdraw His presence and allow for evil so that man can strive to achieve *shleimut.* Rivka Shatz-Uffenheimer argues that Ramhal's views echo the optimism and show the influence of G. W. Leibniz and William King. Her "Moshe Hayyim Luzzato's Thought Against the Background of Theodicy Literature" appears in *Justice and Righteousness: Biblical Themes and their Influence,* ed. H. G. Reventlow and Yair Hoffman (JSOT, 1992).

Several modern thinkers argue that attempts to find rational solutions to the problem of evil are misguided. Rav Yosef Dov Soloveitchik (see *Kol Dodi Dofek* in *Divrei Hagut v Haarakha*) claims that a Jewish response to evil rooted in Halakha does not ask about the reason for suffering; rather, it inquires for the correct response to suffering. Lawrence Kaplan's English translation is in *Theological and Halakhic Reflections on the Holocaust,* ed. Bernhard Rosenberg and Fred Heuman (Ktav, 1992).

David Hartman attempts to find a similar strand of thought in talmudic accounts of suffering. In Hartman's words, the rabbis were interested in religious anthropology and not philosophical theology (*A Living Covenant: The Innovative Spirit of Traditional Judaism,* New York, 1985), ch. 8.

Zvi Kolitz wrote a short story about a Hasid who maintains both his complaint against God and allegiance to mitzvoth. Commentaries on this story are collected in *Yossel Rakover Speaks to God: Halakhic Challenges to Religious Faith* (Ktav, 1995). Emmanuel Levinas's commentary, "To

Love Torah More Than God," suggests that Judaism emphasizes obeying God more than knowing God.

The early twentieth-century world of European yeshivas
also contributed to the literature on the problem of evil.
Rabbi Eliyah Dessler's *Mikhtav me-Eliyahu*, 19–21 (trans. as
Strive for Truth by A. Carmel), reflects a traditional response. Rabbi Avraham Grodzinsky's *Torat Avraham* dedi-
cates a section to virtuous response to suffering. Rabbi
Yerucham Levovitz sees suffering as integral to the nature
of *olam ha-zeh* (*Daat Hokhmah u-Mussar*, 125–131). Rabbi
Eliyahu Lopian's *Lev Eliyahu* ([Jerusalem, 1972], vol. 1, 28–
29) emphasizes the need for suffering to shake a person
out of spiritual stagnation.

Shalom Rosenberg surveys numerous approaches in
Good and Evil in Jewish Thought (Tel Aviv, 1989). Among
the views he scrutinizes are those of Rambam, Rav
Soloveitchik, kabbalists, and Agnon. Rosenberg differentiates between rationalist strands that tend to minimize the
reality of evil and mystical strands that recognize it.

Some rabbinic sources seem to talk about God either suffering along with His people or accompanying them into
exile. Melvin Glatt deals with the former in "God the
Mourner: Israel's Companion in Tragedy" *Judaism* 28
(1979), and Norman J. Cohen discusses the latter in
"Shekhinta Ba Galuta: A Midrashic Response to Destruction
and Persecution" "*Journal for the Study of Judaism In the
Persian, Hellenistic and Roman Period* 13 (1982). Abraham
Heschel understands these sources literally and sees this theology of pathos as fundamental for understanding prophecy (*The Prophets*, New York, 1962). Eliezer Berkovits at-
tacked the anthropopathic tendency in this approach in Dr.
A. J. Heschel's "Theology of Pathos" *Tradition* 6:2 (1964)
(reprinted in *Major Themes in Modern Philosophies of Judaism*, New York, 1974) and a partial defense of Heschel

in S. Carmy, "Modern Jewish Philosophy: Fossil or Ferment?" (*Tradition* 15:3, 147–151).

Berkovits offers a Jewish version of the free-will defense in *Faith After the Holocaust.* He also argues that we can evaluate the theological situation only through the eyes of those who experienced the suffering. Marvin Fox analyzes this view in "Berkovits' Treatment of the Problem of Evil" *Tradition* 14:3 (Spring 1974).

Of course, the Holocaust spawned a great deal of theological reflection. Pesach Schindler deals with Hasidic approaches in *Hasidic Responses to the Holocaust in the Light of Hasidic Thought* (Ktav, 1990). While most writing on the Holocaust occurred years after the event, Rabbi Kalonymus Shapira wrote his *Esh Kodesh* from within the Warsaw Ghetto. For Nehemia Polen's analysis, see his essay in this book and references. He notes a reversal in the *Esh Kodesh.* Traditional sources speak of God suffering in sympathy with the Jewish people. According to Rabbi Shapira, God is the primary object of attack and the people suffer as a result of their identification with Him.

Norman Lamm castigates those who blame the victims as sinners and writes of the experience of *hester panim* (hiding of the face) as a punishment in "The Face of God: Thoughts on the Holocaust" in Rosenberg and Heuman *op. cit.* David Wolpe's "Hester Panim in Modern Jewish Thought" *Modern Judaism* 17 (1997) questions whether the notion of *hester panim* successfully escapes the problems it attempts to avoid. If human sin causes the eclipse, we seem to be returning to *mipnei hattaeinu* ("because of our sins").

Irving Greenberg argues that we must see the Holocaust as a revelational event and speaks of a dialectical theology with moments of faith in response. See "Cloud of Smoke, Pillar of Fire: Judaism, Christianity and Modernity After the

Holocaust" in *Auschwitz: Beginning of a New Era? Reflections on the Holocaust*, ed. E. Fleishner (Ktav, 1977). Michael Wyschogrod strongly critiques this view in "Auschwitz: Beginning of a New Era? Reflections on the Holocaust" *Tradition* 17:1 (Fall 1977). Greenberg's response appears in "Orthodox Judaism and the Holocaust" *Gesher* 7 (1977). Hillel Goldberg comments on this debate and other contemporary responses in "Holocaust Theology: The Survivor's Statement part 2" *Tradition* 20:4 (Winter 1982).

Jonathan Sacks and Eugene Borowitz provide clear and concise summaries of the literature in response to the Holocaust. Sacks' essay appears as chapter 8 in his *Tradition in an Untraditional Age: Essays on Modern Jewish Thought* (Valentine, 1990). Borowitz's essay is chapter 9 in his *Choices in Modern Jewish Thought: A Partisan Guide* (Behrman House, 1995). Borowitz also connects the various theologies with trends in American Jewish life.

Eliezer Schweid's *Wrestling Until Day-Break: Searching for Meaning in the Thinking on the Holocaust* (University Press, 1994) views the question of the Holocaust's uniqueness as fundamental to the recent theodicies (see, in particular, ch. 8). According to Schweid, both the protest theologies that express anger to God and the modern Orthodox theologies that view God as reluctant to intervene in human affairs reflect the Holocaust's impact.

David Birnbaum recently combined the free-will defense with a new conception of providence. His *God and Evil* offers an interesting survey and commentary on various theodicies. Tamar Ross critiques Birnbaum and adds her view on the impact Rav Kook's thought should have on theodicy in *Daat* 28 (1992).

Yehuda Gellman's "Evil and its Justification in the Thought of Abraham Isaac Kook" *Daat* 19 (1987) locates two strands of thought in Rav Kook's writing on evil, primarily in *Orot haKodesh*. Rav Kook, at times, argues for the nonexistence of evil; but on other occasions, he argues that, teleologically, we can justify the place of evil. While the monistic perspective is ultimately true, we currently experience the world in a dualistic fashion. However, Rav Kook does employ the monistic perspective in the here and now in finding the good in many secular philosophies.

General literature:

The problem: David Hume states the theodicy problem and employs it to argue against religion in *Dialogues Concerning the Natural Religion*, chapter 10 and 11. A frequently cited recent version is J. L. Mackie's "Evil and Omnipotence" in *Mind* 55 (1964).

Evil as privation: Some have argued that evil is merely the absence of good and cannot be said to exist. Augustine in *The City of God*, bk. 11, and Thomas Aquinas in *Summa Theologica*, 147–149, adopt the view of evil as privation. A twentieth-century version appears in Karl Barth's *Church Dogmatics* 3:3 (Edinburgh, 1960).

Great chain of being: In the Middle Ages, many thought that the greater the variety of beings existing in the world—even the most lowly and destitute—the better. This has been referred to as "the principle of plenitude." The classic survey is Arthur Lovejoy's *The Great Chain of Being*. A devastating critique appears in Samuel Johnson's "Review of [Soames Jenyn's] Free Inquiry into the Nature and Origin of Evil" (*Collected Works*, vol. 13). Johnson pointed out the mathematical difficulties with an infinite number of beings existing and the lack of succor such a theodicy brings to the destitute.

Best of all possible worlds: G. W. Leibniz maintained that, as the most perfect being, God must by definition create the best of all possible worlds. In *Theodicy: Essays on the Goodness of God, the Freedom of Man and the Origin of*

Evil, he attempted to show how all evil leads to some greater good. Voltaire satirized this last tendency in his *Candide*.

Free-will defense: Another classic theodicy argues that God could not possibly create free beings without allowing for the possibility of their doing evil. This was one of Augustine's explanations for evil in *The City Of God*. Alvin Plantinga's *God, Freedom and Evil* (New York, 1974) represents the most significant current version of the free-will defense.

Return the ticket: In the past two hundred years, many writers have rejected any answer to any of the explanations offered. The classic rejection of all answers is Ivan Karamozov's offer to return the ticket in Feodor Dostoevski's *The Brothers Karamazov*, bk. 5, ch. 4. Albert Camus implies a similar approach in *The Plague*.

Vale of soul-making: John Hick argues that a world of suffering involves greater personal growth than a hedonistic paradise. He contrasts an Augustinian theodicy, which looks backward in history for the source of evil, with an Irenaean theodicy, which looks forward to what will emerge from this evil. His *Evil and the God of Love* (Harper, 1977) provides the best survey for the history of theodicies.

Animal pain and hell: C. S. Lewis (*The Problem of Pain*; New York, 1962) and P. T. Geach (*Providence and Evil*; Cambridge, 1977) deal with two lesser-known aspects of the problem. Lewis argues that animals lack the consciousness that makes suffering unbearable. Geach rejects this view and offers his own explanation for animal pain. Both explain why a merciful God would be interested in eternal punishment for sinners. Lewis returned to the subject in *God in the Dock*.

Recent work: Michael Peterson's "Recent Work on The Problem of Evil" *American Philosophical Quarterly* 20:4 (October 1983) discusses recent work. This includes analysis of God's knowledge of contingent events and definitional questions regarding the nature of free will. Philosophers have debated whether God could have created free beings who would always choose the good. For one side of the debate, see Alvin Plantinga op. cit. Plantinga uses the term "transworld depravity" to indicate that any freely created being in any possible world at some point would go wrong.

Peterson also mentions an important article by Richard Swinburne entitled "Natural Evil" (*APQ*, October 1978). Swinburne attempts to show that the free-will defense works not only for man-produced evils, but for natural evils as well. He argues that human freedom requires nature's stability.

Robert M. Adams has contributed several important articles on the problem of evil. In "Must God Create the Best?" he takes issue with Leibniz. Even if our world is not the optimum world, the creatures in it still would rather exist than not, so God is justified in creating it. In "Middle Knowledge and the Problem of Evil," Adams argues against one aspect of Plantinga's free-will defense. Both essays appear in Adams' *The Virtue of Faith* (Oxford, 1987).

George Schlesinger (*Religion and Scientific Method*, 1977) claims that moral expectations demand not that God grant humans the most happiness possible, but rather that he raise their desirability of state. As there exists no limit to the degree to which the desirability of state can reach, God cannot be expected to give us the most desirable state possible.

Anthologies: Three excellent anthologies with concise introductions and helpful bibliographies recently have appeared. Michael Peterson ed. *The Problem of Evil* (Notre Dame, 1992) differentiates between logical, evidential, and existential versions of the problem. Robert M. Adams and Marilyn M. Adams have edited another anthology with the same name (Oxford, 1990). Lastly, Daniel Howard-Snyder, *The Evidential Argument from Evil* (Indiana University Press, 1996) stresses that aspect of the problem.

Contributors

Yitzchak Blau teaches at Yeshivat Hamivtar in Efrat, Israel, and publishes frequently on Jewish thought.

Shalom Carmy is Consulting Editor of *Tradition*. A student of the late Rabbi Joseph B. Soloveitchik and a veteran teacher of philosophy, Bible, and Jewish thought at Yeshiva University, he has published many essays on these subjects. Rabbi Carmy is the editor of *Modern Scholarship in the Study of Torah: Contributions and Limitations* (Jason Aronson Inc., 1996).

Yaffa Eliach, Professor of Judaic Studies at Brooklyn College, is an author and scholar in Holocaust Studies and the creator of the "Tower of Life" at the United States Holocaust Memorial Museum in Washington. She was the founder of the first Center for Holocaust Studies in the United States.

Yaakov Elman is professor of Jewish Studies at Yeshiva University. He is the author of *Authority and Tradition* and *The Living Prophets.* He is a prolific writer on talmudic literature, biblical interpretation, and hasidic thought.

Aharon Lichtenstein is *Rosh Yeshivah* of Yeshivat Har Etzion and the Gruss Institute, RIETS. He is a frequent contributor to books and journals of contemporary Jewish thought.

Nehemia Polen is associate professor of Jewish Thought at Hebrew College in Boston, Massachusetts. He is currently a National Endowment for the Humanities fellow, working on his translation of the memories of Malkah Shapiro, daughter of the Rebbe of Kozicnice.

Moshe Halevi Spero is Professor, School of Social Work, and Co-Director, Postgraduate Program of Psychoanalytic Psychotheraphy, Bar-Ilan University; Senior Clinical Psychologist and Research Scholar in Psychoanalysis and Religion, Department of Psychiatry, Sarah Herzog Memorial Hospital; Clinical Instructor, Eliezer Ilan Child and Adolescent Treatment Center, Jerusalem, Israel.

Moshe D. Tendler is a senior *Rosh Yeshivah* at the Rabbi Isaac Elchanan Theological Seminary and Professor of Biology at Yeshiva University. He is an authority and author in many areas of halakah and medical ethics, in particular.

Index

About the Editors

Shalom Carmy is Consulting Editor of *Tradition*. A student of the late Rabbi Joseph B. Soloveitchik and a veteran teacher of philosophy, Bible, and Jewish thought at Yeshiva University, he has published many essays on these subjects. Rabbi Carmy is the editor of *Modern Scholarship in the Study of Torah: Contributions and Limitations* (Jason Aronson Inc., 1996).

Robert S. Hirt is the series editor for the Orthodox Forum. Rabbi Hirt has served at Yeshiva University's affiliated Rabbi Isaac Elchanan Theological Seminary (RIETS) for more than three decades and has been vice president for Administration and Professional Education for RIETS since 1985. In 1991, he was named inaugural occupant of the Rabbi Sidney Shoham Chair in Rabbinic and Community Leadership at RIETS. Rabbi Hirt oversees the "Torah U'Mada Project," the purpose of which is to explore the interaction of Torah and *Mada* (secular studies) within the institution and raise the level of discussion about the complexities and challenges that "Torah U'Mada" poses to the community at large. In 1987, Rabbi Hirt coedited Shimon Huberband's critically acclaimed book on the Holocaust, *Kiddush Hashem: Jewish Religious and Cultural Life in Poland During the Holocaust.*